Women and the State

Women
and the State
The shifting boundaries of public and private

Edited by
Anne Showstack Sassoon

London and New York

First published in 1987 by Unwin Hyman Ltd

© Anne Showstack Sassoon 1987

Reprinted in 1989

Reprinted in 1992
by Routledge
11 New Fetter Lane, London EC4P 4EE

Simultaneously published in the USA and Canada
by Routledge
a division of Routledge, Chapman and Hall, Inc.
29 West 35th Street, New York, NY 10001

British Library Cataloging in Publication Data
Women and the state: the shifting boundaries of
    public and private.—(Contemporary politics).
    1. Women—Social conditions
    I. Sassoon, Anne Showstack II. Series
    305.4'2   HQ1121

ISBN 0-415-07908-X

Library of Congress Cataloging in Publication Data
has been applied for

Printed and bound in Great Britain by
Biddles Ltd, Guildford and King's Lynn

For my mother, Sarah Sevell Showstack and for my daughter, Tanya Emma Sassoon

Contents

Part Two   Inside and Outside the Home: Women's Experience and the Transformation of Public and Private

Acknowledgements

I would like to thank all those friends for their conversations. They will know who they are. Laura Balbo has always been extremely encouraging and helpful. So have John Keane, David Beetham, Bob Jessop, Claire L'Enfant, Pat Thane, Suzanne MacGregor, Michèle Barrett, and Mary McIntosh. Martin Jacques put a large effort into editing an earlier version of my piece. Penny Gardiner did an excellent copy-editing job.

Thanks are also due to Mrs Eileen Palmer and her co-workers in the Kingston Polytechnic secretariat for their invaluable help in typing parts of the manuscript. A period of sabbatical leave from the School of Economics and Politics provided time to read and to think at the beginning of putting this collection together. Over the years the interloan service of the polytechnic library has been a great support.

All the contributors have responded to my sometimes minute quibbles. It has been a pleasure to get to know them, and to be able to combine the personal with the intellectual in such an enjoyable way. My mother set me on this path when she gave me a copy of Betty Friedan's *The Feminine Mystique*, while my daughter Tanya has made it all real. So has my husband Donald.

'Women and the welfare state. The transition from private dependence', by Helga Maria Hernes was first printed in *Patriarchy in a Welfare Society*, edited by Harriet Holter (Oslo: Universitetsforlaget 1984), pp. 26–45, reprinted by permission of Universitetsforlaget AS. 'The rationality of caring', by Kari Waerness, was first published in *Economic and Industrial Democracy*, 5 (Sage, 1984), pp. 185–211, reprinted by permission of Sage Publications.

Contributors

Laura Balbo is Professor of Sociology at the University of Ferrara. Her main areas of teaching and research have been political sociology and the sociology of the family from the perspective of women. She is one of the founders of the GRIFF (Gruppo di recerca sulla famiglia e la condizione femminile) of the University of Milan. She has taught in the United States. She is an MP in the Italian Parliament in the Independent Left Group.

Anette Borchorst is a research fellow at the Center for Research on Women (CEKVINA) and at the Institute for Political Science at Aarhus University in Denmark. Her research has been on the situation of women in paid and unpaid work and the relation of women to the welfare state. She has just started a new research project on motherhood, state and living conditions, and she has recently been appointed as one of two co-ordinators of feminist research in Denmark.

Drude Dahlerup, Institute of Political Science, University of Aarhus, Denmark. She has specialized in research on women in politics, the women's movement, theories of women's oppression. She is editor of a forthcoming book on the new women's movement in eleven countries, to be published by Sage. She is active in the women's movement.

Helga Maria Hernes is research director at the Institute for Social Research in Oslo. She has published articles and books in international relations, political theory and women in politics. She is also editor of a series of books entitled 'Studies in Women's Life Course and Living Conditions'.

Chiara Saraceno is associate professor in sociology at the University of Trento, Italy. She has written extensively on the family, women, social policies, partly from a historical and comparative perspective. Some of her work is published by the *Feminist Studies* and *Social Problems*. She is a member of the Poverty Commission at the Prime Minister's office.

Anne Showstack Sassoon is senior lecturer in politics at Kingston Poly-technic, Kingston upon Thames. She has written *Gramsci's Politics*, edited *Approaches to Gramsci*, and published numerous articles. Her recent work on Gramsci has been on the relationship between people and specialists. Her research on women has concentrated on the political implications of women's changed socio-economic role.

Birte Siim is associate professor and director of the Women's Studies Programme at Aalborg University in Denmark. Her research has been on feminist theory, long-term changes in the sexual division of labour and the relation of women to the welfare state. She is currently working on a research project comparing the situation of women in the welfare state in Denmark, England and the US.

Vicki Smith is a graduate student in the Department of Sociology at the University of California, Berkeley, and has researched and written on women's work and feminist theory. Her current research is on changes in the work and organization of middle managers in large corporate firms. She works as the managing editor of the journal *Socialist Review*.

Hélène Strohl is a history graduate. She studied at the École Nationale d'Administration. She is a civil servant in the area of social affairs. She is a member of the board of *Sociétés*, published in Paris by Masson.

Gabriella Turnaturi teaches sociology in the Department of Sociology at the University of Rome. She has published numerous articles and a book on marginalization. She was co-editor of *Donna Woman Femme* and very active in the Italian women's movement. She writes for various magazines and newspapers such as *L'Espresso* and *Il Manifesto* and appears on a radio programme run by women for women.

Kari Waerness works as associate professor at the Institute of Sociology at the University of Bergen in Norway. She has undertaken research in social policy and family sociology with particular emphasis on the role of women, the relation between informal unpaid care in the family and the formally organized health and social services. She has published a number of books and articles on these issues, e.g. 'The Invisible Welfare State: Women's Work at Home', *Acta Sociologica*, Supplement, 1978 and *Kvin-neperspektiver på sosialpolitikken* (Oslo: Universitetsforlaget 1982).

Introduction: the personal and the intellectual, fragments and order, international trends and national specificities

Anne Showstack Sassoon

Any book must be explained and justified in the face of competition for the time, energy, and financial resources of the reader.
How and why did this collection come into being? Four of the
pieces, those by Helga Hernes, Drude Dahlerup, Anette
Borchorst and Birte Siim, and Kari Waerness derive from a
conference.[1]* A number of them, as I shall explain below, are in
dialogue with one another and are involved in an implicit if not
explicit common project. Others were found through personal
contacts. They are being published to make available to a wider
audience stimulating, thought-provoking material which enriches
the discussion about the crisis of the modern state and about
the situation of women and which is both stimulating and
thought-provoking. On the one hand, the *de facto* mainly
male debate about the crisis of the welfare state has all but
ignored women. On the other, debate among women has all
too often ended up in a theoretical and political cul-de-sac.
These pieces open up new horizons. Their publication is
based on the conviction that by starting from the point of view
of women, varied and diverse though it may be, we gain essential insight and knowledge about both public and private and,
above all, about the shifting boundaries between the two. By
analysing the complexity of women's role and the transformations in their lives, by drawing out the contradictory implications
of their socio-economic position, and by raising the contradictory

---

* Superior figures refer to the Notes and references sections following each
chapter.

effects of state policy, we arrive at important features of modern
society and the state.

The personal and the intellectual

Any intellectual endeavour, however, has a personal side, even if
this is rarely articulated,[2] and it takes place in a political and
cultural context, all of which inform the purpose and aim of a
project. Given the varied nature of the pieces here, it may be
useful in explaining their unity and diversity if the collection is set
in its personal, political, cultural context.

My initial impetus to read about women and to listen to what
others had to say stemmed much more from the changes in my
life after having a daughter in 1976, and my contact with the
feminists on the board of a journal,[3] than from academic or
political factors. Although it was possible to relate the work I had
done on the Italian Marxist, Antonio Gramsci,[4] to the debate
which was taking place about the state and about ideology, it was
far from obvious to see how one could think about women from
a Gramscian perspective. In retrospect, however, it is clear that
there is a convergence between a major achievement of the
women's movement and an important aspect of Gramsci's ideas.
The women's movement has insisted that women's personal
experience is political, be it articulated in consciousness-raising
groups or more informally through the kind of networks of friends
and acquaintances which women have always established. It
provides the raw material for intellectual and political work as
well as solidarity. This coincides with a lesson from Gramsci's
writings. He argues that the necessary starting point for a better
understanding of the world must be a critical analysis of people's
common sense.

Gramsci, in a sense, was lurking in the kitchen. My experience
of being a working mother and the experience and ideas of so
many of my friends and acquaintances simply did not correspond
either to much of what was being said in the women's movement
in the 1970s, or to the ideology of femininity and of women's
place as in the home, let alone to what male intellectual work or
male politics was about. These gaps or these contradictions formed
the basis of this anthology. The experience of a few people, of
course, can never be representative, but it is none the less auth-

entic. Joined with an attempt at generalization and synthesis based on critical analysis, it can provide a fertile humus for intellectual work.

Above all, these friends and I were either ourselves combining paid work and other activities outside the home with children and domestic life, or sensitive to the fact that most women have this experience. Some were active in the women's movement. Others were not. Some would not call themselves feminists. They came from different class backgrounds. But all were clear that as things are now organized, life often seem stacked against women. Yet, they were active, lively, and intelligent in different ways. They had a sense of humour. If they had children, it was because they wanted them. Children brought great joy as well as heavy responsibilities. Some of these women were in and out of long-term relationships with men, others with women, most were part of different kinds of families. These various friends and acquaintances hardly saw themselves as victims, although life could also bring pain and distress. I began to reflect on numberless conversations with this unrepresentative sample. It was a period before the current baby boom among feminists, when the family in the abstract was the main object of attack, the state was viewed as above all enforcing the subjection of women, and the call was out that women should be allowed to work.

Most of the debates in the women's movement at the time simply did not reflect this experience, while political and academic discussions usually left women out altogether. I therefore turned to reading whatever I could about the socio-economic situation of the mass of women in Britain, and about their material conditions. And I discovered that most women, like my friends and myself, now had a dual role, in paid work and in the home, and that in fact this role was multifaceted, overriding the boundaries of the various spheres of society.

What became obvious was that the actual situation of the mass of women had gone beyond the terms of the domestic labour debate, one of the most influential theoretical disputes at the time.[5] The merit of that discussion was to focus on the sphere of reproduction and to ask how women's work in the home contributes both to production and to the reproduction of society as a whole. Yet this debate and most Marxist analysis tried to move directly from the theoretical category of mode of production to the socially and historically constructed family. The questions posed became narrowed to how the family helps to reproduce the capitalist mode of production, and in particular, how it physically reproduces the working class. Women's role was reduced to their role within the family. The importance to them, to their families, and to the economy of their place in the world of production was obscured. The historical development of nationally specific, institutional forms and modes of oppression was outside the focus of analysis.

Today most women in Europe and North America combine formal paid work with full adult domestic responsibilities, as well as undertaking other activities. Their socio-economic role hinges fundamentally on what services are provided by the state to substitute for their caring work. The state also supplies many of them with paid jobs. State policy, it is clear, is riddled with contradictions both in intent and in effect. The domestic, productive, state and civil spheres are so interwoven that one cannot be thought about in isolation from another. Personal experience and the socio-economic data about the vast majority of women pointed to the need for a different theoretical approach.

As I read about women, I therefore kept looking for analyses which captured these complexities. I was also struck by the fact that many of these features of modern life connected precisely with the main object of Gramsci's analysis: the intertwining of political and civil society. For Gramsci the most significant historical development of capitalism from the end of the last century is a new relation between public and private, and between the state and society, in which the role of the state expands in response to social needs which are articulated by mass organizations and because of economic development. As the interventionist state develops, the context in which the hegemony of capitalism is reconstituted changes because society has entered into what Gramsci calls an organic crisis. The state, he argues, can no longer be described as the instrument of a class, and state policy, whatever the regime, cannot be understood as the product of a rational design. Social policy is the result of problems and pressures emanating from social development embedded in long-term historical trends which begin under capitalism and which pose questions that extend into socialism. Above all, the precise *forms* of social relations and institutions reflect the concrete history of each country, rather than the requirements of a mode of production. Their historical specificity must be understood as well as the general historical trends which they manifest.

Gramsci's perspective was much wider and much richer and therefore more fruitful than that of the domestic labour debate or of most discussions of the state and women. He was always asking what was new in social and political developments. He tried to understand the contradictory effects of the historical process, to look for new problems and new possibilities in social change. Instead of trying to investigate the contradictory effects of both state policy and social institutions, a static, functionalist approach has tended to dominate. Questions are too often posed in this way: what function does the state have in reproducing the family and hence women's subordination? Or, what function does the family have in reproducing the capitalist mode of production?[6] Overall the discussion about women and the state lacked subtlety. It failed to lead to a differentiated analysis of different national and historical contexts. These were absorbed into an overriding functional model. The novel aspects of recent developments, and the contradictions and complexities of social change and of women's roles and experience remained hidden. Women's creativity and ingenuity were obscured and their wishes and desires reduced to the product of a dominant ideology. A whole series of questions were either not asked or asked as if women were objects or victims: *why* women accept their socially constructed role, what they get out of it, how various social mechanisms bind them but are also changing and providing space for greater autonomy as well as enforcing new kinds of dependence, how the messages sent out about femininity are decoded by women.

The limits of other approaches were a motivation to search for material about women which posed questions in a similar fruitful way to Gramsci, even if it did not use Gramscian categories. At the same time the need to think theoretically about the contradictions inherent in women's situation led to a re-evaluation of Gramsci's work. Did his approach, his categories, have anything to offer to a feminist analysis? The answer was 'yes', if he is understood properly. In addition to his work on the state, the most obvious connection between Gramsci's writings and women might seem those aspects which are related to popular culture and ideology. This is a dimension which is useful but not in the way in which it is usually interpreted. Gramsci has all too often simply been absorbed into a perspective which attributes an all-powerful social control to ruling ideas, norms and practices. The result is to reinforce a sense of victimization. At the same time he is frequently used to legitimize an alternative which is offered to this dominant ideology: a romanticized popular culture. In fact, while asserting the importance of the ideas and the views of the world held by the mass of the population, Gramsci is highly critical of popular culture.[7] What he seeks to investigate are the contradictions within people's 'common sense', and their ability to select among elements of the hegemonic ideology. This ideology, he says, is complex and often contradictory. In order to understand the effects of ideology, he focuses on the relationship between people's material circumstances and social relations, and their ideas.

His approach allows us to go beyond the dichotomy of women as victims versus women as heroines. He is constantly asking the question, *why* do people accept certain ideas? He starts from the premise that if they do, these ideas must reflect material conditions in everyday life which appear to demonstrate their validity. He asks which material structures and practices reinforce the dominant ideology. But, above all else, he is interested in the way people's everyday lives and material practices often simultaneously contradict elements both in their common sense and in the dominant ideas. These contradictions provide the space or the possibility for a political intervention to construct an alternative hegemony, an alternative view of the world. But based on what? Composed of what? Not of the utopian, abstract ideals of isolated intellectuals. An alternative hegemony and alternative structures are only possible historically, he argues, if they are based on the embryonic ideas, practices and institutions which are already in evidence in the lives of the vast majority. Gramsci suggests, in fact, that the material circumstances of the mass of the population are often historically 'ahead' of both popular and dominant ideas. The ideas of intellectuals seeking to change society often lag far behind. The educators need to be educated.

Gramsci is firmly within a tradition of materialism and of mass politics in which material conditions indicate what is possible. His work poses questions like: 'What do the daily lives of millions of people tell us about a new and different society?' 'What can we learn from people's common sense and what is it necessary to criticize and to supersede because it keeps them in a subordinate position?' 'Which alternative structures are already being created which can serve as the basis of an alternative hegemony?' 'How have certain institutions and forms of oppression developed historically in concrete national circumstances?' 'What political programme will maximize the possibility that progressive alternatives are created and that the present dominant ideology and oppressive structures are undermined?' All of these questions are useful for understanding the position of women. They also suggest an important point of departure for intellectual work and political initiatives.

Fragments and order, international trends and national specificities

If Gramsci provided one intellectual stimulus for this collection, the writings of Laura Balbo, Chiara Saraceno, and other women working with a research institute in Milan, the GRIFF,[8] provided the other. The starting point of their work was women's dual role in the domestic sphere and in paid work. It analysed the complexity of women's experience in the family and in society, tracing the web of social relations which constitute women's servicing work. Mediating a wide range of American, British and European literature, their approach corresponded more closely to the experiences of women I knew than many of the debates in the women's movement in Britain in the 1970s. Instead of criticizing an abstract family, the family was viewed in its historical dimension as changing and multiform. Instead of challenging the state in general for oppressing women, the interconnections between the organization of daily life, the family, the labour market and the development of the welfare state were investigated. The point of departure was women's continuing subordination and the implicit and explicit political aim of this work is to contribute to women's liberation. But rather than an ideological attack on the institutions of the state, the world of work, and the family, there is an attempt to trace how the different areas of society are related and ordered through analysing the concrete reality of the fragmentation of women's lives. What shines through is a positive view of women's capacities and their creativity which is at the same time highly sensitive to the constraints placed on women's lives by social institutions and the organization of society in general. It was starting from the work of the GRIFF, plus other contacts in Italy, that I directly or indirectly found most of the material for this book.

Thus, the selection of articles presented here has roots in debates and writing in the women's movement in Britain and in the work of a group of Italian women sociologists. It contains pieces from women living in Norway, Denmark, France, Italy, Britain and the US. It is, therefore, international. But in what sense? And why should readers be interested in articles written in these countries? The international character of this collection derives from the aim of the book: to discuss common themes and trends which are manifesting themselves internationally in a wide variety of countries, and to present a group of essays which are not easily available to an English-speaking audience. Yet international trends manifest themselves in nationally specific forms. Several of the pieces, for example, those by Balbo and Dahlerup, argue that more concrete, historical work is needed to understand the relationship between women and the state and the changes in women's social role. Although most of the articles refer to national data and different historical experiences, the collection is not an attempt to provide an assessment of the situation of representative countries. It is international because the articles come from different countries. They have been selected because they share certain themes: the changing boundaries of public and private, the interrelationship between state, family and labour markets, the complexity of women's role in the home and in society, the need to investigate the contradictions of women's lives.

But, as I will explain below, they do not all agree and the book is divided into two parts. The first part, 'The modern state and contemporary society – new insights and new contradictions' contains a group of articles which all address questions about the state and women. The second part, 'Inside and outside the home: women's experience and the transformation of public and private' is made up of pieces which examine aspects of women's lives in the home, the family and the labour market, which are important socially and politically. In neither section have the articles been selected because they are representative or in order to cover the whole of a topic. They are being published because they are stimulating, innovatory and offer a subtle analysis which has often been missing in feminist writing and in wider debates about the modern state. They open up new perspectives which should provide the stimulus for further discussion and work.

It is, of course, commonplace in books focused on women to connect the private and the public (as undefined as these terms are), or the personal and the political. In this sense feminism, the women's movement and, above all, the lives of women, have gone much further than thinkers like Gramsci or others. But of course the *necessity* of combining the two perspectives, revealed with such great insight by women writers, goes beyond the slogan 'the personal is political'. It derives from the nature of society itself. It is impossible today to think of an area of society or of people's lives where politics or state policy does not have an impact. By the same token, in the modern period of mass politics, the demands arising out of daily life and of every area of society from cultural and sports activities, religious and community organizations, to production, trade unions and the economy are focused on the state and the wider political sphere.

This book is being published in a series of contemporary politics because it is impossible to understand the current crisis of different political systems and of a relationship between state and society which has developed since the end of the last century – that is, the interventionist state and, in its most recent form, the Keynesian welfare state – without understanding social and economic changes. These changes, which state policy itself has helped to produce, are the basis for qualitatively new demands on the political system. A major and, I would argue, irreversible change is women's new socio-economic role in which the vast majority of women have a place in the labour market as well as the home. Moreover, if we start from the point of view of women, heterogeneous though it may be, *because* their role is multifaceted and *because* it reveals contradictions stemming from the new mix of public and private which has developed, we can 'read' these transformations with far greater understanding. So, yes, this collection is for men as well as women. While much of what is discussed here may not ring the same intuitive bell with men, this is all the more reason that they should broaden their horizons and learn from women.

The modern state and contemporary society – new insights and new contradictions

The first chapter, Laura Balbo's 'Crazy quilts: rethinking the welfare state debate from a woman's point of view', sets out many of the themes which run through the collection. She offers it as a contribution to the extensive discussion about the crisis of the welfare state and as part of a feminist project to analyse contemporary society. Her approach is rooted in a subtle and sensitive discussion of what is called women's servicing work and arrives at a complex picture of the web of relationships and institutions which are a mark of modern society. Using the metaphor of patchwork quilts, she analyses the way in which women, through their servicing work, hold together complicated, fragmentary, modern society. One strand of the welfare state debate argues that the fragmentation of modern society renders any attempt at overall understanding and at rational state policy inherently inadequate if not impossible. But Laura Balbo suggests that if we study concrete descriptive evidence of how people live and their everyday coping strategies, we arrive at a more complete picture with a different message. We find, in fact, that it is only through women's cheap, flexible, interchangeable servicing work in which they patch together resources to meet human needs that society holds together. This packaging of resources requires intelligence, planning, creativity, time and hard work. And just as in a patchwork quilt, the end result is design, logic and order. We begin to comprehend how fragmentation, far from being incidental, is a structural requirement and an historically unique feature of advanced capitalist society.

Laura Balbo's approach is also fruitful in what it reveals about women's lives. It is true that some of women's servicing work, for example, domestic labour, is isolated, but much takes place in society at large in the community and through networks of family and friends. Many of the tasks women undertake link public and private. Moreover, the skills needed, from emotional to managerial, are essential in a 'service society'. An implication of this chapter is that many, traditional, private 'feminine' qualities more and more have a public face, as servicing jobs expand either through the state or in the market and as people's lives are increasingly organized in response to the way services are offered. She suggests that women undertake servicing work not just because of their socialization, but because such work arises out of the material conditions of their existence. Although they may in part share the dominant devaluation of the skills involved, they know how important such work is and have at the same time developed an alternative set of values oriented to human needs. They realize that their skills and values are necessary for human survival itself. Far from the family being emptied of its functions by the state, it can be analysed as a producer, processor, and consumer. Women's servicing work also tells us how state services are part of a complex pattern in which there is nothing inevitable about how a particular service is delivered. This pattern and the institutions involved have developed historically and vary from country to country.

The need for concrete studies of historical and national specificities is a theme running through the next three chapters which discuss questions about the welfare state from a feminist perspective by women who live in Norway and Denmark. Why should they be of particular interest? The Scandinavian countries are often viewed as a model of welfare provision and female emancipation. There are in fact considerable differences between them. Moreover, despite the very high labour market participation of women and their relatively high representation in the formal political channels of parliament and local government, they are still discriminated against, are under-represented, and above all have less political power than men. But rather than a cry of despair, these articles offer subtle analyses of the advanced contradictions which are manifest in the present historical period. Rooted in the socio-economic and political realities of Norway and Denmark, they raise issues which are of much more general interest. At the same time the disagreement between them about the effects of state policy should stimulate further debate.

Helge Hernes's article, 'Women and the welfare state: the transition from private to public dependence' raises questions about women and political power, asks why they have so little, and how they can achieve more. She poses these questions from Norway, a country where women's representation in parliament and in government is much greater than others. Yet, in the corporate channel, which has enormous power, it is very low. She argues that, on the whole, women have been the recipients of social policies determined by men, whose organizations – the trade unions, based in the sphere of production, and, as the suffrage was expanded, the political parties – were incorporated into the political system. Social policies had a major impact on women's lives before they became part of the decision-making apparatus. Women have not appeared as a 'problem' which threatens the system until recently: because they have not traditionally been defined as an interest group with separate claims, they have not been incorporated. In fact, she writes, they are frequently mobilized by public policy itself.

In her analysis of what she calls women's three statuses – as citizens with political rights, as clients and consumers of welfare services, and as employees, above all in the state sector – Helge Hernes arrives at an extremely useful picture of a major transformation which has taken place in women's lives which is significant for them and for the political system. Their triple status signifies a shift in their dependence, she argues, from private relations with men to public dependence on the state. An implication is that new lines of demarcation between men and women are being drawn. Women are now much more dependent on state policies than men. This is not only because their direct relationship to the state is different, but because men can achieve economic and corporate power in civil society in the sphere of production and the market. As reproduction 'goes public' which, as she points out is a trend of all western countries which has simply gone furthest in Scandinavia, women are drawn into the labour market. But the political consequences of this are different than, say, the shift of labour from the land to industry. The mere presence of women in the labour market has not resulted in the same increase in power for them that the development of organizations in production and their consequent consolidation and incorporation in the political system did for men. Instead, because women work above all in private, semi-private, and public areas of reproduction, because they have multiple roles, or statuses, and therefore their lives are less coherent than men's, they cannot organize as easily.

We arrive, then, at a picture of fragmentation similar to the one drawn by Laura Balbo. Once more, from a different analysis, we see that changes in women's lives reflect a major social trend: the increase in the role of the state. Their complex relation to the state, and the transformation taking place in the nature of their dependence emphasizes, Helge Hernes argues, the inequalities of power. Yet as the character of this dependence has changed, it is now more visible, and women's economic bonds are emphasized while their social bonds are misrepresented or made invisible.

But, she writes, if women have *little* power, it is decisive that they now have *more* power and that they are in the political arena. They are demanding representation with demands which are qualitatively different from those which the corporate, redistributive state (as she calls it), has traditionally accommodated. This means that women constitute a potential challenge to the political system.

The next piece, 'Confusing concepts – confusing reality: a theoretical discussion of the patriarchal state', is part of a continuing debate about the impact of state policy on women. It puts foward what is bound to be a controversial position. In a wide-ranging chapter which examines a large amount of American and British literature on the concept of patriarchy, the private–public split, and the determinants and effects of public policy, Drude Dahlerup challenges the argument that the state upholds and re-establishes the subordination of women. Her conclusion is that the state is not the main force behind changes in women's lives or in their oppression. Even when all the unintended effects of sex neutral policies are added to the intentional aims of policies directed specifically at women, the importance of public policy toward women, she says, must not be exaggerated. The position of women has largely been a 'non-issue' which has been left to 'nature' or social forces, while public policy is filled with contradictions and unintended side effects, which, however, affect women differently to men. The state, she says, has often been a silent observer of socio-economic development, or blind to the actual transformations taking place. It is frequently slow to react to changes, in, say, women's labour force participation even if, at times – for example, in abortion law reform – it may move ahead of some social forces because of the mobilization of others.

The argument is all the more stimulating because it derives from an examination of a Scandinavian reality where social welfare reform is highly advanced and the role of the state in assuming responsibility for caring has been a precondition for one of the highest rates of female labour force participation in the world. Yet the continuing inequality of women and recent cuts in welfare services have led to a reconsideration of the social democratic tradition and to the question: to what extent can the state be a force for change? Noting the similarities between social provision in the capitalist countries of Scandinavia and in the state socialist countries of eastern Europe, Drude Dahlerup argues that we have to consider the role of the capitalist economy as such, the impact of the industrialization process in general, and the influence of the relative strength of different political forces in analysing changes in women's lives.

The major perspective emerging from this chapter is that these questions can only be answered on the basis of detailed historical studies of the content, scope, and derivation of public policy in different national realities. A theoretical framework is needed, she says, which distinguishes between the enormous changes in the family, in public policy and in women's position, which have occurred from the nineteenth century to the present-day welfare state. For example, women now have new resources for political mobilization and protest and new areas of autonomy as they no longer need a husband to support them to the extent they once did. Simultaneously, the nature of their oppression has changed, she argues, from being personal and structural to being predominantly structural. But here, too, she insists on the need for concrete studies and the development of new terms. For example, she disagrees with Helge Hernes that the word 'dependence' can be used for women's different relations to the state as clients, employees, and citizens and says that women are now also in authority as teachers, civil servants, social workers, etc., over other women. Yet, if the importance of the state must not be over-emphasized, because women's oppression stems from the whole structural setting of society and overcoming it requires simultaneous changes in the different social arena, the question still remains, she says, whether and how the state can be an ally in overturning this oppression.

This theme is all the more relevant in a period when in most countries the women's movement no longer exists in the form it did in the 1970s and early 1980s. In a number of countries, as Drude Dahlerup points out, we now find different manifestations of 'state feminism' such as equal opportunities commissions, ministries for women, and in Scandinavia itself, an evermore substantial representation of women in the formal political institutions. Is this a recognition that women now constitute a separate interest which has to be accommodated? If much power lies elsewhere, in the corporate channels discussed by Helge Hernes, or in the economy, or if the specific independent effects of state policy must not be over-emphasized as Drude Dahlerup argues, the question of the state remains important in the development of any political strategy by women.

Equally important is an analysis of the development and changes in women's relationship to the state in their different social roles. This is what we find in 'Women and the advanced welfare state – a new kind of patriarchal power?' by Anette Borchorst and Birte Siim. They look in some detail at the Danish welfare state and also offer a comparative perspective referring to the difference between Scandinavia and the US and Britain. Using several categories discussed at a general level by Helge Hernes, they investigate the specific consequences of what they consider the contradictory development of the Danish welfare state. Although they disagree with Drude Dahlerup, because they maintain that state policy is of prime importance for women in both its intentional and unintentional aspects, this piece is precisely the kind of concrete, historical analysis of changes in women's position that she argues is necessary.

One of the main characteristics of the Danish welfare state is a partnership between state and family with regard to human reproduction. In Denmark as elsewhere the family is not emptied of its functions. Anette Borchorst and Birte Siim argue that the basis of the Danish welfare state is an institutionalization of women's double role as mothers and wage earners. State policy, then, in a certain sense is in advance of economic institutions for, as they point out, working conditions are not negotiated on this basis and sharp contradictions remain for women between paid and unpaid work. They trace the specific Danish experience of the increase in women in the labour market which was actively encouraged by the state and the history of the extension of child-care facilities which was a pre-requisite. They find that there has none the less been the unintended effect of strengthening male dominance in the public sphere. Moreover recent cuts in services and higher rates of unemployment have led to increasing marginalization of women in the labour market.

Like Helge Hernes they say that women have become more independent of husbands and more dependent on the state, but they suggest that a detailed examination of various welfare states reveals important differences in the degree of dependence related to women's status as employees, consumers of public services, or clients who rely on benefits. In Denmark and Sweden, where public services are considered a right, women are mainly dependent on the state as employees and consumers. In the US and Britain there is far greater reliance on husbands and/or the state for financial resources with the economic and social control and social stigmatization this implies.

In addition to 'deconstructing' the notion of women's dependency, we also find a deconstruction of the relationship between women and the state in another sense. If, as Helge Hernes and Drude Dahlerup argue, the Scandinavian welfare states have institutionalized class conflict in the form of corporatism, according to Anette Borchorst and Birte Siim, the institutionalization of women's double role as mothers and wage earners, combined with social changes, has contributed to diminishing class differences among women. Housework has become standardized as paid help has practically disappeared and the use of household technology has increased, while the double burden of paid and unpaid work is common to women of all classes. Yet they also point out that the expansion of the welfare state has led to new differences between young, well-educated women and less educated, older women, between professional women and unskilled women at the bottom of the job hierarchy, between women employed by the state and women as consumers of services and their clients. Thus the development of the welfare state has led to a new potential unity but also to new contradictions. It has vastly improved women's social and economic position and enabled women to gain more influence as workers and citizens at the same time as the locus of oppression has shifted from private to public.

My own piece, 'Women's new social role: contradictions of the welfare state', restates several of the themes which run throughout the book. These include the interconnections between the division of labour in the domestic sphere, the labour market, state policy, and the changes in the nature of women's dependence. Its approach, however, is particular. While the article discusses empirical material about women's socio-economic position in Britain, what might be called a 'macro' perspective, the concrete illustrations echo my experience and the experience of daily life of many of my women friends in combining paid work with child-rearing and general servicing work. It therefore also follows through the logic of individual women's choices, a 'micro' perspective. A major theme is that women's questions are central rather than marginal to the crisis of British society. I argue that because the vast majority of women are now in paid jobs for most of their lives, that is, at the same time as they have major, adult servicing responsibilities, the contradiction between the organization of work and social needs which has existed since the industrial revolution is now manifest in the everyday lives of the vast majority of the population. I also consider how the welfare state reflects and helps to reproduce a particular form of society and sexual division of labour, while it enters into a long-term crisis as women continue to do service work, but in new conditions. In a sense, the welfare state has sown many of the seeds of its own crisis.

Moreover, these contradictions span welfare state capitalism and really existing socialism. They can only be overcome by going beyond a 'male model of work', a model which assumes that the worker (a-sexed but in fact based on an image of a man serviced by a woman) adjusts personal life to the job rather than the job taking into account personal needs. In this piece, then, there is greater emphasis on the significance of the organization of work than in other articles in the book. The organization of work and the continuing importance of a male wage, even if women do not depend on it to the same extent as they once did, are material constraints on transforming the male role. Simultaneously, however, women's lives have changed to link the domestic world and the world of production. This influx of women into the labour force is a manifestation of a structural change in the economy as the tertiary or service sector develops, and of a fundamental modification of social relations as the vast majority of households rely on women's wages to maintain their standard of living. Yet the domestic sphere, the world of work, and the welfare state are still all organized as if women's role had not changed. Reflecting my previous work on Gramsci, I suggest that this is evidence of an organic crisis – which begins under capitalism and continues under socialism – which can only be overcome as a new mode of production which accommodates social needs is developed, and a new relation between state and society is established which enhances individual and social creativity. Thus the article combines personal experience, statistical evidence, and theoretical speculation. It tries to suggest a Gramscian, feminist materialism.

Inside and outside the home: women's experience and the transformation of public and private

A thread running through the first section of the book is the interconnection between the family, the labour market, and the state, and more broadly civil society. The organization of daily life is now intimately related to politics. The present challenge to state intervention and state services cannot be understood unless the tensions and contradictions which arise in the private sphere are taken into account in the context of the lack of fit between the organization of work, the assumptions of state services, and women's new social role. The second part of the book develops some aspects of this discussion from the point of view of the organization of the domestic sphere. The sexual division of labour in the home where women continue to have the main responsibility for management, domestic labour and caring is a primary constraint on women's presence in the public sphere and in production and on the effectiveness of state services. As the boundaries between public and private change, and women assume a greater role in production, the relatively static relations between men and women in the home come under critical scrutiny. For if neither the organization of work, nor much public policy, nor state services suit women, neither does men's traditional role. A necessary dimension to overcoming women's oppression is, therefore, a change in the domestic division of labour.

In the second section of the book we find an assessment of how women's role in the home is reinforced by material circumstances and the organization of society, that is, the material basis for the ideology and myths which surround women as home-maker. What emerges is a perspective which allows questions about what women get out of their domestic role, why they accept it, and which values are expressed in it which are of general social use. Flexibility, attention to needs, and a sensitivity to the daily requirements of individuals are attributes of women's daily lives which are essential to society. If the rationality and creativity expressed in women's choices and in their caring and service work are appreciated, we can overcome a sense of them as victims. And we can acquire knowledge which is of use in transforming state services and the world of work so that they become more responsive to human needs.

In 'Division of family labour and gender identity', which was written in conjunction with a research project into the concrete organization of family life, Chiara Saraceno provides insight into the various dimensions of the problem of overturning the sexual division of labour in the home. She describes how men and women live asymmetrical but in many ways complementary realities of the family. Thus, they live different lives both inside and outside the home. She examines differences in women's subjective experiences, in their relationship to time and to family tasks, in their realms of freedom and necessity, in the possibilities they enjoy for leisure, self-development and social and political involvement. These differences – their different identities, and their different, supposedly 'natural' inclinations – are all founded, she argues, on concrete factors such as the rigidity of work and other social structures. It is only because women's lives are dictated by 'family time', and their days are as flexible as an accordion that family needs and organization are made compatible with these structures. The contradictions which exist between family rhythms and work rhythms are highlighted by the presence of women in paid work. At the same time, this means that their lives are further fragmented.

Chiara Saraceno also points out that the alternative which exists today between caring provided by the family/woman or by the social services – an alternative which is empirically true – ignores the theoretical possibility of a greater involvement for men. Yet this would necessitate not only the radical revision of work. In a particularly sensitive analysis, she suggests that even if more couples are trying to construct a different division of labour, previous cultural models are of no use. We need, she says, to construct new modes of communication, mediation and negotiation and new relations of reciprocity. But the weight of history, the different interior and exterior worlds lived by men and women, their different family experiences, the loss of traditional sources of security, social identity and recognition, and for men the loss of privilege, all undermine the possibility of creating a new model. An argument which can be derived from this piece is that increased flexibility in work schedules and social services adapted to women's dual role are a pre-condition for a new sexual division of labour but would still not guarantee the social, cultural and psychological changes necessary to transform a realm of necessity into freedom for women. In a period of transition the crisis that runs through society cuts to the heart of the family and slices across the ties that bind men and women.

Women's experience and the social value of flexibility, attention to needs, and sensitivity to the daily requirements of individuals are linked to an important aspect of current debate about state services and the welfare state in 'The rationality of caring' by Kari Waerness. In Scandinavia as in other countries declining confidence in the professionalization and increased socialization of caring has provided a basis for arguments in favour of community care. In reality this signifies shifting responsibility back to women in the family. Indeed, a wider disillusion with state intervention in general can often be related to the experience most people have of professional experts and bureaucracy. Yet according to Kari Waerness, the family, and in particular women, have always continued to perform vital services, and it is unlikely that they could do more. Second, private care often involves oppression, injustice and constraints and is not necessarily of 'good quality'. Good family relations, she says, in fact frequently depend on the development of non-stigmatizing public services. Given women's dual role and a general acceptance that social rights are an inalienable aspect of the status of citizenship, it is unlikely that public services will or could be replaced by private care. Based in part on research on home helps, this piece examines the negative features of professionalization both from the point of view of the recomposition of women's subordination which has accompanied modernization, and the increasing power of the experts, and from the point of view of the quality of care. It is offered as a contribution towards constructing a conceptual framework which can take account of experiences which transcend the traditional and in large part superceded dichotomy between public and private. This is necessary, she says, to improve care-giving services and to reconstruct a basis of support for the welfare state.

The article also has a significant theoretical point to make. If the dichotomy between public and private is empirically false, so, according to Kari Waerness, is a definition of rationality which excludes emotions. Her discussion relates to important philosophical questions and is part of a wider debate about women's culture and traditional values. What is useful in women's experience and what is the product of oppression and subordination? How is it possible to go beyond the limits of a traditional, dominant, male culture without idealizing ideas and values associated with women who have themselves been formed in part by that culture? As Kari Waerness re-evaluates the qualities inherent in women's care-giving work as well as considering its exploitative nature, her argument is not that women's traditional culture is better. Rather, lessons can be learned from women's experience

in the private sphere, she says, which are essential for transforming public services so that qualities which have been lost in
the professionalization of care are restored.

Criticizing the traditional opposition between women's
'natural', 'instinctive', emotional approach and the male, rational,
scientific rules embedded in professionalism, Kari Waerness finds
a different kind of rationality in caring for dependants. This rationality is fundamental for the welfare of dependants but differs
from, and to some extent, she says, contradicts the scientific
rationality which legitimates the power of the professionals. It
involves rules which have to be learned and which, although based
on experience, can also be taught. That is, it is not instinctual or
natural. But unlike scientific rationality, the rationality of caring
implies flexibility and ingenuity and is not premised on excluding
emotions. Thus it is not a question of restoring the responsibility
for caring to an idealized family or women's natural, instinctive
skills but of reorganizing the public care system to give greater
weight to practical experience and personal knowledge of individual clients. She points out that this implies a major political
problem – undermining the authority of the professionals and
the power of bureaucratic control. Yet a critical examination of
women's common sense and experience could contribute to
answering dissatisfaction over current services with a more
flexible, sensitive and caring system.

A perspective which informs all of these articles is women's
continued need and desire to have paid jobs even when they have
children. Indeed in a number of countries, for example, the US
and Denmark, the rate of increase of women in the labour force
is particularly marked with regard to women with pre-school children. This change in the lives of most women is linked to an
international trend in industrial countries which signifies a fundamental shift compared to a generation ago – the increasing
difficulty of maintaining a socially acceptable standard of living
for a household if there is only one wage, typically a male, 'family
wage'. This parallels another international trend which is less
uniform but none the less significant: the increase in part-time
jobs. In the US, Britain and Denmark part-time jobs are a significant factor in the formal labour market whereas in other
countries such as Italy it could be argued that they are equally
significant albeit in the informal or 'black' economy. Moreover,
part-time work is inscribed in deep and fundamental shifts. In

some countries such as Britain and Denmark, the expansion of state services has been an important source of part-time jobs. In most industrial countries the expansion of private market services and retailing are often part of a reorganization of production which increasingly differentiates between a core, or primary labour force, and a secondary sector which is flexible to allow production to respond to irregular demand and which has often resulted in an increase in various kinds of part-time jobs.

Thus, Vicki Smith's discussion of the American reality in 'The circular trap: women and part-time work' is of general interest. In a two-pronged argument, she criticizes advocates of part-time work who suggest that it is an ideal solution for women with children who want to work by analysing how it interlocks with women's subordinate position in the home and reinforces their secondary status in production. At the same time, she examines the demand for part-time work by women and argues that given their *de facto* domestic responsibilities, such access to the labour market (the option to work part time) is important for women. While she shows that management and personnel literature makes clear the utility of part-time labour for the firm while glossing it with benefits for women, she argues that the phenomenon of part-time work cannot only be understood as a case of a capitalist and patriarchal system exploiting women for its own purposes. It is often difficult to appreciate that women want low-paid, unprotected part-time jobs or that they would prefer not to have to work full time when they are raising children, or even that they may never want to work full time given the responsibilities they carry. Her article relates to a recent discussion in the US about women and work. In the debate about achieving equal pay for women in jobs of comparable worth to those traditionally held by men, the question has arisen whether women really want the kinds of jobs that men want. Indeed, how do we know what women's real interests are in the labour market? Is it anti-feminist, or are women the victims of a traditional ideology when they wish to have time to raise children? And what are the appropriate family policies on the part of the state to raise children?

What emerges in this article is the way material and ideological conditions reinforce each other to legitimate women's secondary status. The foundation of the ideology of women's 'natural' relation to the family lies in real conditions. At the same time the expectation prevails that women can fall back on a male wage, despite the insufficiency of a single income to cover household needs and despite the increasing number of women who support themselves and their dependants. What is necessary is an analytical framework for theoretical work and political intervention which takes account of women's needs as they are today while fighting to expand their choices and options. But of course there is also another dimension to an expansion of women's freedom. The most difficult question would appear to be that suggested by Chiara Saraceno: how can the conditions be created to allow, to encourage, to force men to change, to combine their public and private lives in a different way?

When we discuss women's contemporary, multifaceted role, in the world of production, in civil society, and in the domestic sphere, we are implicitly contrasting it to an earlier role and to the view that women are confined to the home. At the same time we are challenging the idea that their 'natural' vocation is as wives and mothers. One way of doing this is to assume an historical perspective, to analyse how women's domestic role has changed, how the ideology of the housewife arose at a particular time, and to ask how the introduction of domestic appliances has affected daily life. This is what the last two pieces do from the particular perspective which runs throughout the book: the interconnections between public and private.

Today the role of the housewife seems to have little dignity, meaning, or social worth. Women more and more take their place in the world of work, struggle to create new areas of freedom and autonomy and refuse to be confined to marriages whose costs are too high. But it is wrong to reason backwards and assume that if now only a few women see being a housewife as a vocation and if once most women did, it is because they are or were simply victims of an overpowering ideology backing male dominance which depended on confining women to the home. Gabriella Turnaturi argues that if the ideology of the housewife and of the home as a haven from a troubled world as it emerged in the United States at the beginning of the century is analysed only from the point of view of women in the private sphere, we miss the way the links between public and private were in fact reinforced, and we fail to see the substantial redefinition of family, home and women's place within it which took place. In 'Between public and private: the birth of the professional housewife and the female consumer', she examines how the private sphere, together with women, are given a social role very much related to developments in the public sphere. Analysing the middle-class American woman's acceptance of a new status as professional housewife, she examines how the attribution of new social and political value to women's domestic role is related to the expansion of state activity and further industrialization. As society appears to threaten any real power for individuals and families to influence their circumstances, there is a perceived need for protection from rapid social change. Traditional institutions, the family and the home, provide elements of continuity and a new basis of social consent, but only in so far as they, and above all women, change and assume a modern, social role.

This is part of a complex process of economic and social change and is achieved with the active participation of women themselves. Contrary to much that has been written, it is argued that the home becomes less separate, alienated or isolated from society as it becomes acceptable to try to apply to the household the principles of efficiency and scientific management being applied in industry itself. The home, which is less and less a productive unit of, for example, clothes or food, now produces something of social value, for example, educated children. As women are forced from the productive sphere and the home loses its productive functions, as the devalued 'feminine' social role of culture and intellectual pursuits appears less and less satisfying, women become increasingly dissatisfied. These 'emancipated', 'uneasy' women, who seek something better, come to be considered a menace. A new, professional, job appeared, performed in and around the home, but based on values outside. This job is that of efficient manager, administrator and rational buyer. It involves planning, organization and intelligence. It both safeguards the optimal functioning of the market and public health and values. To a large extent it is created and justified by women themselves as the only way open to them to play a part in society outside. Yet if they are thus able to achieve a certain social status, it is at the cost of accepting domesticity and their role as housewives.

Shut away in the kitchen. Home as a prison. Bored and devalued. Dissatisfied and depressed. Loss of confidence. These are phrases associated with being a housewife today. Is it any wonder that what used to be considered the mark of achieving a certain standard of living and of social status is now the symbol of subordination and dependency? A few years ago in Rome there was an exhibition called 'The Rational Kitchen'. It linked the ideas of people like Christine Frederick, who argued that the home could be run along the same lines of scientific management as a factory, to the development of popular housing in Germany, Holland and elsewhere in the 1920s and 1930s. To me the models of small rectangular kitchens, with built-in cabinets and a space for everything, appeared boxy, isolated and claustrophobic. Oh, for a modern open plan kitchen linked to the other areas of the house. But wait. Those photographs of the one room in which working-class families lived – kitchen, eating, sleeping space, maybe with a toilet in the corner or in the hallway. How wonderful it must have seemed to move into a new flat, with separate rooms for each function. How happy women must have been to have their own space in the kitchen.

Part of the present political crisis is that people's needs have changed, their demands are different, and their expectations have been transformed as their lived memories are of a welfare state and urban society very different from the period when the foundations and principles of the welfare state were laid. Daily life today has something to tell us about politics. Women's lives in the home, the organization of domestic work, their desire to escape is a political factor. If they need to break out and find fulfilment elsewhere, if they have resisted political moves to send them back home, and if, indeed, the politicians no longer talk in these terms, it is because of irreversible changes in daily life, in social relations, in the relationship between life in the home, domestic tasks and life outside.

As a treat at the end of this book there is a delightful evocation of life today in a fully automated home and a portrayal of what it was like in the 1950s and 1960s in provincial France. Hélène Strohl's 'Inside and outside the home: how our lives have changed through domestic automation' is centred on the new relation between public and private which, she says, women mainly live as a contradiction between motherhood and paid work. The modernization which Gabriella Turnaturi discusses comes later in France and is portrayed differently by Hélène Strohl. She examines whether and how domestic automation has had an effect on the division and the links between home and society which have grown up in the age of the household machine. Today the social dimension has disappeared from domestic life, and there is no innate necessity for women to be at home except for caring for children. She describes the everyday language and reality of what she considers our individual appropriation of domestic technology. Far from standardizing our actions, appliances respond to the specific rhythms of the household. An individual, rational, utilitarian practice with all its responsibilities but also its freedom is substituted for the traditional dictates of community habits. Women wash clothes when the pile gets too high – not every Monday because that is the way it has always been done.

Yet somehow we yearn for that unthinking past. Now that we take machines for granted but no longer remember the hard manual labour they save us, we have constructed a new mythology, she says, of a pre-machine era. If there is nostalgia for a pre-automated past, this past is a myth which is created out of what we feel to be missing in the present. A romantic view is not substantiated by the memories of hard labour of the older generation of Alsatian women she interviewed. But our yearnings do reveal what we have lost. She describes how space inside the home was not divided for instrumental purposes. Domestic tasks such as preparing a meal provided links with the community outside, be it a visit to the butcher or a chat with a neighbour as vegetables were picked in the garden. As she traces how the whole complex of functions are redistributed, she breaks the past into a pre-machine age, an age when machines were first introduced, and the present. She contrasts her mother's generation, who absorbed domestic machinery into the traditional routine, to her own where life cannot exist without a full complement of equipment. Our imagined past in fact tells us something about the present, while the present is the basis of her aspirations for a future when life inside the home will once again be united with the world outside. Perhaps the latest technology will allow us to work from home, or to control our domestic appliances by remote control from a distance.

Women's lives: a prism on the crisis of state and society

For me one of the most striking aspects of Gramsci's work is his insistence on the enormous difficulties we face in achieving a knowledge of reality. Indeed, the only way we can understand how society is changing, what questions are being posed, and what possibilities exist to overcome conflicts and contradictions, he says, is to establish an organic relationship between intellectuals and people, between knowledge and understanding, between knowledge, feeling and passions.[9] Eschewing any populism, his argument is that society is so complex that isolated intellectuals, or politicians, must of necessity depend on information derived from the mass of the population, from daily life. Precisely such a reconstruction of the relationship between specialized knowledge, political programmes, and the lives lived by millions of people is part of the feminist project. The articles in this collection make a contribution to this project. They also provide insights which are essential in developing any political alternative which has a hope of success in countering the neo-conservative attack on the welfare state. For the achievements of the new right and the concomitant crisis of the old and new left cannot be understood detached from the fundamental transformations going on in society. These transformations constitute a challenge to a relationship between state and society, between public and private, between production and reproduction, which has marked a whole historical period. If there is an erosion in public support for the welfare state, for public policy, for state intervention in the economy, it stems from changing needs, changing desires, and changing material circumstances.

Because of the complexity of women's experience, because of the very fragmentation of women's lives, because the changes in their multifaceted role are inscribed in most of the transformations taking place in society as a whole, a critical analysis which starts from women's point of view, as varied as it is, will yield knowledge which is otherwise not available and which is essential to comprehending the current historical period. The feminist project, then, in being for and about women, implies a new world view and signals a watershed. It is an integral part of an historical transition in which contradictions between public and private – which appear in both welfare state capitalism and really existing socialism – are producing needs which are historically unprecedented, and which are inserted in the lives of millions of people. As women become full social subjects, the basis is being laid for historically unique answers to these needs. The task confronting us is to investigate the concrete conditions, in embryo within contemporary society, which can serve as a foundation for these answers; and to create the political conditions needed to allow them to develop. Yet, if these trends are in evidence internationally, the specific, historically determined forms of the relationship between public and private – the institutions, practices, assumptions, and the habits which make up the texture of social, economic and political life – differ from one country to another and require a study of national specificities and of historical differences. This anthology is offered as a contribution to developing new perspectives and enriching the collective efforts of the many people, women and men, engaged in these tasks.

Notes and references

1 'The transformation of the welfare state: dangers and potentialities for women', the Rockefeller Study and Conference Center, Bellagio, Italy, August, 1983, funded by the Council of European Studies and the Rockefeller Foundation.

2 For one of the rare times it has been, see G.A Cohen, 'Forces and relations of production', in *Marx: a hundred years on*, edited by Betty Mathews (Lawrence and Wishart 1983). In a 'Personal interlude', he explains some of the background to his book *Karl Marx's theory of history: a defence* (Clarendon Press 1978).

3 When I was on the editorial board of *Politics and power* (Routledge and Kegan Paul 1978 to 1981) conversations, discussions, and debates with Diana Adlam, Fran Bennett, Beatrix Campbell, Rosalind Coward and Carol Snee were instrumental in opening up the world of feminism to me – as were the conflicts with the male members of the board.

4 *Gramsci's politics*, second edition (Hutchinson 1987); editor, *Approaches to Gramsci* (Writers and Readers Publishing Co-operative 1982).

5 For critical surveys of this discussion see Eva Kaluzynska, 'Wiping the floor with theory – a survey of writings on housework' *Feminist Review*, no. 6 (1980) and Maxine Molyneux, 'Beyond the domestic labour debate', in *New Left Review*, no. 116 (1979).

6 See, for example, Elizabeth Wilson, *Women and the welfare state*, (Tavistock Publications 1977), or Mary McIntosh, 'The state and the oppression of women' in Annette Kuhn and Ann Marie Wolpe (eds), *Feminism and materialism* (Routledge and Kegan Paul 1978).

7 See Alberto Maria Cirese, 'Gramsci's observations on folklore' in A.S. Sassoon (ed.), *Approaches*.

8 See footnotes 28 and 45 on pp. 185 and 186.

9 I discuss this in 'The people, the intellectuals and specialized knowledge', the appendix to the second edition of *Gramsci's politics*. I am preparing a paper to explore further how Gramscian categories are useful for feminism.

Part One

The Modern State and Contemporary Society – New Insights and New Contradications

1   Crazy quilts: rethinking the welfare state debate from a woman's point of view

Laura Balbo

The current debate about the welfare state is inadequate and misleading because it has ignored women and their location in late capitalist society. If we examine women's work and the everyday coping strategies which lie behind it, we gain a better understanding about how society functions as a whole. Yet the concept and analysis of women's work today also needs to be rethought if we are to appreciate fully its relevance for the overall functioning of society. To attempt this double task, we are forced to coin new words or to give conventional words a new meaning, and we are led to look at both everyday phenomena and social organization in a new way. Feminism has often argued that women's experience and women's history can be the starting point for a new understanding of society, and it has often occurred to me that to describe living conditions in contemporary society[1] from a woman's perspective, the images and words of patchwork quilting are most appropriate: the endless sorting out and putting together of available resources, the minute coping strategies, the overall aim of survival, and the imagination, ingenuity and amount of work that these require.

Patchwork quilts – a metaphor

The techniques of quilt-making developed, initially, from economic conditions of extreme scarcity. Although quilting was an activity common to women from all social and economic backgrounds, it is not those who were wealthy or leisured that I wish to consider here. For the immigrants to America, the overworked women in newly settled land, the black women in the South, the poor white women in the mountains of Appalachia, quilting was necessary work, not a hobby. Quilts were needed to make the bed comfortable – this most important and often only piece of furniture in the house.

Much has been written recently to recapture the lives of these American women, through oral history and the history of American folklore and art, and through exhibitions and television programmes. It is the material conditions of these women's lives and the characteristics of their work – this particular and long-neglected aspect – that is so aptly described through the analogy of patchwork quilting; an analogy that is no less apt today to describe women's work in contemporary society. The passages or quotes from books about the history and techniques of quilt-making throughout this chapter serve as illustrations, drawing parallels between the everyday lives, resources and coping strategies of the early quilters and of women today.

This form of presentation, among other things, forces me to move away from the more conventional language of the social scientist and to use new words, indeed new concepts, that I find extremely thought-provoking. Piece-bags, sorting out, piecing, patching and quilting, are all words which suggest parallels to concepts that have been used (by myself and by others) to describe women's work in contemporary society: the servicing, the pooling and packaging of resources, the self-help activities, emotional work and survival networks; how women keep at their endless tasks, how they put their vision into the planning and design of their own and others' lives whose responsibility they carry.

Quilt-making entails hard work, long hours, patience and repetition. As with the work that women carry out within their families, it is mostly individual and isolated, although at times it provides an opportunity for meeting others and sharing activity. Yet it is creative, reflecting women's longing for beauty, and demonstrating their hidden and often unrecognized capacity for self-expression, communication and artistic endeavour.

Quilting was also practical. The quilters patiently preserved all materials left from the family sewing. They could not afford to waste any scraps or worn-out clothing. Out of an apparently immense variety of available fabrics they sorted and selected from what were, in fact, very limited options. They had freedom of design, but the patterns show repetition, regularity and constraints. Part of the work was boring and plain hard work: the lining and quilting, the endless stitching. Behind the beauty of the quilts we cannot fail to be aware of the long hours and the forgotten names: women's work, indeed.

The earliest quilts were known as Crazy Quilts. Women sewed odd-shaped scraps of fabric together and the result tended to resemble a jigsaw puzzle. Whenever times were lean and fabric scarce, women made crazy quilts.[2]

Patching the pieces together: needs and resources

Today, many resources are available in our society, but few live in affluence. As a result of changing economic conditions, life has become difficult for many in the middle class, and although times were hard enough for the poor all through the 'affluent years', they are getting painfully harder. Except for some groups in the population, resources never seem to be adequate in a society which demands that people constantly improve their economic and social conditions. The pressure to meet new needs, to live up to continuously rising standards, has been a crucial aspect of life in western societies in the 1960s and early 1970s. More recently, it has meant coping with the impact of inflation, unemployment and cutbacks in government spending which affect the provision of welfare and public services. In their daily lives the majority are hard-pressed and, like the quilters, juggle a variety of resources in order to survive.

Quilts as they were first made in America were the product of necessity was well as tradition. Factory-made blankets were unavailable . . . fabric was scarce and expensive, and winters were cold. Women had to reuse every available scrap from worn out clothing in their quilts, lining them with worn out homespun blankets, wool, cotton or rags and backing them with muslin or homespun.[3]

Schematically, resources may be goods and services acquired in the market, on the basis of either earnings or cash welfare provisions, or both; and in a welfare system, social services delivered by a variety of public agencies or by firms, as 'fringe benefits', in such fields as housing, education, recreation and health. A number of tasks need to be performed by the family. In today's society resources are channelled to individuals, or rather families, from a variety of external social institutions. They must choose from existing alternatives; 'combine' available resources from various agencies and institutions, whether public or private; 'adjust' them to the specific requirements of each family member, and provide services that are not available through other institutions. These tasks make a crucial contribution to both the quantity and efficient use of available resources and consequently, to the family's standards of living. It is therefore relevant to consider the family as a producer, a processor and a consumer of resources, within the larger system.[4]

Let us pause briefly here, to address a difficult terminological and theoretical issue. The word 'family' is misleading in two ways: first, it is not true that 'nuclear families' – which is what is immediately implied if we use the term – are the 'normal' or even the most frequent arrangement in our society. Second, 'family' is a charged word, which suggests that there is an almost universal form of organization to which individuals belong or ought to belong. I do not intend to deal here with the enormous literature and debate about the family – its history, and its place in contemporary society. What is important is to stress that people live in a variety of arrangements: they are singles, couples, nuclear families, single parents. They are heterosexual and homosexual couples, they live in communes and in institutions. Possibly the most important element to consider in dealing with contemporary society is that for most people arrangements are temporary and tend to change over the life cycle. However, whatever the specific arrangement, important economic and social functions take place within the basic survival units: the pooling and use of resources, self-servicing, and production. No matter how we define them, these units perform a vital function for the mechanisms we have been describing, in that they provide the context – the material and emotional conditions – for survival. 'Survival units' is thus the best term I have found yet, *survival* being the crucial word.

At any given point in the life cycle, for any particular individual or family, there is no nice 'fit' between needs and available resources. In ways which are doubtless very different for people of different social classes and races, everyone has to make the most of whatever is available. How this is done, its significance to society as a whole as well as to family units, gives a deeper and more complex understanding of the role of the state and the way the various spheres of society are pieced together; and this is what we see when we adopt a perspective which puts women's work at the centre of its analysis. For, on the whole, it is women who are primarily responsible for making the choices and arrangements, for finding solutions in everyday life. It is they who are entrusted to 'introduce some elements of order', and 'to create new designs'.

What is involved in women's work? Much planning and imagination is needed. Women make decisions on the basis of how much time they have; how much money; what distances they have to travel; who is available to substitute them, to help, to share; who needs what. There is a design, a purpose and a strategy in selecting and piecing together. Women continuously choose between alternatives, combining whatever variety of resources are available in order to maximize their value. Women must understand and assess each individual's needs, and work out how best to satisfy them. They anticipate, budget, establish priorities. They carry the responsibility for this apparently trivial decision-making process: they work endlessly at their crazy quilts, striving for balance, trying to introduce some method and pattern.

Although the true crazy quilt resembles a jigsaw puzzle in that there is no order or design to the pieces, there seems to have been from the beginning a natural tendency to introduce some elements of order into them.[5]

Frequently there were several quilting designs in one quilt; one for the patches, one between the patches, and one for the border. The quilt makers strove for balance. . . . [6]

Recent research has shown that domestic work, although different today, is no less or less heavy a burden on women than it has been in the past.[7] Estimates have been made of the economic value of this work in terms either of the hours of work provided or of its addition to available resources in society.[8] Because many goods and services are produced outside the family by other institutions (firms, schools, hospitals and so on) and because access to them requires time and flexibility on the part of 'clients', someone has to do the work of dealing with these agencies, adapting to their often complex, time-consuming, rigid and bureaucratic procedures. It is women who keep in touch with teachers and school staff, who take children to clinics and hospitals, who visit welfare agencies to obtain the family's entitlement. It is women who put an enormous amount of time, energy and resources into shopping; into the skill, knowledge and concentration required for decision making; and into the manual work involved in selection, packing, carrying home, and driving back and forth. As Weinbaum and Bridges very forcefully say:

Housewives must work in relation to schedules developed elsewhere, and these schedules are not coordinated with each other. Housewives are expected to wait for weeks for installations and repairs, to wait in lines, to wait on the phone. Changes in the distribution network and the expansion of services demand physical mobility within this less-than-flexible series of schedules. The increase in the number of services as well as shopping centers means housewives spend more time travelling between centers than in producing goods and services. The centralization of shopping centers and services may make distribution more efficient, but at the expense of the housewife's time.[9]

The enormous increase in the provision of services by the state or firms compared to that of the past has not simply transferred tasks from the family unit to other service delivering institutions. Whereas much current analysis assumes that state intervention has 'relieved' the family and taken over many of its tasks, in all cases a lot of extra servicing must be added if public or market services are to be put to use in meeting personal needs. Even services which do save a great amount of women's family labour – such as daycare centres, school cafeterias, adolescents' sporting activities – require a certain amount of extra work: children have to be registered, equipped, taken to the proper location, assisted when they come home.

This need for extra servicing is even more apparent with the growing number of those services which are intended to meet highly specific needs – therapy, counselling, training or leisure activities such as sports and art or music lessons – and which have begun to play an increasingly important role the more service-intensive our 'service society' becomes.[10] The user has to choose a specific service or a specific provider from an enormous variety of possibilities, and this requires information, skill, and entails responsibility. The service as such is usually delivered for a very limited amount of time (a few hours a week) but requires extra time, usually at home, before and after for practising, etc. The typical client very often makes use of more than one of such services: a child will perhaps play a sport, take music lessons, go to the dentist; or a disabled person will go to therapy, spend time on support activities. In order for these services to be taken up, someone has to choose, plan, make appointments, keep the calendar and put in the extra work.

One interesting aspect about how this system actually works is that 'experts' provide the specialized services on the assumption that a lot of servicing is provided by lay people (mothers, wives) who have the responsibility for daily survival: nutrition, healing, nurturing.[11] Let us be sure that we fully understand what this implies, in a context where the majority of adult women are both housewives and workers in the labour force. In describing how contemporary women deal with the issue of time and resources, this aspect needs to be given full recognition: they are dual-life women.

A labour of love

Thick quilts were called comforters.[12]

Love went into the making of these quilts.[13]

It should be obvious that the use of material having an emotional significance added a spiritual and emotional dimension to the quilts as arts.[14]

It is not, however, the double burden that I want to discuss here, or the long hours and continuous stress. Thanks to the insight and cogency of feminist research, these aspects are no longer treated with the neglect and indifference found in earlier 'scientific' studies. (Although it is necessary to repeat our arguments over and over again, lest women's conditions, such as they are, be taken for granted.)

What is important is the peculiar quality which is expected of women in this servicing work.[15] To conceptualize the content of servicing work is not easy: part of it consists of the daily chores of producing goods and services for survival – the washing, scrubbing, cooking and mending (or their contemporary forms) – much of which is hard, repetitive, manual work; part of it consists of the organizational work described earlier, which forms a large component in contemporary society – the keeping in touch with the many outside agencies which deliver services, the sorting out, the piecing and patching, and the creation of orderly patterns.

Last, but by no means least, there is the emotional aspect –

ever-present in all the work that women do.[16] The definition of needs may vary in different classes, cultures and generations: personal needs, because they differ from one person to another, from one stage in an individual's life cycle to another, or even from one moment to the next, require constant interpreting, redefinition and understanding. No amount of resources in quantitative terms is adequate to meet needs unless resources are transformed into the services each individual requires. The recognition of these unique personal needs and the ability to respond to them is what Ulrike Prokop refers to as 'need-orientation'. Although this aspect is more easily seen in nurturing activities – the 'human services' – as one distinct area of women's tasks, she argues that it is inherent in all the work that women undertake. To use her words:

The potential and ability for expressive, non-instrumental behaviour . . . is structurally rooted in the female (rather than in the male) mode of experience. . . . It would be erroneous to attribute it exclusively to processes of the hormone system, to a 'maternal instinct' explicable only in biological terms. Rather, a mode of production peculiar to women defends itself here against the patriarchal and capitalistic environment, a mode of production directed toward satisfaction of needs.[17]

I shall return to the implications of this element in women's experience which acts as a form of resistance to capitalism and patriarchy. But here, I want to discuss some of the implications of Prokop's very acute empirical and theoretical analysis. Women's work is invisible, though its worth is known to all; it is not even considered to be work, for the words which are used are love and self-denial and care for the needs of others. Its value makes it a desirable feature of women's presence in the home and in the workplace, in their relations to the immediate family, and to others in various types of social network, to co-workers and bosses.

Women 'service' when they mother,[18] make love, counsel, assist; when they arrange homes, buy food and cook meals, wash clothes, wait for a delivery, mail out bills; when they take their children to school or go to the surgery with somebody who is sick. Food sold in shops needs to be transformed into meals; cars have to be driven to take people to their destinations; the house has to be cleaned, the TV set fixed when it is broken.

It is not what women actually do that matters: the point is that unless something is added to material goods in order to link them to what a specific individual expects or wants, personal needs are not satisfied. Someone has to see to it that problems are quickly taken care of, and emergencies dealt with; that when someone needs something this is either secured, or compensation found; that longings become wishes fulfilled. Being there to wait, to listen, to respond; to attend to the needs and desires of others; to worry when difficulties are anticipated; to deal with one's own sense of guilt when problems are not successfully resolved: this is servicing. And it is best done if it is not even seen.

There was a time in New England when it was considered positively wicked to indulge in anything from which one derived pleasure for oneself. One might work to please others, but to do so for one's sake was sinful. This woman, so the story goes, had been chided by others, for the time she was spending on her quilts. So she resolved to work on her quilt only on Mondays, which was the hardest day of the week, and only after the necessary chores had been done – the washing, scrubbing, cooking, and mending, and even extra chores she imposed on herself to do on that day. Then only did she feel justified in working on her treasure.[19]

Outside the home: social threads

It has been stressed that much of women's work in the home is carried out, organized and experienced in isolation. As Ann Oakley puts it, 'Research has shown that loneliness is an occupational hazard for the modern housewife. . . .'[20] But there is also an important part of servicing which takes place in the context of extended families, neighbourhood and community groups – women's networks that have been described in sociological and anthropological literature. In working-class communities in the UK,[21] in immigrant neighbourhoods in the US,[22] in black ghettoes,[23] women-centred networks not only reproduce and strengthen bonds of affection and support, but also function to produce, share and exchange resources. The concept of servicing work applies here, too, in that so much organizational and emotional work keeps these networks functioning. Women play a major role in this as part of their everyday survival strategies. They are also aware of and sensitive to the emotional aspects of special occasions; it is women who remember birthdays and anniversaries, who mediate conflicts, and who organize celebrations and family gatherings.[24]

It is relevant to add that the very 'feminine qualities' which make women so highly valued in family work explain why they are also to be found in such large numbers in paid work in the service sector. Female skills in relating to other people, in loving, and in caring for others, are crucial in both their unpaid family work and their paid service work. As a result of their everyday experiences, and their socialization and conditioning, women are professionals at servicing. In the US, the service industry employs the most women, and in health care, the fastest growing field within this industry, women account for 80 per cent of the workforce. In the 1980s women form the overwhelming proportion of workers in a number of occupations: 99 per cent of all secretaries; 97 per cent of all typists; 97 per cent of all receptionists; 97 per cent of registered nurses; 80 per cent of clerical workers; 72 per cent of sales clerks; 98 per cent of private household workers.[25] Not only do women form the majority of workers in the service sector, they also undertake 'servicing' when they are employed in other sectors, or in jobs which are not servicing jobs as such. This has been shown in recent research, particularly in Germany,[26] which suggests that women workers tend to develop – and are valued for – 'feminine' attitudes and behaviour which link them to the particular working conditions of, say, small firms and marginal industries, where women predominantly work. As in their family work, women are not expected to measure the amount of time they give their jobs, nor to question their working conditions in the way male workers do.[27] Low pay, overtime, flexibility and good humour are all aspects of what is expected of these quite special workers.

Unseen and unsung

I have been arguing that there are various implications of a choice of perspective which puts women's work at its very centre. But is this concept – women's work – adequate? Why should we choose it rather than women's role, or position, as a privileged perspective to study patriarchy and capitalism? Marxist theory has considered the concept of work central to an analysis of capitalist society, despite the fact that, in this tradition of thought, women's work

– their labour in childbirth; their unpaid family work; their ubiquitous servicing – has been neither properly analysed nor adequately valued. In fact, most work by women is defined as 'unproductive' – a disparaging term which juxtaposes it to the 'productive', and mostly male, work in society.[28]

At the same time, recent sociological research on housework[29] has helped to rescue this concept out of oblivion, emphasizing the negative aspects of women's domestic labour – as unskilled, repetitive, and devalued; entailing little or no creativity or sense of fulfilment. Finally, feminist theory has argued against the Marxist view of women's emancipation, which is dependent on women entering the world of production, and has explored the many aspects of women's work, from sexuality to motherhood. It has investigated the subtle, sometimes contradictory facets of women's work or refusal to take paid work. In fact, by investigating the specific qualities of servicing work, aspects are brought out which clarify its relevance in the unique historical context of contemporary society. Such work makes a crucial contribution to the functioning of society, but within a patriarchal system which establishes the prevailing criteria for evaluation, its importance is not acknowledged. Not only are women exploited, but their work is devalued, by men, by society at large, and not least by women themselves.

Women bring a variety of skills to their servicing work: independence of decision-making, a vision of the overall purpose, responsibility for its final outcome and for all decisions to be made along the way. Yet its worth is not recognized, nor are the many forms it takes properly acknowledged. Names are forgotten, the enormous amount of time is not appreciated, the skills are devalued. Often women are only allowed to do certain work when all other tasks have been performed: as the New England quilter did on Monday nights.

Although women share these dominant attitudes to some extent, they are also aware of the importance of their work, how it benefits others, how doing it well is something they value for themselves. As Prokop indicates, they have developed their own system of values, and their own unique expertise and skills in the performance of servicing tasks – and whether they give or withdraw their servicing has long been recognized as an element of power.[30]

The women who made quilts knew and valued what they were doing.[31]

If women have this power, or potential power, then 'to force anonymity', to deprive them of names and voices lest they should talk about their work has been a crucial accomplishment. But changing conditions now makes this more difficult, and in our 'service society' contradictory trends are emerging. Not only do women 'value what they are doing', as the quilters did: there is widespread awareness that we only survive as human beings within capitalism and patriarchy because of servicing work, however unrecognized its worth might be in enhancing the quality of our lives. New values and new vanguards[32] act in contemporary society; because the need for and the value of servicing work are now more visible. It can no longer be taken for granted.

A secondary element is suggested by Prokop when she argues that 'a mode of production which is peculiar to women defends itself against the patriarchal and capitalistic environment, which is directed towards satisfaction of needs'.[33] In so far as they are aware of real human needs, and guided by a need oriented logic in their actions, women cannot submit to the logic of capitalism and patriarchy, and in fact are bound to resist it. In other words, in as much as they share what is expected of them – that they should satisfy real human needs – women must fail. What is asked of them in our society is impossible, and they are therefore in a 'no-win' situation. Yet, to a greater or lesser extent, they do succeed: or at least they keep trying. In order to do this, they must expose the contradictions and iniquities in the nature of the social system, and to some extent address them in the concrete experiences of their daily lives.

Again I contend that we all share the view that the prevailing rules must be resisted and defied: were capitalism and patriarchy fully developed, and their values totally accepted, no other values would survive. My argument is that it is simplistic to see a clear-cut juxtaposition of interests between those who take advantage of women's servicing work and those who do it. Women have grounded their own values, and special skills, and even whatever power they have been granted, on the performance of such tasks. Women's work reflects values which are both more progressive than the dominant mode of production, and more backwards – on the one hand they are need oriented, yet on the other they are not part of technological and scientific progress. It is this that

Prokop describes as women's ambivalence, and it forms part of a more general experience. Women's work must be devalued in terms of the dominant interests in the society; but it becomes increasingly clear how other interests also suffer within this process. Servicing allows women, and everyone else, to survive, in spite of and in opposition to capitalism and patriarchy. It is simplistic to say that women can, or even want to, do away with servicing, in its many aspects. Servicing – both to receive and also to provide services, is something we all need. We value reciprocal servicing: we call it love.

Patching, piecing and quilting: strategies for survival in a fragmented society

So far my analysis has focused on women's work, without saying very much about the conditions in contemporary society which account for its main characteristics. Are these specific to our particular historical context? And in what sense do they reflect institutional arrangements in the economic and social structure, the mechanisms of production and reproduction of resources? To deepen our insight into the functioning of society, we need a description of the processes through which resources are produced and distributed, an understanding of the various institutional forms by which society allows people to survive. The image which is suggested is that of a fragmented, intermingled system of resource-producing institutions. The state, the market, family units, and voluntary agencies, are all important components. Let us also suggest that it is an historically unique system, which has yet to be adequately described.

Conventional academic divisions and the prevailing emphasis on specialized approaches have led us to accept distorted views. Some of these emphasize the market as the main arena of production and exchange of goods and services, while others indicate that the welfare state is the main provider. In reality, neither of these descriptions fit: we are located within a highly complex system. To deal with it, we need skills which were not required in the past. Today's intricate patterns of organization in producing, delivering and using resources were previously non-existent. The images of sorting out, patching and quilting suggest strategies for survival in a complex system. In addition, the current crisis has made us more aware of the various institutional components, more thoughtful about the logic of the fragmented patterns: and we raise new questions about the nature of state policy under these circumstances. In order to do this, however, we need a much better description of how this system works. With this aim in mind, it is worth reviewing some recent contributions by various social scientists, which share this image, or have at least contributed to build it by linking areas which were traditionally kept separate.

The most directly relevant theoretical and empirical work comes from a research group at the Joint Center for Urban Studies of Harvard and the Massachusetts Institute of Technology. I shall briefly refer to some of the key concepts suggested by their work, in particular to that of M. S. Miller, Martin Rein, and Lee Rainwater.

In an essay which demonstrates awareness of both empirical findings and of the need for a theoretical reassessment, Martin Rein and Lee Rainwater have set up a 'map' of the variety of resources available in our society.

In modern societies three major institutional frameworks distribute economic resources to individuals and nuclear families: the kinship system, the economy and the state. The concrete expressions of these generalized systems are the family and household, the firm or enterprise or governmental employer, and federal, state and local governments in their relations with citizens.[34]

They then proceed to describe 'the elaborate menu of benefits in the modern welfare state', and deal extensively with the whole area of employer provided welfare benefits. The most relevant part of their argument, in the perspective presented here, deals with substitutions and trade-offs in modes of resource provision. Their concept of resources avoids the fallacy of using any single component of what they call a 'package' as the only or the most important one; on the contrary, they emphasize that

One of the striking characteristics of many kinds of economic resources is that they can be provided either directly in the form of the service or indirectly through money income. An obvious case is food: school meals, business meals, or home meals; and in principle, the government could provide an individual with money or vouchers to purchase his meals in restaurants. Thus different kinds of economic resources can be substituted for each other.[35]

This fact, that resources can indeed be substituted for each other, is something we all know from our daily experiences. Oddly enough, however, economists have been very reluctant to take this fact into consideration, suggesting only that conventional analysis of income distribution and the economic functioning of society is perhaps inadequate. As Smolensky *et al.* suggest, 'appropriately accounting for in-kind transfers alters our view of the size distribution of income'.[36] This is no minor problem, indeed. In addition, estimates of the 'voluntary non-profit sector' have to be considered, adding 'voluntary firms' to the system of resource-providing agencies.[37] Martin Rein, similarly, has dealt extensively with what he calls the 'public–private mix', starting from a critique of much conventional analysis, which, he says,

treats the economy as being composed of two sub-systems: the private sector, where the market and the voluntary sector operate, and the public sector, where the economic activities of government are carried out.[38]

He then stresses the need for a more accurate conceptualization of 'private' and 'public', and argues that in contemporary societies it is the 'mix' of the two that has to be fully taken into account. His own emphasis is on the relationship between wages and salaries, transfers in the welfare system and fringe benefits, suggesting that conventional definitions become 'fuzzy' once we take into consideration the institutional set-up of society resulting from historical change. In his words,

It is widely recognized that the societies of Western Europe and North America have changed over the past centuries from ones in which economic welfare (security and adequacy) were primarily a function of market economy and money wages, to ones in which an elaborate range of both public and private institutions serve as intermediaries between the economy and the family to ensure particular levels of economic welfare throughout the life-cycle.[39]

Looking at the same process from the perspective of those individuals and families who use resources, the same researchers have analysed coping strategies and describe patterns of 'income packaging'. These concepts can most usefully be employed in the context of the previous discussion of women's work. Anderson Khleif, in describing 'welfare families', states that:

Welfare is often part of an overall income strategy. That is, welfare's place in the strategic income planning often seems rather well thought out – not simply an *ad hoc* reaction to crisis, an only alternative, last resort, or a situation of being 'down and out'. When certain families are faced with particular problems, an element of rationality emerges; they find themselves in an economic squeeze, there is a set of resource alternatives, and there are certain family dynamics, goals and values, which are crucial to the process they use for setting priorities and making choices.[40]

Rein and Miller observe how family units 'piece together' a variety of resources:

Aside from the heavily dependent, long-term recipients, welfare women in general counted on welfare for only about one-third of family income during welfare years. . . . Therefore, an additional 66 per cent or more of family income must come from other sources. The earnings of the head of family account for approximately 30 per cent of the family's income; in addition, bits and pieces are put together from the earnings of wives and children, alimony and child support, food stamps, public and private transfers, and work-related benefits. . . . Within these diverse and complex income packages, work remained quite robust for all women except those who were heavily dependent on welfare. . . . [41]

And they specify that 'other sources include: help (reported and unreported) from boyfriends and relatives, free lunches and child-care, small social services payments, and income from earnings on an *ad hoc* or as needed basis'.

One additional comment is revealing: during the years that these women were not on welfare, 'their income packages were surprisingly similar to those of low-income women who never received welfare'.[42] This pattern is very common indeed.

By showing how family units perform tasks that are crucial for survival in this kind of society, these research contributions give support to our previous analysis of the 'patching and piecing' activities of women in their family work, their organizational work. The other aspect, adding work of their own – material as well as emotional – and how much this contributes to the functioning of society and more specifically to the economy, has long been ignored by conventional economic analysis.[43] Prior to recent feminist contributions, very few had paid attention to this aspect.

Galbraith, Burns, Becker, Gartner and Riessman are to be mentioned, not only for addressing these problems[44] but for actually claiming the worth of women's contribution in terms of what has been called the 'household economy',[45] or 'productive consumption'.[46] This is not the issue that I want to address here, however. I wish to develop in somewhat more depth the concept that I find most helpful in considering women's work, that of 'self-servicing'.

As Gershuny has stated, contemporary society is not characterized by the expansion of services. Rather, goods are increasingly manufactured to make self-servicing in the home possible: TV sets for entertainment, washing machines and driers substituting laundromats, and so on. In contrast, cinemas, cafeterias, collective transit systems provide services: but, especially in the United States, the former are by far more frequent. Looking at this process, Gershuny states that,

Instead of capital investment taking place exclusively in industry, and industry providing services for individuals and households, increasingly, investment is transferred from service industries into households, leaving industry engaged in what is essentially intermediate production – making the capital goods (the cookers, freezers, televisions, motorcars) used in the home production of the final product. This is the trend towards the self-service economy, the do-it-yourself economy.[47]

And he concludes that 'final production takes place increasingly in the home'. A table from Scott Burns' *Home, Inc*, helps us to understand how far this self-servicing had already extended at the beginning of the 1970s in the US. And Scott Burns adds,

radios, television sets, clothes washers, refrigerators, irons, vacuum cleaners, and toasters can be found in virtually every home in the USA. In 1971, almost 8 million vacuum cleaners were sold. Merchandisers found ways to sell 4.8 million can openers, 5.5 million powered lawn mowers, 8.5 million coffeemakers, 9.4 million irons, 6.4 million toasters, and almost 4.9 million electric mixers.[48]

So someone obviously uses these gadgets: by implication there are those who supposedly have the adequate skills, the necessary amount of time and, most important, are physically present to organize the functioning of the household through these various appliances, in a way that is both economically advantageous and

Product	Number of wired homes with	Per cent
Television, B&W	65,419,000	99.8
Refrigerators	65,419,000	99.8
Radios	65,419,000	99.8
Irons	65,419,000	99.8
Vacuum cleaners	61,879,000	94.4
Clothes washers	61,814,000	94.3
Toasters	61,748,000	94.2
Coffeemakers	59,650,000	91.0
Irons (steam spray)	59,061,000	90.1
Mixers	55,324,000	84.4
Fry pans	38,019,000	58.0
Color television	33,496,000	51.1
Electric blankets	33,496,000	51.1
Can openers	31,530,000	48.1
Clothes dryers	31,202,000	47.6
Room air conditioners	29,170,000	44.5
Ranges, electric	27,924,000	42.6
Blenders	26,220,000	40.0
Water heaters (electric)	22,156,000	33.8
Freezers	21,435,000	32.7
Dishwashers	19,403,000	29.6
Disposers	18,616,000	28.4

Source: *Merchandising Week*, 28 February 1972

functionally co-ordinated. As Burns says, there are millions of these 'workers without wages': women.

The same component of self-servicing is implied in the use of services. In fact, even though it is true that we increasingly rely upon services rendered by the state or by firms or by voluntary or self-help institutions, these services need to be co-ordinated and labour has to be added to actually use them. One might distinguish between institutions which require little or no integration or support from the client and institutions which deliver services that necessitate a great amount of additional work. Of the former, there are intensive care units in hospitals, providing total care, or daycare centres requiring no involvement from parents during the time the child is at the centre; of the latter, there are those institutions addressing specialized needs for short periods of time, such as psychiatric therapy, art lessons, leisure time activities. Besides that, a great amount of servicing is provided by what is called 'lay-care' in health research, or self-help in related areas.

Speaking of the health system in the US, Levin indicates that studies undertaken during the last decade here and in Western Europe form a picture of health care quite contrary to our accustomed view. We are accumulating evidence that perhaps 75 per cent or more of health care is provided by lay people to themselves and family without professional intervention . . . lay self-care practices are particularly important at the level of primary care. Lay people appear to be almost entirely responsible for their own strategies of health promotion and prevention and control of symptomatic episodes, non-disabling illnesses, and injuries, and the continuing responsibility for chronic conditions. . . . [49]

And he adds that: 'We might refer to the self-help or mutual aid groups as the second level of the lay-care system . . . over 600,000 such groups involving approximately 5 million persons.'[50] By suggesting that, in order to describe how services are delivered and put to use in our society, one needs to look at the plurality of resource rendering institutions and at self-servicing, we arrive at the other side of women's activities. Women's organizational work is a necessary link between various resources and their self-servicing is needed to add the required material and emotional work which make resources in the market or through public agencies actually available.

To briefly summarize: we live and survive by pooling external resources and by adding self-servicing in its countless forms. This aspect has long gone unseen, in superficial descriptions presenting our consumeristic, service society as one in which all goods and services can be either bought on the market or acquired through public agencies. Whatever the case, the assumption is that either the profit market or the welfare market will provide all that is needed to passive consumers – that is, to individuals and family units. What happens throughout the process has never been adequately investigated: I would suggest that women's 'crazy quilts' are crucial as a technique for survival. It is a structural requirement that women be kept busy at their piecing, patching and quilting, given the institutional arrangements that have been described as a 'fragmented society'.

Women, the fragmented society and state action

Women created hundreds of new designs. . . . [51]

By focusing upon the apparently concrete and limited aspect of women's work in our description of contemporary society, we have come to elaborate the image of a fragmented social system: a pattern of production and provision of resources that it is crucial to understand in its overall functioning, and, in particular, in relation to state intervention.

Society can be viewed as a patchwork quilt. Each single patch has a design, an order of its own; but only when one acquires a more general vision does the overall design become understandable: what is common to the different parts, what is unique to each of them, and how they are held together. Some intriguing empirical questions are then to be asked. How is a certain balance achieved at the level of each fragment, be it a family unit, a community, or an organization? And looking at state action, how does the state both use to its advantage the coexistence of different patches, and manage tensions and conflicting interests? And finally, how is it that we have been so unaware of the many aspects of this complex design? Isn't it interesting how we have all shared in the belief that patchwork quilting was a minor artistic form, showing no interest in it because it was women's artifact?

Besides the top designed layer, quilts have two other layers, the padding for warmth and the backing. All three layers are held together by the *quilting*, that is, the tiny stitches which go through all the layers and contribute the lights and rhythms of their own design to the quilt.[52]

The fragmented pattern of provision of goods and services is an institutionalized characteristic of late capitalist societies. This holds true if one looks cross-culturally at countries which are relatively different from one another, such as the USA, Britain, or Sweden. And it appears to be true, to various degrees, of past stages of consolidation/expansion/reformulation of the welfare state,[53] as well as the current stage of crisis.

The apparently enormous variety of available resources and possible combinations is deceptive, even in a wealthy society like the United States. In actuality, people act under all sorts of constraints. The class and race structure of the society and the patterns of segregation and discrimination which are grounded in it; differential knowledge and unequal access ground 'regularities' in the way resources are used. Thus differences exist not only in the amount of resources concretely available to any single individual, but in the kind of resources, conditions, and in the extent to which they are interchangeable with substitutes.

These are structural elements in the society: most important, in the light of the present discussion, it appears that the prevention and management of crises through state action may be easier under such circumstances. The fact that a plurality of resource-delivering institutions exists does not mean that state action is unimportant. In many ways state intervention affects the way these institutions are organized and operate. I have discussed elsewhere[54] how state policies affect the functioning of the family in Britain, the organization of voluntary agencies, and the state regulation of firms and the labour market. But what I stress here is that one ought to investigate the intricacies and interconnections, in order to oppose the image of the state as a monolithic institution with publicly delivered services forming the major component among all those available. One needs to understand the strains and contradictions existing within this fragmented pattern, as well as the necessary efforts by the state to achieve co-ordinated action and some degree of planning. The logic of the fragmented system needs to be investigated. Under these circumstances it is possible for the state to be highly selective: to address certain groups of claimants and not others, to finance certain sectors of the service system but not others; to deliver some provisions or benefits directly, or rely upon the market system, or make use of unpaid (family, voluntary, self-help) services.

And in fact even a very superficial analysis of historical evidence confirms this hypothesis. Looking at different countries or even a single country, over a period of time, one finds that state policies are used very flexibly. Services which were at one point delivered by the state – through nursing homes for the elderly, or mental hospitals, for instance – are being devolved to the community using unpaid family or volunteer work. Care of young children has traditionally been considered the responsibility of mothers, but when women's work is needed in the labour market, employers or state services are pushed to provide daycare. I shall not dwell upon these examples, but I would argue that nothing inherent in any specific service explains the particular historical way in which the service itself is delivered: rather, logic and interests that are generated at other levels of the social and economic system account, partly at least, for any particular choice in its mode of delivery. In all cases – let us repeat it once more – women's servicing work is required, interchangeable (provided within families, through state agencies, by the market according to changing requirements), flexible, cheap. And servicing provides not only a huge amount of work, at little or no pay; most importantly, it represents women's ingenuity in the innumerable concrete ways of piecing and patching resources, their understanding of and response to personal needs, and their ambivalence in dealing with the prevailing rules. Quilt-making is women's work, with little exception.

This does not imply that men cannot, or even do not do some servicing work: in fact, this is an important issue that needs to be explored, and one that I have been unable to do here. What I find useful in the preceding analysis is the way in which it helps to clarify the following points. First, that to assign servicing work to women in the ways which have been described is a structural device in capitalism and patriarchy, though its functions are most often looked at in ideological terms. Second, that what we know about women's work – their attitudes, choices, behaviour – should not just be seen as a result of their socialization and the value system which they are led to acquire: it is part of the material condition of their existence, of the structural set-up of society.

From the perspective of state action, particularly at a time of crisis, women's contribution is crucial in view of the more acute constraints the state has to face. In terms of what has been called the 'accumulation crisis', the more servicing work women provide, the more resources can be diverted from the welfare-service budget to sustain capital accumulation. More specifically, in terms of the 'fiscal crisis', the state budget can be manoeuvred with greater freedom if less pressure is imposed upon the state to provide services within its own apparatus. Or considering the even more general issues raised by the main proponents of the 'welfare state debate',[55] in spite of the persistence of deep inequalities and the recognition, now explicit, that such inequalities are not going to be eliminated; in spite of the open denial of what in the past had been a fundamental pledge – that the state would take responsibility for the basic rights of all citizens – how is one to explain the fact that latent contradictions have not emerged with all their socially destabilizing potential?

Obviously there are no simple answers to such questions. Once more, however, it is worth looking at things from women's perspective. It is crucial to society that they continue to do what they have always done, and are kept busy at their piecing and patching, hard-working and resourceful, in charge of the well-being of those who depend upon them and feeling responsible when they fail. Not only does women's work fill the gaps in available resources within an unequal and fragmented society, the ideology that women are by nature destined to provide servicing is daily reinforced by their concrete experience. It is not only as a result of their conditioning but because of the material conditions of their lives that women are kept – to use a traditional term – depoliticized, unaware of their power, fragmented, and invisible as a collective subject. I would suggest that beyond other more specific goals, the cutting of public services, conservative abortion laws, and ideological support for the family all have this goal in common: to keep women overburdened with the impossible tasks of satisfying needs, to deny them control over their time, energy, or choices, and to make any different pattern impossible to them. Women are indeed under attack. Should they succeed in modifying their position in the existing system, the consequences might be devastating for the continuance of capitalism and patriarchy as we have known them historically.

Notes and references

The analysis I present in this chapter owes much to the research I have been carrying on for many years now with friends and colleagues of the GRIFF at the University of Milan, and at the University of California, Santa Cruz, in 1979 and 1980. Two people in particular, Gloria Watkins and Rosa Maria Zayas, have shared so much of their ideas and experience with me. I hope they will find here something of what I learnt from them. I wish to thank them for their generosity, intelligence, and friendship.

1 My reference throughout this analysis is to capitalism, or as I most frequently say, 'late capitalist societies', both because the literature to which I relate has dealt with this particular system, and because I use empirical references to the US and western European countries in that particular historical stage. I am however most intrigued by the similarities in women's conditions to be found in the Soviet Union and the 'socialist' societies of eastern Europe, and I would contend that it would be very important to include those countries within the analysis suggested here. For this reason, I often use 'contemporary society' as a more general term. In no way am I prepared to deal with third world societies.

2   Patricia Mainardi, *Quilts. The Great American Art* (Miles and Weird, San Pedro, California 1978), p. 18.

3   Mainardi, *Quilts*, p. 9.

4   Laura Balbo, 'The British welfare state and the organization of the family', mimeo (1979).

5   Mainardi, *Quilts*, p. 20.

6   Mainardi, *Quilts*, p. 38.

7   Joanne Vanek, 'Time spent in housework', *Scientific American* (1974).

8   Gary Becker, 'A theory of the allocation of time', in G. Becker, *The economic approach to human behaviour* (Chicago: University of Chicago Press, 1978); Andrée Michel, *Les femmes dans la societé marchandes* (Paris: PUF, 1978), Alexander Szalai (ed.), *The use of time: daily activities of urban and suburban populations in twelve countries* (The Hague: Mouton, 1978).

9   Batya Weinbaum and Amy Bridges, 'The other side of the paycheck: monopoly capital and the structure of consumption', *Monthly Review*, 29 (1976), p. 195.

10 Terms such as 'personal services' and 'service society' are used here without any adequate discussion of their implications. I have dealt with these conceptual problems elsewhere. See Balbo, 'The servicing work of women and the capitalist state', *Political power and social theory*, 3 (1981).

A few general contributions are my main references. See in particular Alan Gartner and Frank Reissman, *The service society and the consumer vanguard* (New York: Harper and Row 1974); Alan Gartner and Frank Reissman, *Self-help in the human services* (San Francisco: Jossey Bass, 1977).

11 Marina Bianchi, 'The servicing work of women', mimeo (1980).

12 Mainardi, *Quilts*, p. 38.

13 Mary McKenry, *Kentucky quilts and their makers* (Luisville, Ky. (3): University Press of Kentucky, 1979), p. 133.

14 Mainardi, *Quilts*, p. 31.

15 Laura Balbo, 'The servicing work of women'.

16 Ilona Kickbush suggests slightly different terms when she states: 'Housework in feminist analysis is not just washing the dishes and ironing the shirts, it is also consumption work with women as the central mediators between the profit market, state services and the needs of the family. And thirdly, it is human services in the form of love, attention, care and sexuality.' 'A hard day's night. On women, reproduction and service society', mimeo (1979), p. 6. Now in M. Rendel (ed.), *Women, power and political systems* (Croom Helm, 1981).

17 Ulrike Prokop, *Weiblicher Lebenzusammenhang* (Frankfurt AM: Aspekt Verlag, 1976), p. 21.
18 A great deal of feminist research has concentrated on the particular and no doubt more important aspect of this complex of activities, which is mothering. I hope it will be evident why I consider it important to carry the discussion to a more general definition, though much of what has been said is relevant to my present argument. I refer in particular to Nancy Chodorow, *The reproduction of mothering* (Berkeley: University of California Press, 1978), and most recently Sara Ruddick, 'Maternal thinking', *Feminist Studies*, 6, no. 2 (1980).
19 L. Ingram Bacon, *American patchwork quilts* (Birmingham, Alabama: Oxmoor House, 1973), p. 116.
20 Ann Oakley, *Housewife* (Allen Lane, 1974). p. 88.
21 M. Young and P. Willmott, *Family and kinship in East London* (Routledge and Kegan Paul, 1957).
22 Lillian Rubin, *Worlds of pain. Life in the working class family* (New York: Basic Books, 1976).
23 Carol B. Stack, *All our kin. Strategies for survival in a black community* (New York: Harper and Row, 1974).
24 Sylvia Junko Yanagisako, 'Woman-centered kin networks in urban bilaterial kinship', *The American Ethnologist*, 4, no. 2, p. 213.
25 Louise Howe, *Pink-collar workers* (New York: Avon, 1977).
26 Marianne Herzog, *From hand to mouth* (Penguin, 1980); Ruth Milkman 'Organizing the sexual division of labour: historical perspectives on women's work and the American labour movement', *Socialist Review*, 10 (1980).
27 Rosabeth Moss Kanter, *Work and family in the United States* (New York: Russell Sage Foundation, 1977).
28 Jean Gardner, 'Political economy of domestic labour in capitalist society', in D. L. Barker and S. Allen (eds), *Dependence and exploitation in work and marriage* (Longman, 1976).
29 Oakley, *Housewife*, and Ann Oakley, *The sociology of housework* (Martin Robertson, 1974); Norma Glazer-Malbin, 'Housework', *Signs*, 1, no. 4 (1976).
30 Lois Beck and Nikki Keddie, *Women in the Muslim world* (Cambridge, Mass.: Harvard University Press, 1978).
32 Alan Gartner and Frank Riessman, *The service society and the consumer vanguard* (New York: Harper and Row, 1974).
33 Prokop, part 2.
34 Martin Rein and Lee Rainwater, 'From welfare state to welfare society' (Cambridge, Mass.: Joint Center for Urban Studies, 1980), p. 4.
35 Rein and Rainwater, 'From welfare state to welfare society', p. 15.

36   E. Smolensky, *et al.*, 'Adding in kind transfers to the personal income and outlay account: implications for the size distribution of incomes' (Madison, Wisc.: Institute for Research on Poverty, 1979).

37   B. A. Weisbrod and Stephen H. Long, *The size of the voluntary non-profit sector: concepts and measures* (Madison, Wisc.: Institute for Research on Poverty, 1977), p. 277.

38   Martin Rein, 'The public-private mix', mimeo (1980).

39   Rein, 'The public-private mix', p. 3.

40   Susan Anderson-Kleif, 'Income packaging and life styles in welfare families', *Family Policy Note 7*, (Cambridge, Mass.: Joint Center for Urban Studies 1978) p. 18.

41   Martin Rein and Lee Rainwater, 'Patterns of Welfare Use', *Social Services Review* 52 (1978), p. 9.

42   Anderson-Kleif, pp. 18–19.

43   Though it is fair to mention that increasingly attention has been paid to the money value of women's contribution to the economy, all that has been said indicates that it is its non-economic value, the non-marketable aspects in it, which are most important.

44   John K. Galbraith, *Economics and the public purpose* (Boston: Houghton 1973); Scott V. Burns, *Home Inc. The hidden wealth and power of the American household* (Garden City, NY: Doubleday 1975); Becker (1978); Gartner and Riessman (1978).

45   Scott V. Burns, *Home, Inc. The hidden wealth and power of the American household* (Garden City, NY: Doubleday 1975).

46   Becker (1978).

47   J. I. Gershuny, *After industrial society? The emerging self-service economy* (Macmillan 1978), p. 108.

48   Burns, p. 33.

49   Levin S. Lowell, 'Self-care and health planning' in *Social Policy*, 8, no. 3 (1977), p. 50.

50   Lowell, 'Self-care'. Reviewing evidence on do-it-yourself activities, Michael Marien indicates that: 'Self-help housing saves American homeowners one-third to one-half of construction costs, self-help health care cuts hospital admissions in half for some chronic illnesses, simple changes in housing design can reduce heating bills by 50 percent, and home gardens can stretch food budgets up to ten percent'. 'Towards a revolution of sciences', *Social Policy*, no. 3 (1978).

51   Mainardi, *Quilts*, p. 3.

52   Mainardi, *Quilts*, p. 9.

53   Hugh Heclo, 'Towards a new welfare state?', mimeo (1979).

54   Balbo, 'The British welfare state'.

55   For these various positions and other interpretations, see Jürgen Habermas, *Legitimation crisis* (Boston: Beacon Press 1975), and

Manual Castells, *The economic crisis and American society* (Princeton, 1980); James O'Connor, *The fiscal crisis of the state* (New York, 1974); Claus Offe, 'Advanced capitalısm and the welfare state', *Politics and society* (1972); Claus Offe, 'Structural problems of the capitalist state: class rule and the political system. On the selectiveness of political institutions', in Klaus von Beyne (ed.), *German political studies*, vol. I (Sage Publications, 1974); Alan Wolfe, *The limits of legitimacy, political contradictions of contemporary capitalism* (Free Press, 1977).

2 Women and the welfare state: the transition from private to public dependence

Helga Maria Hernes

Introduction

To many observers the Scandinavian state represents the modern welfare state in its archetypical form. In this chapter some of the institutional and organizational aspects of this state form are analysed from a feminist perspective (as well as being written from a Scandinavian one). While feminists from other western countries often look upon Scandinavian women with a certain mixture of envy and admiration, a closer analysis reveals patterns of under-representation, discrimination and subordination very similar to those found elsewhere. Although the generally low level of social inequality, combined with a highly developed and universal social insurance network, assures Scandinavian women a comparatively high standard of living, this is not synonymous with power nor with the ability to shape and influence their own status, despite the fact that the ability to influence one's status is considered an integral part of personal welfare in all Scandinavian welfare thinking. This chapter therefore addresses itself to issues of Scandinavian women's political and economic power and only indirectly to their social welfare.

Historical and social development

Historically, the nineteenth-century industrial revolution drew men from agriculture into wage labour, and this process was followed by a period of political incorporation of working-class men through the labour movement's two organizational expressions, namely the trade unions and socialist parties. There is only one process, at least in the Scandinavian context, of similar magnitude and impact, and that is the expansion of the public sector after 1945.[1] It is this process which drew women into the labour market on a large scale, albeit often on a part-time basis, and fundamentally affected families and their relationship with the state. Before turning to the major theme of this chapter, namely political development as it affects women, I shall briefly summarize the major trends in the Scandinavian family as a socio-economic institution.

The family is a changing institution both as a unit of production and in terms of lasting ties among individuals. The increase in divorces, decline in births and delay of childbearing, as well as a slow decline in the number of hours spent at housework, are one indicator. Yet more women than ever before become mothers, and the remarriage and cohabitation rates among divorced people are high.

The labour market ties of women, especially of young mothers, combined with a network of cash and service transfers, have served to undermine the economic importance of the family for women by weakening men's provider status. Economic developments, especially inflation and increasing housing costs and aspirations, have also made the one-provider family less feasible economically.[2] Social policy has intervened and is bringing women slowly towards a modicum of economic independence, although this is as yet neither an openly stated policy-goal nor a reality. In fact, where poverty exists in certain parts of Scandinavia it is concentrated among women, especially as heads of households. The major reasons for this are that a large number of women work part time and that women work mainly in low wage occupations. The combined effect of these two phenomena accounts for most of the existing income inequalities in Scandinavia today.

As an institution, the family is now even less private in terms of public control, intervention and support than it has been in the past. Yet, as this chapter will argue, the expansion of the public sector can in many ways be described as the family 'going public' to borrow a term from economics. This is true partly because of intervention policies, but even more as a result of political developments. The transfer to the public sector of such traditional tasks as socialization, education, and the care of the sick and aged has resulted in the professionalization and expansion of the kinds of work and care which, during the nineteenth and part of the twentieth centuries, was provided by extended families, clerical and secular volunteer organizations and local communities.[3] To describe the process in this way does not necessarily contradict those analysts who claim to see an increasing intimization of the family, or its withdrawal into emotional privacy.[4] On the contrary one could claim that the declining economic relevance of the family increases its emotional centrality and may thus contribute to its instability in the long term.

Political development

As stated above, political developments in the shaping of the modern Scandinavian state involve two processes, partly overlapping in time: a mobilization and incorporation of new participants into the political process, and an expansion of the tasks of the modern state. The combined effect of these two processes will be discussed here in the context of Nordic developments.

The extension of the suffrage to all men, and the rise of socialist parties and trade unions, established and institutionalized political divisions and lines of conflict which still persist. These divisions have made their mark on both the corporate and the parliamentary systems of representation. The franchise was extended to women early in this century. But the vote did not bring any appreciable changes in the overall picture for women. There followed no noticeable increase in the number of women representatives for any political party in decision-making bodies. As late as in the 1960s, women representatives were still extremely scarce.[5] By 1980, although men and women participated in elections and in political protest activities to more or less the same degree, considerable differences still exist in their relative representation in governing assemblies. There has been a remarkable increase in women's representation, especially in parliaments in the 1970s, yet the interpretation and analysis of the causes of this remain to be established theoretically and empirically. Women's entry into the public sphere can be ascribed partly to economic development, partly to pressure brought to bear by women themselves, and partly to government measures.

The other developmental process involves a transition from the liberal, limited state to a state which undertakes an increasing number of functions which used to be either regulated by the market,[6] or performed within the family and volunteer organizations.[7] Regulation and control of the market and the system of production have affected men more directly than women, whereas regulation and control of the family has affected women more directly than men.

The Scandinavian state form has several descriptive names; the name welfare state is the one used most often, yet I prefer to call this state 'the corporate, redistributive state' in order to describe its corporate organizational base (corporatism), and its central tasks of distribution and redistribution.[8] The parameters for distribution and redistribution policies have increasingly been determined within the framework of the corporate system, where women have had an even more marginal role to play than in the parliamentary system. The term 'state' as used here comprises governmental institutions, both elected and administrative, at a local and national level.

Changes in political and economic participation and in the state's area of competence have determined general political development in this century. This chapter suggests the beginnings of a framework for an empirical and theoretical analysis of the relationship between these two processes which have influenced, mobilized and partly incorporated women politically. The two developments are intimately related to one another, since the expansion of state tasks is partly synonymous with the growth of the public sector. In addition these developments have been planned and executed by a male-dominated establishment.

Corporatism as a mode of interest intermediation, redistribution and policy formation is a male world of civil servants, organizational leaders and technical–professional experts which defines an ever increasing part of the public interest. It is also an institutionalized form of group access rather than individual access to politics. As a matter of fact these 'groups', i.e. organizations and professions with political clout, have very clear gender profiles. This helps to explain, in part, women's slim chances of entering the network of political power. The organizational gender profile in Scandinavia, where we find men in economic and professional organizations with representation in the corporate bodies such as commissions and boards, and women in humanitarian and volunteer organizations without political access, is politically more consequential than in other less corporate systems. It is the powerful organizations and institutions rather than voters and political parties that have become the central gatekeepers in the Scandinavian state system, and these have not been as willing as political parties to recruit women or take up women's issues. Of all the channels of access to the political decision-making centres the corporative one is the least 'participative', the most hierarchical and oligarchical, and the most elitist.[9]

To look at Nordic corporatism from this perspective clarifies certain general trends: associations of employers and trade unions occupy 'points of far greater strategic importance for most of the battles of industrial societies than those that any other interest group can seize.'[10] These usually have few women members, and practically no women in their leadership. Those organizations where women are in the majority neither threaten the central bureaucracies' independence nor exercise any important influence and control. They have very few representational rights in terms of access. Women and their organizations are, to use Claus Offe's terms, 'policy takers' at the grass root levels. Men are represented through class organizations which have access to the political 'market'.[11] In the political process, women are recipients and men are participants. The very narrow representational base of interest representation which corporatism implies underlines and strengthens power inequalities between women and men. In corporate systems economic and political status and power are collapsed, manifest and visible.[12] From this perspective one can describe the Scandinavian state form as a tutelary state for women, since they have had a minimal role in the actual decision-making process concerning distribution. This is, of course, related to and conditioned by their weak market position and their mooring in the family. With regard to representation another significant factor is that a 'women's policy' and 'women's politics' have not been regarded as politics based on particular and separate interests until very recently. Women's policy was integrated into family and social policy and was thus of 'general' interest.[13] Women's absence from the political arena was therefore not regarded as a problem. Expansion of state tasks has to an increasing degree also affected women directly rather than just indirectly, but in different ways to those of men.

Under the aegis of social democratic governments, the extension of citizens' entitlements and participation rights has largely occurred in relation to the individual's status in the labour market, a process which, among others, has given the Scandinavian states their distinctly corporate profile. The fact that this corporate profile is also a patriarchal one is related to several factors, among these the concensus between working-class and bourgeois men about the proper place of women.[14] But there are also other historical forces at work. The production process and labour market became the objects of public regulation and support, in the form of subsidies, earlier than the reproduction process which occurred within the bounds of the family and in private agencies. Working men thus became direct and women indirect recipients of public actions and controls, subsidies and interventions. But women's massive entrance into the labour market during the past two decades – mainly into the steadily growing public sector characterized by service occupations – has contributed to their partial political incorporation. In terms of numbers, women employees now dominate the public sector and have a practical monopoly on the lower echelons and branches of the public and private tertiary sectors.

These differences between employment in the sectors of production and reproduction, important as they are, are not the major reason for women's lack of political and organizational clout. The differences in political power and in standards of living between men and women can also be ascribed partly to structural differences in labour market participation rates and patterns. Many women work part time and are therefore not as 'interesting' in terms of membership recruitment and activization for labour unions. Women work in the politically weak service sector. Very few women have positions of authority and leadership at work or in organizational life. This also applies to areas where women dominate in terms of numbers. While all these factors combine to explain some of the reasons for women's political powerlessness, I want to pay special attention here to the male world of 'production' and to the female world of 'reproduction' and their respective sectors.

Women have become clients and employees of a highly developed welfare state with a large public service sector. Their client and employee status is defined by a corporate political system in which they do not participate on a level of citizenship equal to that of men as a group. Yet women's client and employee status in Scandinavian systems is highly dependent on and defined by the corporate system. It is to a discussion of women's three statuses – as citizens, clients, and employees of the state – that we now turn.

Women's citizen status is determined in the state as a political arena and as the scene where conflicts over distribution policies are fought. Women have less power than men in parties, trade unions, the central bureaucracies and universities. Women's employee status is to a large extent determined in the labour market, about half of which is in the public sector, the arena for public consumption and indirect distribution. Women have lower worker status than men and their employment is often directly determined by public decisions. Because of their role as mothers, women's client status is more fragmented than men's. In addition, women are more likely to be clients than men, a fact which is partly explained by their longevity and partly by their higher rates of illness. Women are thus dependent on the state as provider of services and transfers, and as the scene for public redistribution.

Women as citizens, clients and employees of the state

It is this chapter's main thesis that women's lives are more dependent and determined by state policies than men's. There are several reasons for this which can be summarized as follows: first, women are more closely integrated into private and public reproduction than men, in other words into the family and the public sector – the two settings where reproduction occurs and is regulated. This affects their client and employee status. Second, women do not have the same organizational buffer as men between themselves and the authorities which can articulate and defend their interests. For example, they cannot depend on trade unions in the same way as men can. This affects their citizen status. Men's status, income and influence are to a larger extent determined by the market. It is toward the market and industrial production, and thus toward men, that labour unions concentrate their efforts.[15] Third, one possible working hypothesis might be that it is the state, more than the market, that creates and reinforces differences among women. Women's interests, which are tied to their three statuses, are not defended to the same extent as men's by interest organizations; and it is the state which, through its equality policy, now attempts to pave the way for women into the political representative system. Norway has the most developed equality policy in this respect.

The combined effect of these three factors could lead to a situation where women more than men will support and be interested in public growth and regulation, since their status, income, and influence are positively affected and dependent on a stable public sector. Our discussions of women's dependence, then, will take place within the boundaries of the public sector, the corporate system and public policy concerning women, three different aspects which, however, are necessarily connected and not always totally distinguishable.

Market and state can thus in some ways be regarded as gender specific arenas for action and problem-solving. Yet this is also an oversimplified picture since the 'men's' market is heavily dependent on state subsidies in order to survive. The tension between the productive and reproductive spheres is both primitive and complicated. It can be explained most simply by pointing out the fact that the one sphere's activities are considered a contribution, while the others are considered as costs in relation to the national product. Roughly speaking one can say that men dominate on the income side and women on the expense side, partly because much of women's work, both paid and unpaid, is either not counted in the national product or because it also counts as public expense in the form of transfers. This is further underlined by economic theory which misrepresents the public sector's contribution to, and large investment in, the private sector, and strongly overestimates the private and the industrial sectors' contribution to the public good. The invisibility and misrepresentation of women's work is thus both a question of unpaid work – which women's research has pointed to at great length – and of paid work in the public sector – carried out predominantly by women – as a contribution to the producing sectors' productivity and efficiency.

In Scandinavian countries the transition from women's unpaid family work to paid work has, to a greater extent than elsewhere, also been synonymous with their employment in the public rather than the private sector. In principle this work can be and in many other western countries is organized privately. I refer here to schools, hospitals, nurseries, homes for the aged, etc. In Sweden more than 50 per cent and in Norway about 50 per cent of all workers in the public sector are women. Service work in general is dominated by women in both the private and public sectors. In

Norway, 80 per cent of all women who have paid work (90 per cent in Sweden) do private as well as public service work of some kind, as cleaning women, saleswomen, hairdressers, in travel bureaux etc. In all western countries one sees a trend of reproduction 'going public', but in Scandinavia this has to a greater extent than elsewhere meant its *'Verstaatlichung'* – its taking over by the state. It is this aspect which interests us in this chapter. This process is by no means finished, complete or one-dimensional, and as Laura Balbo, among others, argues in this volume, it is this incompleteness of the process which makes life difficult for women. The difficulty lies, in the Scandinavian system at least, in the fact that the expansion of public consumption and public services, which has brought women into the public realm as workers, is not necessarily synchronized with the expansion or the scope of redistribution and improved social services which is mainly addressed at and builds upon an idea of women clients as mothers and housewives. This lack of synchronization and great fragmentation of partly contradictory rules, regulations, transfers, and support systems has its final cause in women's absence from and distance from policy-making arenas.

Yet women's absence from the public discussion of more or less ideological matters reflects itself also in the 'crisis of the welfare state' debate. To the extent that the welfare state's 'crisis' is regarded as *financial*, women will be affected more than men by attempts to solve the crisis through budget cuts. To the extent that the 'crisis' is regarded as a crisis of *legitimacy*, it is women who, through their demands and their support, can maintain belief in the state as opposed to the market as problem solver. If one regards the 'crisis' as mainly a problem of governmental *overload*, women will be affected if one solves the problem by transferring services back to the family and to the market, a process which would affect women as employees and clients.

A relationship of mutual dependency develops between women and the state, and this can in part be explained by the fact that the market as an institution has played a more marginal role in most women's lives compared to the family and the state. Of course women also have a long history as underprivileged workers subject to the ups and downs of the labour market in the private sector. Yet their 'special' (i.e. non-male) worker status has strengthened their ties to the state. The incorporation and *'Verstaatlichung'* of social reproduction involving continual daily renewal has created paid work for women in the social, health and educational sector. Biological reproduction over generations has been affected and controlled by social and family policies which have defined women's client status through transfer payments and services. Neither the process of 'job creation' in the service sector nor the process of becoming clients have given rise to patterns of organization as strong and as integrated as men's participation in industrial production. Nor has it resulted in representation in political bodies or in positions of authority as it has for men, i.e. the integration of working men's organizations into the political system.

In contrast to the development of organizations connected to the sphere of production where a trend toward consolidation and corporation has been evident, the transfer of reproduction to the public sector has been accompanied by fragmentation. The transition from family and volunteer organizations to state, i.e. from private to public control, has progressed unevenly so that organization of all the various private, semi-public and public types of labour is difficult. Women's roles as worker, paid or unpaid, as client of the state, and as consumer of public services, are much less cohesive and more fragmented than is the case for men. Tove Stang Dahl's model showing the tripartite arrangement of maintenance and dependence within the family illustrates this situation.[16] The lives of individual women are influenced not only by the husband's income, but also by his and their own status as employees, and by their positions as mothers. For women with family obligations the time budget is at least as influential as the financial budget and is often even more disjointed. Fragmentation with regard to central spheres of activity and areas of responsibility is more prominent in the lives of women than in those of men, and this disunity is again reflected in their own organizations which, so to speak, incorporate their lack of influence and powerlessness.

Women's low citizen status is reflected in their limited level of representation in, and their absence from, decision-making bodies. This, together with their increased dependence on state authorities, which reflects the transition from private to public patriarchy, is important from the point of view of power. The central questions in this context are these. What are the interests of women and where and how can they be incorporated? How can politicization of reproduction be utilized as a basis for organization? Has the difference in status between the productive and the reproductive sphere arisen from sex-determined contradictions, and are these then of a temporary or a permanent nature? Is gender now the most basic conflict dimension? And if gender rather than class is regarded as a central conflict dimension in politics, what does this mean in terms of its incorporation into the corporate power structure? It is to this question we must turn in order to discuss the organizational aspects of women's citizen status.

Scandinavian corporatism is the product of protracted social democratic rule, an institutionalization and legitimation of the class conflict at its most civilized and refined. Yet from the point of view of new groups, new issues and new alignments wishing to enter the political scene, it is important to point out with the Norwegian social scientist Johan P. Olsen that 'cleavages, identities, and powers have to a large extent been taken as given'.[17] And women pose a great challenge to the political system both in terms of the demands of representation of individuals and in terms of the new issues.

In Rokkan's work incorporation refers mainly to the inclusion of new groups after these received the right to organize themselves and to vote. He does not connect this process to the extension of policy areas.[18] Incorporation describes the organizational structure of mass participation, which leads to an integration into political life and later to representation in decision-making organs and culminates in the conquest of power positions so that the working classes' representatives become policy makers. State regulation of new areas – the development of welfare policies – are in Rokkan described implicitly as a result or consequence of mobilization. It is argued in this chapter that, at least with regard to women, mobilization and politicization of new policy areas alternate with each other, so that women's mobilization to a great extent can also be interpreted as a result of this politicization. It seems clear in any event that the sequence of these events is different for women than it was for men.

Neither incorporation, i.e. combining in large women's organizations, nor the suffrage have in the case of women led to their integration into the political system, but more often to separation and separatism. Women's large organizations, despite their size and level of activity, were not regarded as politically relevant and were placed in the cultural category or 'segment', to use Rokkan's schematic description of the different sectors in society. Women's organizations incorporated the complementary role and the activities of women which belonged to the traditionally private sphere. These organizations were not, like the economic interest organizations, drawn into the corporate network, not even after their areas of concern and work became subject to more and more regulations and controls. Housewives have therefore remained politically less active than most other social groups, while women workers did not get integrated into trade unions' decision-making forums on an equal footing with men. Women have therefore had difficulties in getting represented in decision-making forums. Their organizational experience was not considered politically relevant on the national level, although it was to some extent at a local level.

Women became a part of the representational system only very slowly, yet they more and more often became the object of tax and social policies which they themselves were not invited to shape politically. Areas which are of direct concern to women's lives became the object of political decisions before women themselves were a part of the decision-making apparatus. This was not considered problematic because women were not defined as a relevant interest group with separate representational claims. One could therefore state that women became mobilized by public policies, while Rokkan postulates that in the case of men they had time to organize and integrate into decision-making bodies before this development of the state's welfare policy began in earnest.

Summarizing the changes in the relationship between state, market and family which have characterized much political development in the post-war period, one can say that these changes have brought into focus two dimensions which can give and have given cause for political conflicts. Until now, however, these are only intermittently regarded as gender relevant or gender specific. I am referring to the two types of mutual dependence which have shaped women's lives: that between public and private reproduction (the family and the state), and that between production and reproduction, roughly the primary and secondary in the tertiary sectors of the economy, with much of the latter in the public sector. Both forms of mutual dependence can give rise to the development of political interests on the part of women and shape their profiles as citizens of the modern state. Both have tended to increase women's dependence on the state rather than the family and the private labour market.

Women's political history is closely tied to the second phase of the welfare state, a phase which has weakened men's provider role by strengthening women's client status and employee status. In this context it is irrelevant whether and to what extent this was the intention. Women's collective status along all three dimensions (citizen, client, employee) is of course lower than men's. Yet it is of decisive importance that women have made the transition from being powerless to having little power. These are two significantly different stages of political development. The difference lies in the fact that women are in the political arena rather than outside it. They participate without having influence commensurate with their social contribution. They participate in political battles which they usually lose, partly because they are outnumbered. Yet the most important reason for 'losing' is probably the fact that few political battles or conflicts appear clear cut gender issues. Gender is in other words often not an explicit, legitimate, conscious political dimension in politics. The next two sections will discuss to what extent this has been changing in Scandinavian politics.

Women's dependence on the state

The transition from private to more public forms of dependence accentuates inequalities in terms of power which have existed in the family based on men's provider status and has moved them to the public sector where they become a part of organizational hierarchies. Incorporation into the public sector of reproductive activities has not led to women taking public control of those sectors dealing with reproduction. The mutual dependence between production and reproduction has become more visible in the public sector than it was before, but the unequal distribution of power between women and men has been confirmed and even ossified. Dependence seems to change its character when it becomes public and subject to regulation and support. Moving dependence between individuals and groups to the public sector makes it more visible and seems simultaneously to emphasize the economic bonds and to misrepresent or make invisible the social bonds between these individuals and groups. What is most important in our context is the fact that one's status as citizen is strongly affected by one's status as participant in the labour market and as client of the welfare system. This process seems also to have had mobilizing effects on women, especially because their integration and incorporation has not only had positive consequences for them.

The welfare state as we know it today in northern and central Europe has in its second wave of incorporation of formerly unregulated activities affected women more than before. The first wave of reforms affected mainly market activities and thus mainly men, leading to extensive organizational developments especially in the form of trade unions and employer associations. The second wave has incorporated reproductive areas, such as maternal health, childcare, care of the aged and sick, etc., socialization and schooling. All this work used to be carried out by women within the family or by charitable private organizations run by women. Women have thus had great experience in self-organization both across and within their own classes. This shift from the private to the public network of dependency and mutual help has not been complete in all areas and one still relies heavily on the family to provide basic services as well as to organize the use of such services. This work is still mainly carried out by women. It is unclear whether this incompleteness of the shift from private to public is meant to be permanent or not. Volunteer organizations have suffered varying fates, to which we will return below.

This development means a shift from private to public dependence for women when it comes to financial support and services. Women are no longer solely dependent on a private provider and begin to direct their demands for support and services to the public sector. State intervention in the form of support and control is the result. Welfare states differ according to the extent of their support system. Most have childcare programmes, yet by no means on the level with East European policies. The major development from the point of view of women's economic independence from individual men, has been the direct receipt of wages, transfers and services. However, there are great differences among types of dependencies among groups of women. The major point is a loosening of private ties of dependence and a strengthening of public ties of dependence. In none of the western welfare states are women as involved as men in the politics of redistribution. The organizations which control these policies are organizations tied to production not to reproduction. The system of corporate policy making which is characteristic especially of the

Scandinavian states strongly underrepresents women in the decision-making process.[19] Women have become clients without having gained the status of citizen. Women outside the labour market, especially poor women, have extremely low status as citizens. It remains to be seen whether increased labour market participation will increase women's political participation and power. Most politically relevant forms of organization have had their basis in the labour market. The women's movement has not.

The growth of the public sector as a labour market circumscribed by the state is another aspect of this development, especially relevant for women since they have filled many of the jobs created. Women are, in other words, also dependent on the state as a major employer and their interests are clearly tied to growth in the public sector for this reason as well. Most of the professions and semi-professions connected to the public sector are dominated by women and it is the contention of this chapter that this also affects women's relation to the state. As professional employees of the state women become advocates of women as clients and the process of their professionalization will be affected by this. As citizens they will be required to take a stand on political decisions affecting their status as employees and the social services provided through their work. Here the three roles can come most clearly into conflict with one another.

Women and political power

We have argued in the foregoing (perhaps somewhat too strongly) that women have been the object of welfare policy and not its creators. Yet women's organizational history shows the role they played in setting the groundwork for much later welfare policy.[20] We have also argued that state policy has contributed to mobilizing women politically. Yet if through its policy of redistribution and through the growth of the public sector the state has had a decisive effect on the mobilization of women, then women's organizations and the new women's movement have concentrated on giving this mobilization form, scope, political content, and direction. We return now, therefore, to a short discussion of women as political actors.

Political participation occurs in three different arenas: in elected bodies dominated by political parties and legitimized through constitutions and the democratic process; in corporate bodies dominated by economic organizations and public bureaucracies, legitimized through custom and long social democratic rule; in political movements characterized by *ad hoc*, issue-oriented political activities, not legitimized or institutionalized yet popularly accepted. Any discussion of women's political power must take into account these different types of institutional and organizational settings. Women's chances of gaining power are very different in these settings and not surprisingly it is in the arena with least institutional power, namely the movement arena, that women are most active participants.

When I speak of political power for women I am referring to two aspects and expressions of power: the influence over policy issues and the control of power positions. These two are of course related, yet women's organizations differ in their emphasis and strategy. The new women's movement has been most interested in influencing the political agenda through political agitation and other forms of movement politics. Trade union women and professional women have been interested in gaining access to the corporate centres of decision making. Party women of all political persuasions have been interested in increased political representation for women. Surprisingly, there has been little conflict among these three different groupings, in part because there exists overlapping membership especially on the left. Overlapping membership and agreement on basic issues have formed the basis for alliances among groups of women. These potential and real alliances form a countervailing power against women's alliance with and dependence on the state which we have analysed in the first sections of this paper.

Given their weak power position as a group, women will remain the less powerful partner in any alliance with the state as long as their status as citizens does not improve. Given the present power constellation such an alliance will prolong and strengthen women's client status at the expense of their citizen status. This is true even though women may conquer some few key positions within the central bureaucracy.

The women's movement has chosen separatism, i.e. alliances among women, as its basic strategy. The reason for this is the strong belief that separatism is essential for establishing a common consciousness, a common identity and autonomy as a group. Recent Scandinavian women's movements have all been leftist oriented and have chosen to co-operate with less radical women on single issues rather than co-operating with other more male-dominated social movements. This trend is now being reversed by the peace movement. There has been a division of labour between feminists and other politically active women and trade union women. Feminists have 'specialized' in defining issues and arguments while party and trade union women have been willing to fight for political representation in decision-making bodies and there to launch feminists issues. It is obvious that both have been forced to make political compromises through these alliances. Yet there has been basic agreement that sexual politics (abortion, violence against women, incest, pornography) and what has been termed the 'organization of daily life' (symbolized mainly by the fight for a six-hour workday, by childcare demands and the fight for equal wages) are the basic issues. One has agreed about basic issues and disagreed about final goals and strategies. I would argue that this agreement among women of rather different persuasions has its ultimate cause in Scandinavian welfare policy which has shaped women's common client status in strong pronatalist protection policies. Women are now uniting to gain control over those issues which affect them most.

Yet obviously arenas, issues, and strategies are connected. Issues concerning sexual politics have originated in the women's movement but have made their way into party politics at an amazing speed. They are ideological issues par excellence. 'Organization of daily life' – issues are much more costly economic issues which challenge the major participants in corporate politics, namely trade unions and employer organizations. The attempt to restructure the basic division of labour between family and labour market on the one hand, and women and men on the other, now cuts deep into the political agenda and is at the core of gender politics in the corporate system. Conservative women and radical feminists co-operate on issues of sexual politics; socialist feminists and social democratic women co-operate on issues such as the six-hour day and threats to the welfare system due to the economic crisis. These are thus the beginnings of a 'gender-bloc', women fighting for women's issues across other political divisions.

Yet a 'gender-bloc' as an integrated dimension of the core political system dominated by men is far from being a reality. Women's issues are most visible and apparent in movement politics and least visible in the corporate system of social and economic planning. Within the confines of the corporate system women are still mainly the object of policy, and dependent on the foresight and benevolence of male decision makers. Yet the separatism of the women's movement has proven to be an effective strategy in terms of influencing the political agenda. The integration strategy of party women has led to the world's highest rates of parliamentary representation for women. However, not even in the Scandinavian context is there as yet clear evidence of what women's entry into the public realm and their increasing political participation will bring in terms of political changes.

There has been scholarly and public debate during the past decade as to whether the 'post-industrial society' harbingers a change in public values away from an emphasis on productivity and growth towards concerns with the quality of life. It will be interesting to see whether women's participation in politics and their attitudes towards political issues are more representative of these 'post-industrial' values than men's and whether this has had any political effect. There is some evidence that women give stronger priority to social policy than men, and that they have different attitudes towards defence policy and spending than men. But women have not yet had enough positions of political power to affect political outcomes. In terms of values it seems quite clear that the modern welfare state, with its incorporation of activities which until recently were limited to the confines of the family, will have to deal with the question of emotional health to a greater extent than it did before. Public concern with neighbourhood organization and local networks is some indicator of this development. Among popular movements the women's movement has been the strongest exponent of a less rigid division between the private and the public sphere. The policies and economic developments which have brought women into the public sector were largely controlled by men. These same policies contribute to women's mobilization and will in time affect their status as citizens and give them political power. Only then will their effect on the contents of policies be discerned and differences between men's and women's political priorities be revealed.

Notes

This paper is a substantially revised edition of my article 'Offentliggjøringen av familien' which appeared in a festschrift for Professor Harriet

Holter, Oslo 1982. I want to thank Hilde Bojer, Harriet Holter, Anne-Lise Seip, Kari Skrede and Natalie Rogoff Ramsøy for their comments.

1   Daniel Tarschys, *Den Offenttiga Revolutionen* (Stockholm: Liber 1978); Jürgen Kohl, 'Friends and problems in postwar public expenditure development in Western Europe and North America', in Peter Flora and Arnold Heidenheimer, *The development of Welfare States in Europe and America* (Transaction Books: 1981).

2   Kari Skrede, 'Family policy in relation to changes in family structure and the distribution of income', Notat 83:1 (Oslo: Institute of Applied Social Research 1983)

3   Helga Maria Hernes, *Staten: Kvinner igen adgang?* (The state: no access for women?) (Oslo: Universitetsforlaget 1982); Flora and Heidenheimer, p. 8.

4   Harriet Holter, *et al.*, *Familien i klassesamfunn* (The family in class society) (Oslo: Pax 1976), Hildur Ve Henriksen and Harriet Holter, 'Family policy in Norway' in Jessie Bernard and Jean Lipman Blumen, (eds), *Women and social policy* (Sage 1979).

5   Harriet Holter, *Sex roles and social structure* (Oslo: Universitetsforlaget 1970): Elina Haavio-Mannila, 'Sex roles in politics', *Scandinavian Political Studies* (Oslo: Universitetsforlaget 1975).

6   William J. Baumol, *Welfare economics and the theory of the state* (Cambridge, Mass.: Harvard University Press 1967).

7   Hernes, *Staten;* Helga Maria Hernes, 'The role of women in voluntary associations', (Strasbourg: Council of Europe, 1982); Flora and Heidenheimer.

8   Hernes, *Staten;* Hernes, 'The role of women'.

9   Reginald J. Harrison, *Pluralism and corporatism* (George Allen and Unwin 1980), p. 187.

10   Suzanne D. Berger, (ed.) *Organizing interests in Western Europe* (Cambridge University Press 1981), p. 13.

11   Claus Offe, 'The attribution of public status to interest groups: observations on the West German case', in Berger, p. 138.

12   Hernes, 'The role of women'.

13   Henricksen and Holter.

14   Heidi Hartman, 'The unhappy marriage of marxism and feminism', in Lydia Sargent (ed.), *Women and revolution* (Boston: South End Press 1981).

15   Adam Przeworski and Michael Wallerstein, 'The structure of class conflict in democratic capitalist societies', *American Political Science Review*, **76**, no. 2 (June 1982).

16   Tove Stang Dahl, 'Women's right to money', *Working Papers in Women's Law*, no. 1 (Oslo September 1982).

17 Johan P. Olsen, *Organized democracy* (Bergen: Universitetsforlaget 1983), p. 31.
18 Stein Rokkan, Introduction to Seymour Martin Lipset and Stein Rokkan, *Party systems and voter alignments* (New York: The Free Press 1967) and Stein Rokkan, *Citizens, elections, parties* (Oslo: Universitetsforlaget 1970).
19 Helga Maria Hernes and Kirsten Voje, 'Women in the corporate channel', *Scandinavian Political Studies* (1981).
20 Hernes, *Staten;* Hernes, 'The role of women'.

References

Balbo, Laura, 'Crazy quilts', in this volume.
Baumol, William J., *Welfare economics and the theory of the state*, Cambridge, MA: Harvard University Press 1967.
Berger, Suzanne D. (ed.), *Organizing interests in Western Europe*, Cambridge: Cambridge University Press 1981.
Cameron, David R., 'On the limits of the public economy', *Annals*, AA PSS, **459**, January 1982.
Dahl, Tove Stang, 'Women's right to money', Working Papers in Women's Law, no. 1, Oslo: September 1982.
Flora, Peter and Arnold Heidenheimer (eds), *The development of welfare states in Europe and America*, London: Transaction Books 1981.
Haavio-Mannila, Elina, 'Sex roles in politics', Scandinavian Political Studies, Oslo: Universitetsforlaget 1975.
Hancock, Donald, 'The political management of economic and social change: contrasting models of industrial society in Sweden and West Germany', *Annals*, AA PSS, **459**, January 1982.
Harrison, Reginald J., *Pluralism and corporatism*, London: George Allen and Unwin 1980.
Hartmann, Heidi, 'The unhappy marriage of marxism and feminism: towards a more progressive union', in Lydia Sargent (ed.), *Women and revolution*, Boston: South End Press 1981.
Henriksen, Hildur Ve and Harriet Holter, 'Family policy in Norway', in Jessie Bernard and Jean Lipman Bluman, *Women and social policy*, London: Sage 1979.
Hernes, Helga Maria, *Staten: Kvinner ingen adgang?* (The State: No Access for Women?) Oslo: Universitetsforlaget 1982 (a).
Hernes, Helga Maria, *The role of women in voluntary associations*, Council of Europe, 1982 (b).
Hernes, Helga Maria and Kirsten Voje, 'Women in the corporate channel', Scandinavian Political Studies, 1980.

Holter, Harriet, *Sex roles and social structure*, Oslo: Universitetsforlaget, 1970.

Holter, Harriet, *et al.*, *Familien i klassesamfunn* (The family in class society), Oslo: Pax 1976.

Kohl, Jürgen, 'Trends and Problems in postwar public expenditure development in western Europe and North America', in Peter Flora and Arnold Heidenheimer, *The development of welfare states in Europe and America*, London: Transaction Books, 1981.

Jonung, Christina, 'Kvinnorna i Svensk Ekonomi', Lund, 1982. Nationalekonomiska institution, Særtrykk nr. 50.

Offe, Claus, 'The attribution of public status to interest groups: Observations on the West German case' in Suzanne Berger (ed.), *Organizing interests in Western Europe*, Cambridge: Cambridge University Press 1981.

Olsen, Johan P., *Organized democracy*, Bergen: Universitetsforlaget 1983.

Przeworski, Adam and Michael Wallerstein, 'The structure of class conflict in democratic capitalist societies'. *American Political Science Review*, **76**, no. 2, June 1982.

Rokkan, Stein, 'Introduction', in Seymour Martin Lipset and Stein Rokkan, *Party systems and voter alignments*, New York: The Free Press 1967.

Rokkan, Stein, *Citizens, elections, parties*, Oslo: Universitetsforlaget 1970.

Skrede, Kari, 'Family policy in relation to changes in family structure and the distribution of income', Oslo: Institute of Applied Social Research, Notat 83:1.

Tarschys, Daniel, *Den Offentliga Revolutionen*, Stockholm: Liber 1978.

3   Confusing concepts – confusing reality: a theoretical discussion of the patriarchal state

Drude Dahlerup

The concept of patriarchy

Some of the most important theoretical discussions in women's studies today are centered around the concept of patriarchy. Ten years ago we all talked about 'women's oppression', and in the 1960s the feminist movement and feminist scholars – at least in Scandinavia – started talking about '*mandssamfundet*', the male society. Yet none of these concepts was invented in the 1980s, 1970s, or 1960s respectively, and individually, feminists have used them in previous periods. It is only during this second wave of feminism however, that these concepts have come into more common use. Feminist scholars and the feminist movement in general now use these concepts in the theoretical discussions about the basis for women's subordinate position as a second sex – stressing male domination as an integrated *system*.

Originally, the concept of patriarchy was used to denote, for example, a society ruled by elderly men, or more simply, the feudal rule of the father as head of the household over 'his' woman, children, labourer and servants.

In the present discussion, however, the concept of patriarchy is used to denote the subordination of women, and it is on this interpretation that the following discussion is based.

Patriarchy is the opposite of matriarchy, the third possibility being a truly egalitarian society in which no gender/sex dominates the other. The present and historical prevalence of patriarchy is overwhelming. Rosaldo and Lamphere conclude:

Everywhere we find that women are excluded from certain economic or political activities, that their roles as wives and mothers are associated with fewer powers and prerogatives than are the roles of men. It seems fair to say then, that all contemporary societies are to some extent male-dominated, and although the degree and expression of female subordination vary greatly, sexual asymmetry is presently a universal fact of human social life.[1]

Anthropologists differ in opinion about the existence of early matriarchal societies. Several scholars support the theory that matriarchal societies of some kind existed in the Mediterranean area three to four thousand years ago. Yet the basic problem is that of defining a matriarchy or patriarchy. Is a matrilocal society, that is, a society in which the bridegroom moves to the house of the bride's family, a matriarchy? Or is it a matrilineal society, in which property descends from mother to daughter?

No matter what the anthropologists conclude, the idea of possible matriarchal societies somewhere in history is stimulating, since it challenges the idea of women's subordination as natural. Even if no true matriarchal society, nor any true egalitarian society can be found, the variations in men's and women's positions in various known cultures throughout history are big enough to prove that patriarchy is a cultural, not a natural phenomenon.

Definitions of patriarchy

Let us turn to recent definitions of patriarchy. Goldberg defines patriarchy as 'any system of organization (political, economic, industrial, financial, religious or social) in which the overwhelming number of upper positions in the hierarchy are occupied by males'.[2]

Other scholars include the relation between men in the definition. In her well-known article about 'the unhappy marriage' of marxism and feminism, Heidi Hartmann defines patriarchy as 'a set of social relations between men, which have a material base, and which, though hierarchical, establish or create interdependence and solidarity among men that enable them to dominate women'.[3] Brita Gulli argues that men's domination of women does not rest on solidarity among men, but rather on competition among men.[4]

Common to all definitions of patriarchy is, however, the focus on men's power, authority or dominance over women.

Contrary to Goldberg's definition, which is purely nominal, Hartmann's and Gulli's definitions include the question of the basis of patriarchy. What is patriarchy's foundation? The new discussion of patriarchy focuses on that particular question. But before we proceed to those problems, some methodological questions must be raised:

Patriarchy – a universal concept?

The present discussion aims at constructing a *real definition* of patriarchy – a concept which includes some statements about the why and how of patriarchy. The first question is, however, whether we are trying to construct a universal concept of patriarchy, that is, a concept that will cover all kinds of oppression of women in all kinds of societies. This would be an effort to conceptualize male dominance over women not just in feudal and capitalist societies, but also in developing countries and in the countries of state socialism such as in Eastern Europe and the Soviet Union.

The fact that male dominance seems to be somewhat universal speaks in favour of constructing a universal concept. A universal concept of patriarchy implies that male dominance is not just an effect of, for instance, capitalist society, or a left-over from feudalism, but an independent structure of its own.

The problem with such a universal concept is that it might obscure the tremendous variations in women's positions and in the forms of male dominance. This is the reason why Sheila Rowbotham rejects the notion of patriarchy as an ahistorical concept, the construction of which hinders, rather than helps, our understanding of the relationships between men and women.

'Patriarchy' implies a structure which is fixed, rather than the kaleidoscope of forms within which women and men have encountered one another.

She adds that the concept of patriarchy does not carry any notion of how women might act to change their situation.

Nor does it even convey a sense of how women have resolutely manoeuvered for a better position within the general context of subordination – by shifting for themselves, turning the tables, ruling the roost, wearing the trousers, hen-pecking, gossiping, hustling or (in the words of a woman I once overheard) just 'going drip, drip at him'.[5]

This criticism may be relevant in some cases. But in my opinion, an ahistorical approach is not an inevitable consequence of choosing to construct a universal concept of patriarchy.

Let me first stress that a universal concept of patriarchy does not imply that all societies are and always have been patriarchal. Rather, it is a universal concept to cover all societies of male dominance. Second, a universal concept of patriarchy indicates that we in our research are trying to understand some of the common elements to all societies of male dominance. But we must not stop at that. The next step is to develop a *typology of patriarchies*. Unless we develop an understanding of different types of patriarchies, we risk ending up with biology as the only determining factor. Consequently, in the present discussion of patriarchy, one will find concepts like 'capitalist patriarchy', 'feudal patriarchy', 'patriarchal horticultural societies/matriarchal horticultural societies', 'welfare state patriarchy', or 'reorganized patriarchy'.[6]

The crucial question is to understand how patriarchal structures interact with changing socio-economic conditions: to understand why, how and in what forms male dominance is restructured and re-established even during fundamental economic, social, political and cultural changes.

The general assumption behind the discussion of present-day patriarchy is that even if women have been oppressed throughout history, patriarchy today is not simply a historical left-over. The subjection of women is not just the last kind of inequality to be removed, as John Stuart Mill thought, but an integrated part of the structure of present-day society.

According to Veronica Beechey, the concept of patriarchy is used in a different way by radical and revolutionary feminists (like Kate Millett) and by marxist feminists (like Juliet Mitchell, Zillah Eisenstein, and Heidi Hartmann). While radical feminist scholars are searching for the autonomous basis of the oppression of women, marxist or socialist feminists analyse not simply 'patriarchy', but the relationship between patriarchy and the mode of production.[7]

To me it seems essential to study both the common features of all patriarchal societies and the way in which male dominance and the subordination of women is integrated with the socio-economic structure of any given society.

The socialist–feminist discussion of patriarchy started as a criticism of the shortcomings of marxism in dealing with those kinds of oppression (like that of blacks and women) which are not directly based on the extraction of surplus value. It is also a criticism of the assumption by classic marxists (in the sparse writings of Marx and Engels on women, but even in Clara Zetkin's writings) that the contemporary oppression of women is derived from capitalist production and will disappear quite easily in the socialist mode of production.

Socialist feminism tries to combine the radical feminist view and the neo-marxist view. The theory is that the oppression of women is the result of an integration of a patriarchal and a capitalist power system that leaves women at the bottom in terms of power, status, income, etc. My conclusions for future research are, therefore, these: first, the rather universal character of male dominance makes it appropriate to work with a universal concept of patriarchy – but only if followed by a typology of patriarchal societies, based on genuine historical and comparative research. Second, the scattered examples of *types* of patriarchies, mentioned in the literature so far, are mostly classified according to a mode of production (capitalist patriarchy, feudal patriarchy). The argument is that the way production is organized seems to be decisive for women's position, as it decides whether women's childbearing capacities become a handicap or a source of power and prestige.

So far so good. But why construct a typology of patriarchy, which rests exclusively upon variations in the mode of production? This does not enable us to distinguish – which we should – between the position of women in say, the Victorian period of the nineteenth century, in the 1950s or today, in the 1980s.

While our classification of patriarchy may be based on modes of production it must also incorporate several other factors which shape women's lives. One of the most important of these is whether or not women are able to control their reproductive forces through contraception, abortion or other measures, as a woman's whole life situation is structured according to whether she can control the number and timing of her children or whether her life is an endless row of pregnancies, childbirths, miscarriages, ill health and many infant children.

Patriarchy – a concept for society at large

'Look at all these women who completely dominate their families', some people say. 'How can you then call it a patriarchal society?'.

The answer is that in our society on average women earn much less than men, that in general women advance less than men and hold inferior jobs, that women carry a double burden of work, are raped, battered, and subject to physical violence by men and to sexual harassment at work; that political institutions, the political parties and the trade unions are dominated by men and finally that girls and women are deprecated by men – and by themselves. Girls' and women's lower self-esteem is general. These are some of our reasons to label it a patriarchal society.

'Patriarchy' is a concept for a society *at large*. Within an overall patriarchal society, the relations between men and women may vary according to personal characteristics, but also according to *arena*. So, women may in general or in a great number of cases dominate the family arena within the framework of an overall patriarchal society.

Whether to call the overall structure 'patriarchal' or not rests on the 'sum' of structures and relations in a society – but not a sum in the mathematical sense. The crucial point is which forces are the dominant ones in a society. To mention one example: if women in general were dominant in an extended productive family, e.g. a farm, within a society in which farmers were independent and self-sufficient, then this would not be a patriarchal society. But women may dominate the social relations and even the major decisions in a family of say four people in a three-room flat, where the economy is based on the wage of the husband and maybe also the wife. In this modern case the family life is to a large extent structured by outside forces, which neither the wife nor the husband control.

But let us not forget that of course it makes an important difference for women whether there are some areas which are based on the dominance of women or maybe even based on egalitarian relations between the sexes. It has been an important improvement in women's lives that the patriarchal *pater familias* who, up until about twenty years ago ruled over *his* family and *his* house or flat, is being dethroned in most western societies today.

But when are patriarchal structures and relations so fundamentally changed that patriarchy in fact withers away? Few will find it difficult to label the society of the Old Testament patriarchal, just to mention one obvious example of a society openly oppressive towards women (and many men). But are we in the western world now in a period of transition away from patriarchy?

I believe we are. But we still have a couple of hundred years to go, and the movement might even experience some setbacks.

Until now, we have talked of various types of patriarchal societies. But what about the differences between women in the same society according to ethnicity and class? The notion of specific oppression of women on the basis of class or race must not be forgotten in the new discussion about patriarchal societies. Patriarchy does not have the same effect on all women. Some basic features are the same for every woman, others are very different. In some cases the only common factor is that women of every class, race and ethnicity are relatively worse off in terms of income, power and status than are men within the same class, race, or ethnic background. Runa Haukaa argues that women's relations to patriarchy vary according to class, age, and status as housewife or employed outside the home.[8]

The basis of patriarchy

Vicky Randall identifies many different aspects of women's status, 'such as their control over their economic product, their say in household decisions, the extent of their property rights, sexual autonomy, public esteem and public authority'.[9] And, I would add, control over their working conditions.

Patriarchy is here seen as an integrated system of male dominance. Goldberg focuses on the question of whether the upper positions in the hierarchy are mainly occupied by males. Rosaldo has emphasized the 'culturally legitimated authority' as predominantly male.[10] Whatever definition is used, it has something to do with *power*, *authority* and *control*.

The present discussion is not about the origin of women's subordinate position. Such a genetic explanation would have to discuss factors like women's childbreeding and childbearing functions, differences in physical strength, internalized personality types – all in connection with the modes of production, the organization of labour and the emergence of private property. These are not the questions in this chapter. Here the questions are these: What is maintaining women's position as the second sex? Is there a hidden power structure which, no matter how things change, keep women in a subordinate position?

It has been suggested by several theorists that the basic element of patriarchy is men's control over women's *labour*. Others argue[11] that the basis is men's control over women's *sexuality*.[12] Men's physical control over women, including physical violence, may be at least as important.

In my view, however, there are some problems connected with the notion of men's control over women, especially when describing society today. Women's oppression is not just a consequence of men's control over women, even if that is a fact. Women are also deprived of control and power, not by any individual man or groups of men, but rather by the whole structural setting of society. Women may have no control over their working conditions, but in a society of wage earners, it does not follow from this that *men* have that control. Here the basis of women's subordinate position is the *segregation of work between the sexes*.

Consequently, it is necessary to distinguish between men's personal control over women and the structural subordination of women. Structural subordination, however, will often (but far from always), show itself in personal relationships, e.g. in the relation between a woman worker and her foreman, between husband and wife, between schoolboys and schoolgirls.

The socialist–feminist analysis is basically an analysis of the *structural* oppression of women: the sex-segregated labour market; women's double burden of work, most of which is unpaid; women as a reserve labour force; the wage gap between men and women; the effect of the socialization process on girls and women; women's relative powerlessness in traditional politics, etc. The possibly oppressive behaviour of individual men is not the focus, just as the best marxist analysis of capitalism tries to move away from the portrayal of capitalism as an evil old man with a black top hat.

We may have been so eager to get away from the notion of women's oppression being the effect of personal relationships between evil men and good women that the relation between men and women has been almost neglected. Heidi Hartmann brings this element back again: *under patriarchy women give service to men*. This gives men an active interest in maintaining patriarchy.[13]

The content and extent of the services may vary by class or ethnic or racial group, but the fact of their receipt does not. Men have a higher standard of living than women in terms of luxury consumption, leisure time, and personalized services. . . . Men have more to lose than their chains.

Hartmann talks about the 'role of men – ordinary men, men as men, men as workers – in maintaining women's inferiority in the labour market',[14] and about the interest men have in the personal service women give them in the family (sex, household work, comfort, legitimate children).

Do all men benefit from living in a patriarchal society? Empirical analysis on the level of specific societies is needed in order to answer that question. It follows from my definition of patriarchy as a concept for society at large that individual men might live in a subordinate position to their wives or to a woman employer.

It is more important to notice, however, that the concept of patriarchy used here implies that patriarchy is a totality of structures, processes, relations and ideologies, which might not benefit men, nor women and children.

Let us take the example of divorced middle-aged men in the modern welfare state. The division of emotions and the division of work between men and women in this society makes this group of men a risk group with very high unemployment rates, alcohol problems and high rates of suicide. The modern patriarchal society implies living conditions which are unfortunate for women, men and children – even if many men in their everyday life benefit from women's services and from women's adaptation to men's needs.

It has been argued that historically we have witnessed a change from *personal patriarchy* to *structural patriarchy*. Harriet Holter calls this a 'reorganized patriarchy' and argues that this shift from direct, personal forms of dominance to indirect or structural ruling of weaker groups and classes is a general trend brought about by capitalist industrialization.[15]

I have but one objection. The fact that male dominance was so visible and personal say three hundred years ago should not make us forget the overwhelming *structural* patriarchy of that time. Let me mention the fact that most women in a feudal society could not support themselves unless enrolled in a household as daughter, wife or maidservant. Or let me mention the shame and the economic disaster that forced an unwed mother to kill her newborn child. Those are severe examples of structural oppression of women.

Harriet Holter argues that in western societies there have been other changes in the form of oppression than the change from direct, personal (and structural, I argue) forms of dominance over women, to impersonal, indirect or structural oppression. There is also the change from *visible* to *invisible* oppression. Today the process of dominance is invisible and may be unintended, but the results are in some respects more visible. Then we see a change from *physical/material* to *psychological* oppression, and last, but not least, we have witnessed a change from *legitimate* to *illegitimate* oppression.[16]

In the western world today it is illegitimate for a man to beat up his wife, and sex discrimination is forbidden by law. The structure and processes maintaining oppression are, however, by and large legitimate, as Harriet Holter states.[17]

It is not unusual to find theoretical literature which argues that the family is the basis of patriarchy. Or the statement could be that the specificity of patriarchy lies in the relations of reproduction. In this way we get a dichotomy: class exploitation in production, patriarchal oppression in reproduction.[18] It is not, however, as simple as that. To mention an example: as wage earners, women are oppressed, not just as workers, but also as women (low pay, limited promotion, sexual harassment, subordinate jobs in relation to male workers.) Women's relatively weak position on the labour market is connected with women's family obligations. And women's relative powerlessness in politics has something to do with the fact that women have less experience of leadership in their jobs or from organizational life and that they have less leisure time than men.[19] Further, following the fact that a woman usually has a lower income than her husband, it is she who stays at home when their common child is ill, which in turn is a handicap to her in her job. And one could go on like this.

Unlike the marxian concept of class exploitation, which is defined exclusively by the relations of the classes to the means of production and the extraction of surplus value, the oppression of women does not derive from a single set of social relations but from a complex system of interrelated structures and relations.

This interrelated structure also explains why it is so difficult to change women's subordinate position. In so many cases improvements in women's position, e.g. women's access to new types of jobs, have resulted in the creation of new hierarchies and new forms of segregation which leave women at the bottom. The gender–power system of other relations and structures will quickly turn new advantages for women in one social arena into new examples of low pay and low status for women's work, paid or unpaid, in another, which again lowers women's self-esteem and deprives women of the necessary resources to revolt.

This understanding does not imply that patriarchy is an inevitable social structure. History has proved that structures are changeable. For women, strength gained in one arena, e.g. parliament, can be used to work for changes for women in other arenas, e.g. on the labour market or in the educational system. The real opportunity lies in simultaneous changes in several arenas of society at the same time in order to break the integrated patriarchal system of male dominance and female subordination.

The patriarchal state? A theoretical discussion

Theories of women's oppression tend to deal with the relation between the family and the sphere of production, almost forgetting the existence of the state. In the same way as it took some time for marxist theory to discover the role of the modern state, so it did for feminist theory. From a Scandinavian point of view it seems mandatory to include the role of the state, since the state is now integrated into all social relations in modern society. The distinction between private and public has become blurred.

Few theorists of women and the state make use of the concept of a patriarchal state. At this point most people seem to prefer other concepts to cover their theories of the role of the state *vis-à-vis* the oppression of women. Zillah Eisenstein, however, talks about the 'capitalist patriarchal state' and in this volume Anette Borchorst and Birte Siim use the term 'the new social patriarchy' about the welfare state's relation to women.

First we must clarify whether we are searching for a universal concept of the patriarchal state. Using Goldberg's purely nominal definition of patriarchy makes it easy to identify the patriarchal state as any state in which the overwhelming majority of upper positions in the state apparatus are occupied by men. If one chooses more substantial definitions of patriarchy, a patriarchal state could be defined as any state or political superstructure that functions mainly in the interests of men. Or, phrased another way: the patriarchal state is a state that maintains or actively supports the oppression of women. As discussed earlier in this chapter, such universal concepts only become useful when completed by *a typology of patriarchal states*. I feel uncomfortable using a concept of the capitalist patriarchal state without sub-divisions to cover the enormous differences between, say, the nineteenth-century state and the modern welfare state. The new discussion of the relation of the welfare state to women is based on the recognition of these differences.

The basic problem in defining whether or not a state is patriar-chal derives from our lack of a clear definition of patriarchy as such. Even if we skip the term patriarchy, the problem still remains of how to understand and define the mechanism that seems to maintain women in a subordinate position. Until we have developed a better understanding and definition of women's oppression, it is impossible to develop a theory of the state *vis-à-vis* women (the patriarchal state).

These difficulties become clear when reading existing analyses of women and the state. Here the same state action may be considered oppressive of women by some scholars, and liberating by others. Often feminist analysts fall into the functionalist trap so well known in marxism, that all actions of the state contribute to oppression, because it is a patriarchal state; a class/gender version of Robert Merton's universal functionalism![20]

My conclusion is that, for the time being, I would prefer to drop the concept of the patriarchal state and wait for more empirical research about the role of the state *vis-à-vis* women. Since no one has suggested that the oppression of women derives solely from the state, and since the general issue of women's position and status has mostly been a non-issue in western poli-tics,[21] the question of the role of the state should be put this way: what part does the state play in establishing, sustaining and changing systems in which women are oppressed and subordinate to men, such as the family, the labour market and the educational system?

The public/private split: some critical comments on recent theories

The split between a public and a private sphere has been the subject of several recent studies, for example the works of Susan Moller Okin, Zillah Eisenstein, and Jean Bethke Elstain,[22] who all deal with older as well as new political theory.

The central argument of these studies is this: the split between a public and a private sphere reflected in most liberal thought is one of the foundations of patriarchy or male dominance over women. The split between public and private is, so it is argued, a split between state and the family, and ultimately a split between the domain of men and the domain of women. Although all discussions acknowledge the many historical variations in what is considered private and what is considered public, some kind of universality is attached to this conception of a split. Eisenstein states that even though the *political* differentiation of the family and the state does not develop until bourgeois society is established, feudal society still recognized the public domain as male and the private as female. According to Eisenstein, 'there is no constant meaning to the terms *public* and *private* other than their sexual identification, and even this identity takes on particular meaning within the specific culture and society one is examining'.[2]

I find this discussion very important for the study of the role of the state in maintaining or changing women's position. I am, however, uncomfortable with the very general character of these statements of a public/private split. In the following I will raise some critical questions for further investigation.

What is the public/private split really about? I see at least two separate, but interlinked aspects: women's exclusion from the public sphere; the scope of government action. The latter aspect concerns the extent and limits to state interference; the question of what is politics and what comes on the public agenda, all well-known issues in political science.

What is the private/public split – a motive? A hidden assumption beneath action? An ideology? A judicial distinction? A description of the reality or simply justifications for interference/no interference? Is the private/public split a consequence of some other structuring principles of society (for instance the development of the forces of production), or is it in itself a structuring principle?

The public/private split does not always equal a male/female distinction. In the emerging liberal states as well as in classic liberal philosophy, women were excluded from the public sphere – and that exclusion was no mere coincidence, but in fact a part of the very foundation of the early liberal state.[24] But even if participation in the *public* sphere was limited to (some) men, men were not seen as absent from the sphere of the *family* in the eighteenth and nineteenth centuries. In liberal theory, the new public sphere was a sphere for male heads of households. The public sphere was ruled by men, but so was the family. Women had one sphere, men two – at least.

Susan Tenenbaum, who has written a critique of the new theories of the public/private split, states that Hegel, for instance, centered his discussion about altruism within the family on the *male*. In her article she argues that the conclusion in the literature about the public/private split in political theory rests on a very selective reading which has excluded theorists who offered a more subtle or positive view of woman's domestic role and/or who proclaimed the relevance of domestic values to public life – like Montesquieu, Mme de Staël and Jane Adams.[25]

The main question is that even if the dominant sphere for women is the family, the power relations of this very family may vary considerably. Are women locked in a strictly patriarchal family, or is the family women's (only) base of power and control? Historically, the family has been a patriarchal family, legally and in reality, long after the family stopped being the main unit of production. But today's family looks very different from the nineteenth-century family, and that has to be taken into account. Moreover, the fact that today women still have the main responsibilities for family work does not totally exclude women from political participation, even if that is still an important factor behind women's lower political participation. The character of housework has changed dramatically during the last hundred years, and women's new control over childbearing has meant that the family does not swallow women up for their whole life as it used to do.

What is the 'private' sphere? I have problems with the notion of private, and especially with restricting that notion to the family or household. It is not just the family which is private. In a capitalist society, the main part of production is also private. The industrialization process separated the family from production (except for the petit bourgeois families) and made a large part of the working population wage-earners in the new sphere of private enterprises.

Inspired by Jürgen Habermas,[26] I have illustrated the plurality of spheres in the following table.

We should make clear what kind of 'private' sphere we are talking about in a given context. Private sometimes means what is intimate, or closely associated with the family. Sometimes it

Private sphere	Private sphere of public life	Public sphere (*the state*)
Private production The family	Organizations Cultural life Mass media	State apparatus State production

refers to private enterprises which in fact are only 'private' for their owners, not for their workers.

The boundaries between these spheres are getting more and more vague, and the relative size of the spheres is changing. In the western world, the intermediate sphere of an arena of public debate developed in the nineteenth century. (Note that 'public' has also different meanings, one referring to the state, another that which does not belong to the family, or to private production.) Today, the interventionist state interferes considerably with the family and private production, and simultaneously the interest groups and the state are becoming increasingly involved in corporate decision-making structures.

What is the negation of the private/public split? The split between a public and a private sphere is considered one of the foundations of the subordination of women. But what if that split did not exist? What is the negation of that split? Concerning women's political participation, the negation of the exclusion of women is women's total integration into the governing of the state – or into a different kind of state. But what about the scope of government? On this point there is no agreement in the literature.

Some theorists of the public/private split have made the relevant point that as a consequence of the split (or as an expression of it), the state has not interfered with intrafamily relations, especially not with sexual relations in the family. The new women's liberation movement has, by its statement 'the private is political' challenged this 'privacy', making violence and rape in the family and men's exploitation of women's services in general, subject to public debate and to collective action. Reluctantly, the state is beginning to touch these problems. But is state interference necessarily good?

State interference in family relations is not new. Before the advent of liberal democracy laws frequently regulated sexuality, demanded women's obedience to their husbands, and established rules for the husband's rights to corporal punishment of the members of his household, including his wife. So, state intervention may be damaging for women – or the opposite.

In the present discussion of the private/public split, two points of view are presented: one is that the intervention of the state sustains the oppression of women; the other is that the state, by leaving intrafamily relations to the 'private' sphere, contributes to the continuing oppression of women. This disagreement leads to one conclusion, that discussion must be more specific as to which kind of state is interfering with which kind of society.

My conclusion from this short discussion is that instead of a very general debate of a private/public split, I would prefer specific studies of the scope and context of government action and its consequences for the position of women. A historical and comparative perspective would clarify this discussion. To mention one example, in Denmark, the number of state-supported daycare facilities has expanded, especially during the 1970s, so that in 1984, 42.3 per cent of all children aged 0–2, and 57 per cent of all children aged 3–6 had a place in a day nursery, kindergarten or were cared for by a child-minder. These facilities were regulated by the authorities, who subsidized about 70–90 per cent of the costs. In the United States, childcare is still almost exclusively a private problem. Our theory should be able to explain such differences.

In the present situation of serious cuts in the services of the western welfare states, the debate about the boundaries between public and private has been revived. Conservative governments have invented a new word: 'privatizing'. Although based on solid ideological grounds within the Conservative movement, it is nevertheless mostly used as a justification for cuts which will transfer some of the responsibilities of the welfare state on to women in private homes. So private/public splits *are* significant, but it is an important task to clarify what these mean in practice.

Determinants of public policy concerning women

The relation between women and the state has several aspects that need to be examined:

determinants of public policy concerning women

effects of public policy on women

the feminist movement and its troublesome relation to the state[27]

women's low, yet increasing political participation and
  representation.[28]

We will focus on the first two aspects. Women's position in society
has never been a major issue in western politics. On one side we
have a women's movement engaged in a constant struggle to make
women's subordinate position an issue in its own right. On the
other side we have a political system which has only dealt with
these questions piecemeal as side-effects of other issues or has
simply neglected the matter. This negligence is related to the
feminist demand of changing women's position, but also to the
question of how various policies affect women in their present
situation.

In general, women's social position and the relation between
the sexes have been left to social forces outside the political sphere
– or simply considered a matter of nature.

One could add the category of 'women' to the criticism of the
pluralist perception of the political system: some people and issues
are systematically excluded from the political system, either by
direct action by those in power or by the whole structural setting
of society.

This is a description of the general picture. The next step is to
study the many variations in this pattern – variations between
states, variations over time, and variations according to class and
race within one society.

What is the state?

Empirical studies about the relation between women and the state
must break down the perception of the state as one unified block.
A general study of the functions of the state seen as one block of
power can be justified, but if political actors, like political parties
and the women's movement, or questions of intentions and
motives are involved, a more specific understanding of the state
is necessary. We must look upon local, regional as well as national
politics. And we must look at conflicting interests within the state.

Expressions such as 'the state wants to' or 'the intention of the
state is' – can be found in research, the general approach of which
is otherwise a study of unintended effects of state action. 'The

state is at present looking for new forms of patriarchal control', Zillah Eisenstein writes.[29] In my opinion, such statements do not help our understanding of what is going on.

The state is *an expression* of social conflicts in society at large. It is an arena for social conflicts and conflict reconciliation. Interests may be expressed through political parties, interest organizations, corporate business, solid movements etc. Some interests, however, do not find expression within the political system. The political system is then an expression of the most powerful (although antagonist) interests, but it is not a mirror of all social conflicts. Some interests or conflict dimensions are not visible in the political system.

While the class war has been 'institutionalized' especially in the Scandinavian countries in the form of corporatism, the conflict or potential conflict between men and women, following their very different social positions, has not been subject to institutionalization. Recent years have shown a new, albeit modest change in this pattern: with the Equal Status Councils, Equal Opportunity Commissions and the like, established in most of the western world during the 1970s, these questions are for the first time built into the state apparatus itself.

What is public policy concerning women?

The history books of the women's movement tell only the story of those kinds of public policy which deal explicitly with women. This is a logical consequence of the fact that the autonomous women's movement has mainly engaged itself in such questions, sometimes supported by women from the political parties and the trade unions. To exemplify this kind of public policy towards women, an outline of the Danish legislation most explicitly directed towards changing the status of women is given in Figure 1. This type of legislation is well known in most western countries, where it has been passed during the last hundred years, often in the same order.

As one can see, this type of public policy towards women is on the whole progressive, e.g. its aim is to remove old injustices and to give women the same formal rights and access as men. So why all this talk about the state being oppressive towards women? If we focus alone on these measures – and that is what many people do – we see that the state has acted for the equality of women.

Figure 1   Danish legislation explicitly aimed at changing women's position. An outline from the 1850s until today.

1850s	Equal right to inheritance for sons and daughters Legal authority to unmarried women Freedom of trade for unmarried women and widows
1860s–70s	Women's access as teachers to employment in public schools and women's access to the university
1880s–90s	Married women's right to command over her own earnings and her own property Right for unmarried mothers to get alimony in advance from the authorities, in case the father fails to pay. To call in the money from the father now becomes the problem of the authorities Access for women to several new types of education and jobs
1901	First protective legislation for working women: four weeks maternity leave (extended through the century). Ban on women's work at night never passed in Denmark
1903	Co-education in secondary schools (in the countryside a longer tradition for co-education)
1903–15	Right to vote for women (unmarried and married) to parish councils (1903), Social Aid Boards (1907), local councils (1908), parliament (1915)
1919–1920s	Equal access to public offices except military positions and priesthood (1947) Equal pay for women and men in public service (but bonus for breadwinners was introduced now, not to be abolished until 1958) New marriage law: spouses now share custody of their children
1930s–50s	Few laws on the status on women as such, but social legislation to support the family and mothers, e.g. aid to mothers and pregnant women, extension of maternity leave, health visitors, home help, the right of illegitimate children to the name of the father and inheritance of the father
1960s–70s	Large increase in the number of public daycare centres

1965–74	Commission on the status of women
1970, 1973	Liberalization of the Abortion Law (1970), followed by a law of free abortion on request (1973)
1976	Equal Pay Act (1973 equal pay part of the general agreements)
1975	Equal Status Council
1978	Equal Treatment Act – prohibits discrimination in hiring, promotion and dismissal on account of sex
1981	Equality consultants in every regional labour market administration
1984	Extension of maternity leave to six months after birth. Introduction of paternity leave
1984	A woman keeps her own family name when marrying, unless she explicitly opts for the name of the husband. The same goes for the husband. Before this, women got the husband's family name, unless she explicitly stated otherwise – a symbolic change
1985	Law requiring balance according to gender in all public commission and boards, 'as far as possible'.

Note: Only laws not administrative provisions are included here. Many details are omitted.

In fact, we see a progressing line of laws to remove injustice and to further equality. The women's movement, which has fought so hard for all this progress, has many reasons to celebrate what it has achieved. But this outline is, however, only one part of the whole picture of state action towards women, which must be completed with several other types of analyses.

The second step is to study the effect of legislation and other public measures which are apparently sex-neutral, but which nevertheless have different consequences for men and women because of their different social positions: for example traffic planning, tax policy, housing policy, labour market policy, and also family and social policies. Even if family policy does not deal explicitly with women's position, it may rest on certain hidden assumptions about 'women's proper place' and may in fact result in unintended changes.[30] So the study must include, for instance, old age pension schemes, the actual effect of the educational system on girls and boys – in short, all types of state intervention. By widening the approach in this way, the evaluation of the effect of public policy on women obviously becomes more complex and offers no simple conclusion.

The third step is to include studies of lack of reactions on the part of the state. Since the position of women has often been left to the forces outside the political system, the issue has mostly been a non-issue. This has been the case when the women's movement has demanded state interference without success, as with wife battering.[31] In many cases important social changes have not been followed by necessary intervention by the state. To mention one example: the state did not react to the problems of poor children being left alone when their working-class mothers went into the factories. Protective legislation for women never solved any problems, and the state did not engage in the unsuccessful efforts to secure working-class men a family wage. So, the state did not take any efficient action to help with the childcare problem. But neither did the state respond to the demands of a ban on working-class women working outside their homes. All western states were silent observers to these fundamental changes brought about by the industrialization process, and it was not until middle-class women entered the labour market in the 1960s that the state – and only in some countries – took steps to build daycare centres on a massive scale.

The origin of public policy towards women

Several approaches may be applied to the study of what determines the sum of public policy concerning women in a given country or group of countries. One approach is to focus on how the issues are raised, the agenda-building process, and the decision-making process. This approach usually, but not necessarily, involves studies of political actors; in this case, the political parties, the women's movement, the trade unions, and the proceedings of government. This approach will tell something about the goals and strategies of the political actors, their conflicts and co-operation. Another approach deals with the same question of conflicting interests, but from another starting point. From the effects of public policies on various groups, the scholar tries to trace the covert or overt interests involved in state action. This type of approach is usually immune to aspects of actors, arguments, motives, even if the two mentioned approaches might in fact complement each other.

In the following I shall mention some examples of studies of the determinants for the actions of the state *vis-à-vis* women.

Capitalist interests

Several theorists argue that the root of public policy concerning women is the development of the economy. The provision of daycare facilities and maternity leave, even free abortion, is explained by the need of capital for cheap female labour. Elizabeth Wilson[32] argues that the modern welfare state regulates the family to keep its capacity to reproduce labour. Protective legislation for women has been explained by the fact that the reproduction of the labour force was threatened. These approaches form part of the general marxist critique of the welfare state, the emergence of which is explained primarily by a need for capital for reproduction of the labour force and for preventing the working class from revolting. Jennifer Schirmer follows this line in her critical book on women in the Danish welfare state.[33]

Even if the development of the economy no doubt plays a major role for policy outcome, including that which most affects women, I would warn against the economic reductionism which is the basis of Wilson's and Schirmer's arguments.

The development of the productive forces and changes in the organization of the labour process no doubt constitute the framework for state intervention; and indeed, in the mixed economies of the western nations the state is itself more and more involved in these processes. So maybe we should talk about needs which derive from changes in the production process rather than about pure capitalist interests when studying the relation between economy and policy outcomes.

But the development of production cannot explain all variations in policy outcomes among nations. To mention an example, why has the US, contrary to Scandinavia, almost no public daycare facilities nor any general regulations giving women maternity leave? These measures are most important in order to make it possible and legitimate for women to work outside the home.

Differences in production do not fully explain these variations. Factors like the strength of the labour movement, social democracy and the relative strength of the women's movement and of women in the political parties have to be taken into account.

The astonishing similarities between the capitalist countries of Scandinavia and the state socialist countries of eastern Europe when it comes to social policy and policies directed especially towards women, make it important to distinguish between what is the effect of the capitalist economy and what is in fact the effect of the industrialization process in general, combined, maybe, with the relative strength of the political forces on the left.

State interests

In her stimulating book *Women and Politics*, Vicky Randall tries another approach. Critical of those efforts to explain public policy concerning women mainly as the interest of capital or men (patriarchy), she discusses the role of 'state needs', distinguishing between state needs, which are common to all states, and features of particular political systems which modify them.[34]

Vicky Randall states three 'state needs': the first is the promotion of economic prosperity or growth. The almost inherent need for the state to pursue this aim affects women highly through employment policies and also through population policies. Similarly, Randall argues that the two other main state needs, a secure international position, and internal political order and stability, result in policies with great impact on women's position. Thus the state needs and supports the family as a stabilizing element of society. Randall makes some very interesting points here. My problem with this scheme is that the kind of policy that follows from these 'state needs', in terms of sustaining or changing women's subordinate position, is not obvious.

Patriarchal interests

Few will maintain that patriarchal interests, that is male interests in sustaining women in a subordinate position, are the determining factor behind all public policy. But the question must be raised as to what extent patriarchal interests influence public policy – in various historical periods and in different countries.

We have many examples of earlier legislation openly serving

the interests of men by demanding women's obedience to their husbands or fathers. Older marriage laws were often extremely sexist. The Code Civil enacted in 1804 by Napoleon in the period of reaction after the Revolution, defined the relation between men and women in this way: '*Le mari doit protection à sa femme, la femme obéissance à son mari*' (The husband owes his wife protection, the wife obedience to her husband). The Code Napoleon also stated (this was not new) that inquiry into who was the father of an illegitimate child was prohibited.

Many countries previously had rules that judged adultery much more harshly for women than for men. French ruling men once passed a law saying that adultery was a crime if committed by the wife, but for her husband only if the mistress was brought into the family home! Such laws were obviously written by men in their own interests, and whereas they no doubt corresponded to the social relations and norms of contemporary society, they nevertheless provide examples of public policy arising from male interests in subordinating women.

During the twentieth century, public policy in all western countries has increasingly taken the form of sex-neutral measures. Simultaneously, the oppression of women has changed from personal and structural to predominantly structural, all of which implies a new interest in studying the indirect effect of public policies. In the 1970s and 1980s, a new wave of special state measures to further the equality of the sexes has been introduced following the renewed feminist debate, the UN decade on women and the coming of the new feminist movement. Following the general trend of stronger direct state intervention, the action programmes of the new 'state feminism' have replaced the old, more modest political tradition in this area with its focus on the removal of formal barriers for women.

The effects of public policy on the position of women derive from the sum of various measures behind which lie different, often conflicting interests. Several theorists have dealt with the conflict between capital interests and patriarchal interests, for instance the conflict between capitalist (and state) interests in women's labour power and patriarchal interests in keeping women under control in the home. In this case, patriarchal interests lost.

Zillah Eisenstein twists the old discussion of the relative autonomy of the state *vis-à-vis* the economy into one of the relative autonomy of the state *vis-à-vis* patriarchy. Is it possible for

the modern state to act against the fundamental patriarchal structures that maintain the services of women to men? Is it possible
that the state can act against even the combined patriarchal and
capitalist interests in keeping women as cheap labour in a sex-
segregated labour market? If anybody can, I will argue, it is the
state.

Women's interests

Few observers believe that the modern state has a general policy
in the interests of women, even if one may find this line of argument among some groups of men who have gone through tough
divorces! Most people will argue that the state acts sex-neutrally,
which the majority of feminists will deny.

In the case of free abortion, which was introduced in many
western countries in the 1970s as a result of strong feminist
pressure, state action seems to have preceded those social forces
that so far have determined women's position. Most feminists will
see this as a clear victory that shows the strength and potential
strength of women if they are united. But others have rushed in
with a negative interpretation, stating that free abortion came at
the time it did because women's stable labour force was needed
by the employers. But if this is so, why do some countries get free
abortion in times of economic crises and massive unemployment?

In my opinion, history shows that women have achieved some
victories, often in alliance with progressive men. But until now,
women have not succeeded in making the state give priority over
other well-established interests to schemes which would fundamentally change women's position. Only the increasing influence
of feminism both inside and outside the political system would
make this possible. Part of the feminist movement has always
considered this strategy relevant and has focused on increasing
women's political representation and putting pressure on the
political institutions. Others, especially in the women's liberation
movement in its first years, did not believe in either the willingness
or the ability of the state to create fundamental changes for women
in their everyday lives.

My conclusion is that no single factor can explain public policy
towards women, nor other kinds of policies for that matter. We
should add a study of the impact of the women's movement and
other political actors to the discussion of structural explanations.

State policy towards women has, in my mind, always been full of contradictions, and the pressure from the women's movement – even if only a marginal political force – has contributed to these contradictions, when successful!

Present state policy in most western countries illustrates this point. On the one hand, cuts in welfare programmes (un)employment policies, etc., seem to hit women especially hard. Simultaneously, equality policies – equal pay acts, equal opportunities laws, and affirmative action programmes – are in progress in the very same countries.

The effects of public policy on the position of women

Let us now change perspective and ask what effects the sum of public policy has on women's position in a society.

The state as the oppressor?

Mary McIntosh concludes that the state does play a part in the oppression of women, 'not directly, but through its support for a specific form of household: the family household dependent largely upon a male wage and upon female domestic serving'. She suggests that the analysis should focus on the effect of state policies on those systems in which women are oppressed, first and foremost the family and the labour market.[35]

Elizabeth Wilson's discussion of the welfare state and women concludes that this modern state offers not just a set of services, but also an ideology about the role of the family and of women. Her very negative evaluation of the welfare state concludes that this state establishes a certain structure of the family in which the man is the breadwinner, and the woman depends on the man for support.[36]

In her analysis of politics and women's status in Britain, Vicky Randall examines the effect of state action on six aspects of women's status: marriage; women's control over their own bodies; women's role as mothers; income; employment; education. The conclusion of her short survey is that although British policies towards women reinforce women's traditional role as mothers and housewives, at the same time such policies have made possible some widening of women's life options in the twentieth century

and indeed, may have played some small part in the emergence
of the women's liberation movement.

The scale against which the effect of state policies is measured
is based on goals like independence for women and women's
control over their own lives, including their work situation, self-
realization and dignity (especially a goal for the women's rights
movement in the nineteenth century). Here again we are at the
core of the problem: how do we define the oppression of women,
and what is the negation of that oppression? These definitions are
the Alpha and Omega to a theory of the state versus women.
They are not necessarily *the* definition, but must be openly and
clearly defined by every study wishing to measure state policy as
it affects the status of women. For example, Joey Sprague[38] has
written an interesting analysis of theories of a patriarchal state.
Criticizing the instrumental concepts of the state, she develops
Claus Offe's structural analysis of the class-specific selectivity of
the state into an analysis of what one could call the gender-specific
selectivity of the state (the patriarchal state). It is a very interesting
approach. But it is when she comes to the analysis of actual
patriarchal state policies that the problems begin. Some of the
measures which she, without hesitation, uses as expressions of
patriarchal selectivity are debatable. The best example is the case
of protective legislation. She has no doubt that protective legislation contributed to the oppression of women through its 'tremendous impact on long-term job segregation on the basis of sex' (pp.
10–11). In my opinion, however, protective legislation was not
especially important for the creation of the present segregation of
work by sex.[39] Another point is that many feminist women within
the labour movement did see protective legislation for women
as something good and progressive, while the middle-class-based
women's rights movement in most countries (not in Germany,
however) went strongly against protective legislation especially
for women. In Norway, the social democratic women's movement
demanded protective legislation (without success), whereas in
Denmark women from the labour movement successfully opposed
the measure in a rare coalition with the women's rights movement.
Summa summarum: even feminists may have different opinions
about whether some policy contributes to the oppression of
women or not.

Again, I will warn against these very general statements about
the effect on women of state policies. I find it very difficult to

conclude whether or not the state has sustained the oppression of women. Evidently the state has not been able, or willing, to try fundamentally to change women's subordinate position. But some states have been more active than others, especially in some developing countries. Moreover, state action may have different effects on women of different class and race.

More empirical studies are needed of public policies and their effects on women's position in a historical and cross-national perspective. Studies must be conducted concerning various aspects of women's position before we can conclude on the combined effect. Let me here just mention one other example of the difficulties of evaluating the effect of public policy on women's status.

Dependence on the state

Has the state contributed to sustaining women's oppression by supporting a family system based on a male breadwinner and a dependent housewife, as McIntosh states?

In my opinion, state policies towards the family have changed considerably during the last hundred years, not least in Scandinavia. In general, women are less able to support themselves than men are (due to lack of education, low pay, part-time work or housework and responsibility for small children). But today, women do not need a husband to support them to the extent they did in earlier times. In a long process of change, the state has taken over the support of women who cannot support themselves, and consequently many women are now economically dependent on the state instead of a husband. This at least makes it possible for a woman to leave a husband, or to remain single if pregnant – and that is new.

Scandinavian family legislation has, since the 1920s, been based upon the mutual obligation of spouses to support each other. Consequently, social benefits depend on the income of one's husband/wife/cohabitator. Simultaneously, however, quite a lot of social transfers are now granted to the individual, not to the family. This is the case with unemployment benefits, which, although now somewhat reduced, are very extensive in all Scandinavian countries. Partly as a result of long-standing pressure from the women's rights organizations, the tax system is becoming increasingly based on 'splitting' the husband's and wife's income.

The dramatic increase in women's employment outside the home, combined with the safety net of the Scandinavian welfare system, has in fact shaken the patriarchal family previously based on the economic power of the male breadwinner. The state has not had the lead in this process, but it is part of this 'individualizing' of family members. There are tremendous differences between the nineteenth-century peasant family, bourgeois family, and working-class family and corresponding families today. Even the power structure of the family of the 1930s was much different from the present, and we have to develop concepts which are able to grasp these differences. One such concept is the change from personal and structural to structural patriarchy.

Some studies conclude that in fact women have just moved from dependence on husbands to dependence on the state, while their subordination remains. I will argue that this shift has in general improved women's position and has given women new resources for mobilization, protest and political influence. Moreover, I prefer not to use the same word, dependence, to characterize both an interpersonal and a structural relation.

In her contribution to this volume, Helga Hernes writes that women's lives in the welfare society are more dependent and more determined by state policies than men's. Women have become dependent on the state as clients (especially as mothers), as employees in the public sector and as citizens (women have less political power than men in the corporate system). The sum is that women have moved *from private to public dependence*. Dependence changes its character when it becomes public and subject to regulation and support, Helga Hernes argues, but does she imply that women are better off under these new conditions? It seems to be her conclusion that the unequal distribution of power between men and women is upheld – and may be strengthened.

Also in this volume, Anette Borchorst and Birte Siim develop this line of argument further. They discuss women's dependence on the state as employees, clients, and consumers (e.g. of public day-care). They, apparently, reach a negative conclusion, in that they talk about a 'strengthening of male power on a more structural level'.

This is an important discussion, but maybe again the level of generalization on behalf of all women is too high. At any rate, it is problematic to use the same term, 'dependency' for a woman's relation to the state as, for example, nurses, old age pensioners or patients. This analogy is more confusing than illustrative.

It is characteristic that these more pessimistic lines of argument forget to mention that women have become not just clients, employees, consumers and citizens in relation to the state, but also exercise public authority over other women – and men, e.g. as teachers, lower level civil servants, daycare workers, doctors, nurses, and social workers, etc.

Conclusion

Recent theories of women and the state discuss what direction public policy concerning women is taking in the western world: can we see stronger support for equality of the sexes and for women's self-determination, or does the sum of state action, intended or unintended, reinforce women's subordinate position and create new forms of male dominance?

It is amazing how different the conclusions are to the above mentioned, predominantly theoretical, analyses of the relation between women and the state. My conclusion is that we need more empirical research based on various approaches to the study of this complicated relation. We need more research into the role of the state in developing countries, and we need empirically grounded cross-national research on the effect of public policy on women's position in comparable western countries.

My analysis so far has four conclusions. First, the state has not been the main force behind the last century of fundamental changes in women's position as such and *vis-à-vis* men. These dramatic changes are the result of the industrialization process and the socio-economic changes following the development of modern capitalism. In general, the development of capitalism is mainly the effect of independent economic forces, and has not been decided upon in political institutions. But in matters of women's position, the state has been mostly passive, at least until very recently. Indeed, the state has contributed to new opportunities for women, which the private sector would never have provided. But in general, it is the socio-economic forces that have shaped women's new lives, the state merely following suit.

Second, compared to many other political issues, the question of women's subordinate position in society has been a 'non-issue' in western politics. Women's status has never been a main issue on the party platforms, in electoral campaigns, or in any government manifesto. Nor has any government coalition fallen apart because of disagreements on the role of women in society. Generally speaking, the political parties have avoided politicizing the issue. Women's status has been left to nature or to privacy. For more than a hundred years, the women's movement has challenged this trend and asked for state action to the benefit of women, but in only a few periods of history has it met with any success.

Third, one has to distinguish between the intended and unintended effects of public policy on women's position. Deliberate policies have mostly concerned formal rights for women, and have not changed the fundamental structures which make women's lives so different from men's. The unintended effects are mostly side-effects of seemingly sex-neutral public measures, which nevertheless turn out to have different consequences for women and men. In a few words, what help is it to have the right to equal pay, if a woman loses her job because public industrial support goes to male-dominated industries, or because import deregulation ruins the textile industry?

Fourth and last, we may be entering a new era of more direct and intended intervention on behalf of women. There is also a growing awareness of the side effects for women of seemingly sex-neutral public measures. The massive entrance of women into paid employment has forced the state to react, and the revival of the women's movement has made feminist pressure somewhat successful – or, as in the United States, has stirred up large anti-feminist forces. At any rate, feminist issues have become more visible on the political agenda, and a new, although modest 'institutionalization' of the gender conflict is taking place in the form of Equal Status Councils, Equal Opportunity Commissions and the like. Whether this new 'state feminism' will be able to grow strong remains to be seen.

Notes and references

1 Michelle Zimbalist Rosaldo and Louise Lamphere, *Women, culture, and society* (Stanford: Stanford University Press 1974), p. 3.
2 S. Goldberg, *Male dominance: the inevitability of patriarchy* (London: 1979), p. 25.

3   Heidi Hartmann, 'The unhappy marriage of Marxism and Feminism: towards a more progressive union' in Lydia Sargent (ed.), *Women and revolution*, (Boston: South End Press 1981), p.14.

4   Brita Gulli on 'patriarchy' in *Paxleksikon*, 5 (Oslo: 1980), pp. 99–102. *Paxleksikon* is a new and exciting effort to construct a leftist encyclopaedia. It has come out in six big volumes in Norwegian.

5   Sheila Rowbotham, 'The trouble with "Patriarchy" ', *New Statesman*, December 1979.

6   See Hartman, Zillah R. Eisenstein (ed.), *Capitalist patriarch and the case for socialist feminism*, (New York: Monthly Review Press 1979); Harriet Holter, *Patriarchy in a welfare society* (Oslo: Universitetsforlaget, 1984).

7   Veronica Beechey, 'On Patriarchy', *Feminist Review*, no. 3 (1979), pp. 66–82.

8   Runa Haukaa, 'Interessemodsetninger mellåm kvinner', in Harriet Holter (ed.), *Kvinner i fellesskap* (Oslo: Universitetsforlaget 1982), pp. 42–53.

9   Vicky Randall, *Women and politics* (Macmillan Press: 1982), p. 15.

10   Michelle Z. Rosaldo, 'Women, culture, and society: a theoretical overview', in Rosaldo and Lamphere, p. 21.

11   See Catharine A. MacKinnon, 'Feminism, Marxism, method, and the state, an agenda for theory', in *Signs*, 7, no. 3 (Spring 1982), pp. 515–44.

12   Control over women's labour has in various periods coincided with control over women's sexuality. This has been evident where the family is the main unit of production (like in farming). But it is striking that the move among working-class men at the beginning of industrialization to have women's work in the factory forbidden by law, was often followed by arguments about how dangerous factory work was for morality. At its famous Gotha Congress, 1875, the big and influential German Social Democratic party wrote in its programme: 'Ban on child-work and all women's work, that is dangerous for the health and for the morality'. Wilh. Schröder, *Handbuch der sozialdemokratischen parteitage von 1863 bis 1909–1910*, new edition, (1971), pp. 165, 468. The decision was in fact a compromise, since some had suggested a total ban on women's work in industry. By the way, Marx criticized these paragraphs.

13   Heidi Hartmann, 'Capitalism, patriarchy, and job segregation', in Zillah Eisenstein (ed.), *Capitalist patriarchy and the case for socialist feminism* (New York: Monthly Review Press 1979), p. 208. Hartmann directs this criticism against classic and neo-marxism, but in my opinion this criticism also holds true for the first stage of marxist feminism.

14   Hartmann in Sargent, pp. 9 and 33. Even if I like the approach, it

does not mean that I will buy the theory of the *family wage*. I think
that a family wage (a wage for the husband, which was enough to
support the whole family) for the working class and for poor people
in farming has never existed, except for skilled workers in a very
short period, in Denmark from, say, 1930–60. I am not sure whether
the whole theoretical construction will fall apart, if a family wage
did not exist in reality, but only as a wish among working-class men
– and women.

5 Holter, *Patriarchy*.
6 Harriet Holter, 'Om kvinneundertrykkelse, mannsundertrykkelse og
   herskerteknikker' in Tordis Støren and Tone Shou Wetlesen (eds),
   kvinnekunnskap (Oslo: 1976).
7 Holter, *Patriarchy* p. 20.
8 'Reproduction' is one of the most confusing terms. Veronica Beechey
   mentions (p. 78) at least three meanings of the term: *1* social reproduction of the total conditions of production, *2* reproduction of the
   labour force, *3* biological reproduction. Incidentally, Engels did *not*
   call biological procreation 'reproduction' in his famous statement of
   the basis of the materialistic conception of history. In fact, he said
   that 'die Produktion und Reproduktion' of life had two aspects:
   creating food, cloth, tools, dwellings on the one hand and 'Produktion' of human beings on the other. Friedrich Engels, *Uhrsprung
   der Familie, des Privateigentums und des Staates*, 1884, *Marx-Engels
   Werke*, **21**, pp. 27–28.
9 The differences between men's and women's political activity cannot,
   however, be explained totally by women's fewer resources. Socialization, expectations, the female/male culture are factors too.
10 Robert Merton, *Social theory and social structure* (Glencoe, Illinois:
    1957).
11 Drude Dahlerup, 'Overcoming the barriers: an approach to the study
    of how women's issues are suppressed from the political agenda', in
    Judith Stiehm (ed.) *Women's views of the political world of men*.
    (New York: Transnational Publishers 1983).
12 Susan Moller Okin, *Women in western political thought* (Princeton
    New Jersey: Princeton University Press 1979). Zillah Eisenstein, *The
    radical future of liberal feminism*, (Longman 1981); Jean Bethke
    Elstain, *Public man, private woman. Women in social and political
    thought*, (Princeton, New Jersey: Princeton University Press, 1981).
13 Zillah Eisenstein, *The radical future*, p. 26.
14 Teresa Brennan and Carole Pateman, 'Mere auxiliaries to the
    Commonwealth: women and the origins of liberalism', *Political
    Studies*, **27**, no. 2, (June 1979) and Helga Maria Hernes, *Staten –
    kvinner ingen adgang?* (Oslo: Universitetsförlaget 1982).

25 Susan Tenenbaum, 'Woman through the prism of political thought'
    Polity, **15**, no. 2 (Fall 1982), pp. 90–102.
26 Jürgen Habermas, *Strukturwandel der Offentlichkeit*. (Berlin, 1974)
27 See e.g. Drude Dahlerup (ed.), *The New Women's Movement
    Feminism and political power in Europe and the USA* (Sage Publi
    cations. Forthcoming 1986).
28 See Elina Haavio-Mannila (ed.), *Unfinished democracy. Women in
    Nordic politics* (Pergamon Press, 1985); Joni Lovenduski and Jil
    Hills, *The politics of the second electorate* (Routledge & Kegan Pau
    1981).
29 Eisenstein, *The radical future*, p. 221.
30 See Sheila M. Rothman, *Woman's proper place. A history o
    changing ideals and practices, 1870 to the present* (New York 1978)
31 The women's rights organization in Denmark, Dansk Kvinesamfund
    founded 1871, demanded state action against wife battering in the
    1880s, without much success. This is still a feminist claim, maybe a
    little more successful today due to the activities of the new women'
    liberation movement.
32 Elizabeth Wilson, *Women and the welfare state* (Tavistock 1977).
33 Jennifer G. Schirmer, *The limits of reform. Women, capital and
    welfare* (Cambridge, Mass: Schenkman 1982). After a period o
    praise to women's position in the Scandinavian 'model' (inspired by
    the Swedish government's policy to spread information about the
    best of that country in English), a new wave of American literature,
    critical of the Scandinavian experiences is coming into the market,
    see for instance Hilda Scott, *Sweden's right to be human* (Allison
    and Busby 1982).
34 Randall, *Women and politics*, pp. 129f.
35 Mary McIntosh, 'The state and the oppression of women', in Anette
    Kuhn and Annmarie Wolpe (eds), *Feminism and materialism.
    Women and modes of production* (Routledge and Kegan Paul)
    p. 255.
36 Wilson, *Women and the welfare state*.
37 Randall, *Women and politics* p. 108f.
38 Joey Sprague, *Toward a theory of the patriarchal state*, unpublished
    paper (Madison, Wisconsin: University of Wisconsin-Madison 1981).
39 Protective legislation for women was widely discussed in all western
    countries from the end of the nineteenth century to the Second
    World War. Only some countries passed such legislation, for instance
    bans on women working at night, on Sundays and in mines. While
    Sweden got a ban on nightwork, no protective legislation for women
    (apart from maternity leave) was passed in Denmark and Norway.
    In the discussion in the US, many have argued that protective legis-
    lation laws backed by court decisions have played an important role

in shaping the sex-segregated labour market. The Norwegian and Danish cases may question that assumption, since we have a heavily sex-segregated labour market without ever introducing protective legislation especially for women.

4 Women and the advanced welfare state – a new kind of patriarchal power?

Anette Borchorst and Birte Siim

Women's position in society has changed fundamentally during the last twenty to twenty-five years, especially in those countries where welfare states have been most expansive. In this chapter we analyse the contradictory aspects of this process in Denmark. The Danish and Swedish welfare states belong to the most advanced in the world, and are often perceived as a model for other countries, particularly when it comes to the situation of women. We therefore find it important to analyse the Danish model focusing specifically on women's situation.

One of the main characteristics of the present Danish and Swedish welfare states from a woman's point of view has been the development of a partnership between the state and the family in relation to human reproduction, especially care for children, the sick, the elderly and the handicapped. Earlier, caregiving functions were performed mainly by women in the family as unpaid work. The new partnership was formed during a period of integration of large numbers of women into paid work. The expansion of public responsibilities for care-work was a prerequisite for this integration. We argue, however, that it was based on an institutionalization of women's double role as mothers and wage-earners. State policies still relied on women's responsibility for the psychic and physical well-being of the family members.

The integration of women into paid work on a large scale has become a common feature of the western world. It has, however, been most extreme and permanent in countries where the shift from private to public responsibility for human reproduction has been most radical, that is, in Denmark and Sweden.

Although the situation of Danish and Swedish women has changed fundamentally, we argue that they are still subject to male domination and part of a hierarchical, patriarchal sex-gender system. It is important to note, however, that male domination has been transformed. We argue that there has been a shift in the locus of female oppression from the family and the private sphere to the public sphere. In other words what has been called family patriarchy has been weakened, whereas social patriarchy – that is, male domination in the public sphere – has been strengthened.[1] The cutbacks in the welfare state and the growing unemployment which has accompanied the economic crisis have also made the limitations to strategies of sexual equality more visible. In the following we develop our arguments about the changes in patriarchal power and discuss our conclusions; and finally we outline the strategic perspectives of the Danish model from a feminist point of view.

The homemaker–breadwinner family

Women's integration in the public sphere has been a long and complicated process related to the social and economic development of capitalism. With the development of the modern welfare state this process has, however, acquired a number of characteristics which have qualitatively changed women's position in society. This integration has, however, been different in different countries.

In Denmark women were not pulled into or pushed out of the labour market in such large numbers during and after the Second World War as they were in countries actively engaged in warfare, for instance the United Kingdom and the USA. Denmark was occupied by the Germans, but Danish men were not sent away as soldiers to any great extent.

During the recession and special ideological climate of the cold war in the 1950s the family was ideologically strengthened. Married women's labour force participation rates fell from 27 to 23 per cent from 1950 to 1960; the number of full-time housewives increased as the birthrate rose in the first half of this period. The role of the mother and housewife was praised and regarded as the crucial element of female identity. Correspondingly a man was considered a good husband if he was able to support himself and his family with his income alone. In this period the ideological and economical polarization between the homemaker–

breadwinner and housework–wagework division and between women's and men's activities was the strongest it had ever been.

The institutionalization of women's double role as mothers and workers

In the 1960s women's situation changed radically and at the same time the family institution underwent profound alterations. The north-western part of the world experienced the beginning of an economic boom. Demand for labour increased, and in the early 1960s 'full employment' was reached in Denmark. There was a growing demand for labour that could no longer be met by the existing labour force, and many efforts were made to find new reserves. There have never been large numbers of foreign workers in the country, and there was only a minor increase in workers coming from abroad in this period. The group of full-time house-wives was seen as the solution to the scarcity of labour, and great efforts were made to get them into the labour market. Employers' interest in women's labour and the old feminist movement's demand for sexual equality (which was also fought inside the political parties) merged, and together with public authorities they tried to motivate married women to take gainful employment. In 1965 a state-owned research institute was asked to question housewives about which measures would make them take paid work. The results indicated that particularly part-time work and an increase in public childcare facilities would increase the number of married women in the labour force,[2] and during the 1960s these measures were actually promoted. Part-time work was extended to many areas of the labour market, and public responsibility for the care for preschool children during the daytime was increased substantially.

The number of full-time housewives started to decline, and the number of married women in the labour force increased drastically. Thus the labour force participation rate of married women rose from 23 per cent in 1960 to 49 per cent in 1970 and 57 per cent in 1974. This increase was parallel to a similar development in Sweden, but the participation rate of married women in Sweden was even higher in this period. In Finland married women had had permanent labour market experience for a much longer period, but in Norway there was no significant rise in the participation rate of married women until the end of the 1970s and the 1980s. The percentage of part-time workers among married women in the labour force in Denmark was about 20 per cent in 1960, in 1970 it was 46 per cent, and in 1974 52 per cent. It appears that apart from Finland, the countries which have the highest participation rates for women also have the highest level of part-time work.

The extension of the female labour force in Denmark stemmed at first from the entry into the labour market of women who were formerly full-time housewives, but later on it was due to more fundamental changes in women's life perspectives. The generational profile of the female labour force altered because younger women came into the labour market with still higher activity rates.[3] More women experienced wage-work as a permanent part of their adult lives, and more women received higher education. The gender division of housework, however, did not change radically in spite of this process. Women still have the chief responsibility for unpaid work in the family, especially for the care of the children. This means that housework is still an important part of women's lives and identity. The new development, however, means that women on a much larger scale than before have experiences both from the public sphere and the private sphere. One main problem is that working conditions on the labour market have not changed. They are not negotiated on the basis of women's double responsibility, but are still based on a male norm, i.e. on individuals who have no responsibility for housework and care-work once the paid working day is finished. As a consequence everyday life for a large number of women is characterized by sharp contradictions between their paid and unpaid work, and they have to tackle them individually.

In the 1970s a new phenomenon appeared because Danish women no longer took time off from work when they had small children (except for maternity leave). Now women with small children have the highest labour force participation rate of all women. Thus in 1978 81 per cent of women with one child were in the labour force. This is different from the situation in, for instance, Norway and the United Kingdom, where older women have the highest participation rates.

Apart from illustrating the changes in women's ideas about motherhood, the high level of paid work among mothers of small children also indicates the economic necessity of women's paid employment, especially in families with small children. Investigations of family budgets in Denmark have shown that housing expenditure particularly puts a strain on the economy of such families,[4] as due to higher demands for housing facilities and the special financial system of privately owned houses, housing expenditure is often at its highest when the children are young. Consequently the need for both paid and unpaid work tends to grow for parents of small children, and simultaneously the sexual division of work becomes more profound. Women stay in the labour market when they have children, but they do more part-time work the more children they have, and the smaller the children are, when the burden of house- and care-work gets heavier. Conversely men do less housework, but take on more paid work, the more children they have.

Changes in male domination in the family and in family patterns

Family life in the 1960s in Denmark became very different from that of the 1950s. The fertility rate fell drastically from 1966 to 1970 and has continuously had a falling tendency till today. The same tendency has been visible in many European countries, but it has been particularly strong in Denmark. In 1983 the gross reproduction rate in Denmark was 672, whereas it was 780 in Sweden, 800 in Norway and 850 in the United Kingdom and Finland. The gross reproduction rate is defined as the number of daughters that will be born alive to 1000 newborn girls during the reproductive period of their lives (ages 15 to 49) under the assumption that none of them die and that the age-specific fertility rates continue to be the same for the year concerned. The immediate fall in 1966 in Denmark was caused by the release of the contraceptive pill, and the legalizing of free abortions in 1973[5] has surely contributed to this process. Safer contraception has given women more control over their reproductive capacities and has helped them to separate sexuality from reproduction, but this can only partly explain the falling birthrate. The change in women's social and economic situation and the new ideas of women's role in society must also be taken into consideration, when explaining why women often choose education and gainful employment instead of having more children. It is, however, also important to pay attention to the fact that women often express the wish for more children than they actually have.[6] We interpret this as an *illustration of the incompatibility of mothering and wage working*. This contradiction has existed ever since the expansion of wage work with the rise of capitalism, but it is a historically new situation that women today prefer and have the choice of wage work and education to mothering.

Another new phenomenon appeared when marriages became less stable and permanent. The number of formal marriages began to decline in Denmark in the middle of the 1960s and has continued to fall. In the same period an increasing number of couples decided to live together in informal marriages without a licence and the total number of these 'paperless marriages' doubled from 1974 (when they were first registered) to 1981. The number of paperless marriages has been rising in all the Nordic countries, but they seem to be especially numerous in Denmark. To complete the picture, the number of divorces began to rise drastically in Denmark at the end of the 1960s and at the beginning of the 1970s, and has remained at a comparatively high level ever since.

What we have seen is a set of almost simultaneous and interwoven factors pointing in the same direction: marriages have tended to become less formal and less stable and families have become smaller. This development has apparently been greatest in Denmark. It is difficult to tell which are the causes and which are the consequences of all these changes. One important fact is that women became more independent of marriage and their husbands when they acquired a more permanent income of their own. Another important factor is the ideological break with the traditional homemaker–breadwinner family, which the new feminist movement particularly represented. The movement arose at the end of the 1960s and was very critical of the social isolation and economic dependency of full-time housewives. The young, relatively well-educated women who dominated the movement thereby dissociated themselves radically from the lives of their mothers. The scope of the changes in family patterns reflects, however, the fact that these ideas were spread far beyond the movement's own immediate circles.

The drastic increase in divorce was a result of both the transformation of the sex-gender system and the new ideas of women's tasks. The continuously high divorce rate reflects the fact that family life has not stabilized. An investigation of divorces in Denmark in 1980 shows that the contradictions between women's paid and unpaid work have become a new source of conflict in families, at least in women's opinion. It is mainly women who decide and take the initiative to divorce, and they often point specifically to problems with the division of work. Men, on the contrary, often give infidelity of their partners as the main reason for marriage break-up. The investigation concludes that men's and women's experiences with marriage and divorce often are two different phenomena.[7]

The economic power relations in the family have changed, but unfortunately we do not know much about changes in the psychological power relations in families. An investigation from 1965 indicates that the most democratic and equal decision-making structure exists in those families in which both husband and wife have an income of their own.[8] As to the sexual power and domination of men, we find it difficult to arrive at any general conclusions. Women's sexuality has surely become more visible and there has been more focus on and to some degree support of women, who have been subjected to sexual maltreatment from fathers, husbands or relatives. We are, however, not able to tell whether rape, violence in marriage and incest have diminished or not. Our hypothesis is, however, that the social and economic independence that women have gained *vis-à-vis* their husbands has limited male dominance in the family on a more general level.

The growth of the welfare economy from a woman's perspective

The modern welfare state in Denmark has a long history, but the development of a comprehensive welfare economy dates back to the beginning of the 1960s. The gradual development of the welfare state in this century has been closely connected to the growing influence of the Social Democratic Party. The Social Democratic Party has been in government since the end of the 1920s, as in Sweden, although always in a minority position and dependent on alliances with other political parties. Since the 1930s a Social Democratic model of a welfare society has become the dominant political form of state intervention.

In the 1960s state intervention was extended to new areas of society – both in relation to the economy and in relation to human reproduction. The Social Democratic Party combined support for the capitalist accumulation process with a substantial social reform programme for the working class in order to alleviate some of the social inequalities created by capitalism. From the 1960s the Danish and Swedish welfare states began to distinguish themselves from other welfare states like the British, influenced more by liberal ideas, and the Danish and Swedish welfare states became a model for the most advanced welfare states in the west.[9]

One important characteristic was the dramatic expansion of the social, health, and educational sectors with their corresponding expenditures and the creation of a welfare economy as an important part of the total economy. Another important characteristic which distinguished the Scandinavian welfare states from other welfare states was their distinct corporatist profile.[10] This corporatism was built on an institutionalized collaboration between the dominant classes. Huge and extremely hierarchical, male-dominated organizations representing different class and professional interests obtained increasing power and influence. Working conditions were negotiated by these organizations, and conflicts between employers' and workers' organizations were settled by a formalized system of rules with state representatives functioning as neutral arbitrators.

This expansion of the welfare economy and of the sphere of government intervention has had very different consequences for men and women. On the one hand the expansion of the welfare economy in relation to human reproduction has been an important precondition for married women's integration into the formal labour market and for their growing social and economic independence in relation to men. The state has, through its policies, ideology, and different forms of legislation, helped women to become integrated as employees. The state has also helped women accomplish important reforms like free abortions and the removal of explicit sex-discriminating rules.

On the other hand the state has basically supported the hierarchical gender division of work and has continued to limit women's power and influence in the public sphere through the structure and policies of the corporatist system. In this way the development of the Danish welfare state has been a very contradictory process for women. We argue that the Danish welfare state has not been neutral to women, rather it has contributed actively both to facilitate women's integration into the formal labour market and to institutionalize and legitimize women's double roles as mothers and workers. We therefore disagree with the conclusion that women's position is determined primarily by economic forces, especially the need for women's labour power. Instead we find that the state is an important mediator between the needs of the economy and the interests of different political actors. This does not necessarily mean that state policies have had the *explicit* and *conscious purpose* of reproducing the hierarchical gender division of work and male domination, which has not been the case in Denmark, where the institutionalization of women's double roles as mothers and workers has had the *unintended* effect of strengthening male domination in the public sphere.

The limitations of state policies in obtaining sexual equality have become more visible during the economic crisis with mass unemployment. In Denmark there have been no explicit attempts to push women out of the labour market, but cutbacks in public expenditure are clearly working in the direction of marginalizing women in relation to the labour market. In the following we shall explore the contradictions in public policies towards women in more detail and outline our conclusions about a strengthening of what has been called social patriarchy.

One crucial factor in the analyses of women's relation to the welfare state has become *the question of women's political power*. The breakdown of the breadwinner–homemaker family has increased women's independence from their husbands and has at the same time made women more dependent on the state as employees, clients and consumers of public services.[11] We argue, however, that there are important differences in the degrees of dependence in the different welfare states connected to differences between their status as employees, consumers and clients. We find that women in the Danish and Swedish welfare states are subject to a different form of dependency than women in welfare states such as those of Britain or the United States. The large state sector means that women have primarily become dependent on the state as employees and consumers of social services and only to a smaller extent as clients. The opposite is the case in Britain and the US where women to a larger extent are still dependent either on their husbands or on the state as clients.

In the following we shall look into women's different roles as employees, consumers and clients in more detail.[12]

Women's role in human reproduction

The substantial extension of public services in relation to human reproduction in Sweden and Denmark has had a great influence on women's lives in the sense that it has relieved them of some of their responsibilities in the family, especially the care of children, the sick and the elderly. We consider this process as one of the necessary prerequisites for the integration of married women in gainful employment. It is true that women have been integrated on the labour market in countries where there has not been an increase in public responsibilities for care-work. This was for example the case in the United Kingdom in the 1970s and in Norway in the late 1970s and the 1980s, but the point is that the integration has not happened on such a large scale as in Denmark and Sweden.

Yet, in contrast to the dominant belief, we do not find that as a consequence of the expansion of public services families were emptied of their functions in Denmark and Sweden in the 1960s and 1970s. On the contrary it has been estimated that work in the informal sector still accounts for about one third of all economic value.[13] Housework like cooking, cleaning, washing and so on did not diminish radically, but was rather reorganized by the introduction of new products like semi-manufactured food and new household technology so that it could be done more intensely at evenings or at weekends. The average time spent on housework per day in Denmark only fell from two hours and thirty-eight minutes in 1964 to one hour and fifty-two minutes in 1976.[14] The time spent on care for children, the sick and elderly persons of course diminished due to the growing number of creches, kindergartens, hospitals, and nursing homes for the elderly, but the public services were never intended to cover all the needs of dependant persons. Individual needs were furthermore not automatically met by the public service, but they had to be made accessible to individuals. Moreover, a whole range of new functions related to the growing need to contact public authorities and professionals arose. All these new functions were still mainly performed by women, serving as the necessary link between the family and the state.

The life situation of men was affected by these changes, particularly in family patterns, but not so thoroughly as for women, and the growing participation of women in paid work was not followed by a corresponding increase in the participation of men in unpaid work. The daily average time spent by men on housework per day only rose by eleven minutes for blue-collar workers from 1964 to 1976, and by thirteen minutes for white-collar workers. Thus in relation to human reproduction it was not so much the division of work between men and women in the family that changed, but rather that between women and the state. Accordingly, the integration of women into gainful employment and the weakening of women's economic dependence on men was based on an increasing dependence by women upon the state for public service. Women thereby became more closely linked than men to the state as consumers of social services.

Ideologically the substantial increase in public services related to health, social, and educational areas was closely connected to Social Democratic ideas of equality between classes. Public service was no longer considered as charity but was now regarded as an individual right. It often required no or only partial payment from the consumer and was financed by general income taxes paid according to a proportional system. This is one of the main characteristics which distinguishes the Swedish and Danish welfare states from, for instance, the British and American, where a much greater part of the welfare services has remained means-tested.

In our research on the impact of state policies upon the economic and social situation of women, we find that childcare policies have been one of the factors which has influenced the position of women most fundamentally during the last twenty years.[15] Motherhood and mothering have been difficult to combine with wage-work because of the patriarchal split between the private and the public sphere. The public sphere has been structured by a male norm which means that wage-work and participation in public life on the whole is difficult to combine with the responsibility for, for example, preschool children. The care of other dependent groups also influences women's position in society, but compared to the situation of British women the care of elderly persons and invalids has a much smaller significance for the position of Danish women.

In the 1960s dramatic changes were made in relation to the motives behind childcare policies in Denmark. Earlier a rather high level of public support had been given to childcare and education. It was, however, a condition for state subsidies that institutions mainly accepted children from low-income families, i.e. families in which mothers had to work because of economic necessity. In the middle of the 1960s legislation was passed formulating radical new purposes for childcare institutions, among other things, in order to get more women in paid employment. They were now aimed at all children in principle and educational or pedagogical motives like play and social interaction were given a very high priority. As a new phenomenon state subsidies could be given to daycare in private homes, but it was considered as a provisional arrangement until there were sufficient institutions and professionals to cover this need. This legislation caused a substantial increase in the number of creches for 0–2-year-olds, kindergartens for 3–6-year-olds, and a minor increase in the recreational centres for 6–12-year-olds outside school hours. In 1972 16 per cent of all 0–2-year-olds were enrolled in public daycare and childcare institutions, and 31 per cent of 3–6-year-olds. These percentages increased gradually through the following years, and 1984 they were 42 per cent for the 0–2-year-olds and 57 per cent for 3–6-year olds. They are the highest in the Scandinavian countries, and, especially for the 0–2 age group, among the highest in the West.

This legislation was supported by almost all the political parties in the parliament (*folketinget*). Many of the right-wing parties were motivated to vote for it because of the increasing supply of married women in the labour market that would result, but they preferred daycare to institutions. The Social Democratic government was conscious of the influence of the legislation upon the situation of women, but argued explicitly for an increase in the public response for preschool children, and considered institutions as the necessary frame for it. Thus childcare institutions were not formally related to the needs and interests of women, and childcare was not integrated as part of the legislation for sexual equality, which was passed in the 1970s.

During the 1970s attempts were made to reduce public expenditure, especially related to public service, but it was not until 1974, with the economic crisis, that any greater change in public services became visible. Childcare institutions became one of the favourite targets for cutbacks. At first there was no fundamental break with the incentives of the 1965 legislation, and the number of places in daycare and childcare institutions still rose, but gradually educational standards deteriorated and care gained higher priority, whereas pedagogical purposes are rarely mentioned in government notices. What has also happened is that admission to childcare facilities has been still more closely linked to the employment situation of the parents.

The general tendency is towards privatization of responsibility for dependant groups, and political attempts are being made to introduce new combinations of public and private care for children, sick and elderly persons. This destructuring of the welfare state was introduced by the Social Democratic government in 1980 and was connected to a strong criticism of the existing welfare services.[16] This was followed up and intensified by the right-wing coalition, which came to power in 1982. Reduction of public expenditure especially related to social, health, and educational areas has now become the first and foremost endeavour of the government.

The depreciation of public service is affecting women's lives more than men's, as their burden of unpaid work gets heavier, and their possibilities for staying in gainful employment diminish. The dependency of women on the welfare state has thereby become more visible. One cannot say, however, that for instance childcare is being used as a direct tool to control the position of women. Compared to the less advanced welfare states the Danish still offers a high quality public service.

The sex segregation of employment and unemployment

Danish society has been characterized by economic crisis since 1974. This has not sent women back to the kitchen or resulted in an increase in the number of full-time housewives, and in fact their number has continously been falling. Women's labour force participation rate has, on the contrary, been rising from 55 per cent in 1974 to 64 per cent in 1984, and it is thus approaching the level of participation among men, which was 78 per cent in 1984. This illustrates how fundamental the changes in women's life-perspective have been, and is also reflected by the fact that very few people argue publicly that women should go back to the kitchens. It is obvious that family patterns are still unstable and that marriage does not give women a life-long possibility of economic support.

The participation rates do not, however, reflect the level of employment, and unemployment has been increasing from 2.1 per cent of the labour force in 1974 to 10.5 per cent in 1984. From 1977 women have been relatively harder hit by unemployment than men, and sex differences in unemployment have been widening since then. In 1984 10.5 per cent of men and 12.7 per cent of all women in the labour force were registered as unemployed. There are also sex differences in unemployment in the sense that women are unemployed for longer periods than men, and they have more difficulty in finding permanent jobs after having been unemployed. It is especially older women, women without vocational training and mothers of small children who are exposed to long-term unemployment.[17]

If women are more seriously hit by unemployment than men, one may ask, why has the number of full-time housewives not been increasing in Denmark? This is explained by the fact that more women have insured themselves against unemployment, and therefore receive unemployment benefits and are registered as unemployed when they lose their jobs. Another important factor is that Danish labour market policies and rules for unemployment have been characterized by the Social Democratic commitment to secure employment. This has resulted in rules which allow the unemployed to remain in the unemployment system (and receive unemployment benefits) for a longer period than in other countries. When rules of insurance are fulfilled, totally unemployed persons can receive unemployment benefits for a period of two years and five months, and before being relegated to the social welfare system they are entitled to a job offer (for seven months in the public sector and nine months in the private sector). This enables them to stay in the unemployment system for another period.[18] The legislation regulating unemployment insurance (which is constituted by a public–private organizational mix) has, however, slowly deteriorated during the last ten years, especially after the change of government in 1982. The right-wing government is obviously not so committed to secure employment as the Social Democrats and has tried to widen the differences in living conditions between the employed and the unemployed in order to 'make it payable to work'. The changes and reductions mean that more people will be expelled from the labour force in the future. Although most of the rules still are formally sex-neutral, some of the cutbacks clearly hit women more than men.

The differences in unemployment are linked to the differences in men's and women's relation to human reproduction, and they are also related to the sex segregation of the labour market. This segregation functions both on a horizontal dimension, in the way that women and men have different kinds of jobs, and also on a vertical dimension in the sense that they occupy different positions in the job hierarchy. *Horizontally* women concentrate on very few areas like jobs in offices and shops, public care-work and private service. In 1978 the ten largest occupations for women included 68 per cent of all women in the labour force, whereas the ten largest occupations for men only included 37 per cent of men.[19] This illustrates the fact that men are much more spread across different job areas than women. Moreover a much larger proportion of women are public employees. Accordingly women are also more dependent on the welfare state as employees then men are. This has become especially visible during the increasing attempts to reduce public expenditure, primarily in the social and health sectors. The vulnerable position of women also becomes clear when new technology is being introduced, because it is often women who are made redundant. The question is whether women will be able to get some of the new jobs that technological changes create.

Vertically women are concentrated in positions at the bottom of the job hierarchy. Even though women have increasingly been employed as professionals at medium and top positions in the hierarchy, the majority of women are still employed as unskilled blue-collar workers or low position white-collar workers. Differences in vocational training can of course to some extent explain this situation, but the sexual hierarchy is also found despite the level of education. Finally, working hours also constitute a matter of extreme sex segregation. Almost 45 per cent of women work part time, whereas almost all men work full time. Apart from being the individual solution for women coping with contradictory demands from paid and unpaid work, part-time work is also preferred by employers in many areas and forced upon women who actually want full-time work.

The sex segregation of the labour market seems to be a common characteristic almost everywhere in the world, but we have been struck by the fact that the sex segregation has been exacerbated since the 1960s both horizontally and vertically whereas the number of women in the labour force has risen markedly. Countries with the highest participation rates for women seem also to have the strongest sex segregation of the labour market.[20]

The hierarchical character of the homemaker–breadwinner model has accordingly been replaced by another hierarchy in paid work, and we see this as a reflection of the strengthening of male power on a more structural level, although it is important to notice that the hierarchical relation between male and female labour in the work place often has a very personal character.

The question is whether the policy of sexual equality has affected this situation. In the 1970s it became apparent that the strategy of ensuring sexual equality merely by integrating women in gainful employment, which was given a very high priority in the 1960s, had not been successful. From this time there has been a growing focus on the sex segregation of the labour market, and attempts to integrate women into men's jobs or 'non-traditional jobs' has been the overall, dominating theme in sexual equality measures. As far as we can see only those strategies for sexual equality which are acceptable from a male point of view are carried through. This means that attempts to change the male-dominated areas so that girls' and women's values and experiences are integrated are doomed to fail. Instead the problem is perceived as the failure of women to choose the right education and jobs, and the strategy is mostly based on attempts merely to integrate women in the male-dominated areas. The limits of state policies for sexual equality are also related to the fact that they do not seriously face the problems of combining paid and unpaid work. Some of the women who have jobs inside the state apparatus, and who are dealing with the special measures for women in their work, are trying to challenge these attitudes. It is unlikely that they will succeed unless there is a political agreement to change the structures of work conditions in both paid and unpaid work.

Women's dependency as clients

The breakdown of the earlier breadwinner–homemaker family has reduced the role of the husband as an economic provider for women in the family. The changes in family patterns and the growth of the dual-earner family, however, has not meant that men and women today have equal opportunities to provide for themselves and their children. As a result women have come to rely on three different sources of income for their survival: their own wage-work, public services and welfare benefits from the state, and their husbands' wages.[21] Why is it that the economic position and economic opportunities for men and women are still unequal?

First of all, women and men have different relations to the labour market. The sex segregated labour market, meaning low wages and low influence for women in relation to men, combined with motherhood and women's role in mothering, is one important reason why women have lower earnings and substantially higher expenses than men. In Denmark during the 1960s and 1970s there has been a substantial rise in women's wages relative to men's, and by 1977 women's relative wages to men's in industry were almost 90 per cent. The gradual weakening of a solidaristic wages policy which aimed to reduce differentials between men and women during the economic crisis and mass unemployment has made women's relative wages fall slightly after 1977. They still, however, made up more than 85 per cent of the average male wage in industry by 1984.

Second, the more dynamic family patterns – the increased number of divorces and remarriages – means that a growing number of women live alone for some period of their lives. After a divorce it is more often women who get custody over the children, even though there is a tendency among the well-educated young families that men become increasingly involved as parents. The combination of being responsible for paid and unpaid work in the family makes the group of single mothers very vulnerable and research has pointed out that this group has some of the worst social and economic problems today.[22] During the 1970s it became accepted that many women chose not to marry and not to have children, or wanted to live alone with their children. It has, however, during the same period become increasingly difficult to provide for a family with only one income. This is especially true if you happen to be a low-income group, because the social norm today is a two-income family. Therefore single mothers rely heavily on the state for economic support, and the amount and kind of support received from the state becomes crucial for them.

In Denmark single mothers have very high labour activity rates compared to women in other welfare states. This is on the one hand an expression of the fact that they only have their own earnings to support themselves, but as a consequence they have come to rely heavily on public services and support, for example in relation to childcare. One third of the group of single mothers belong to the group of unskilled low-income workers, and the rest of the group belong to the group of white-collar workers, but the majority rely on different kinds of state benefits and services. Single parents in Denmark receive relatively generous support from the state compared to Great Britain. They receive a supplement to the universal family allowance, which is means-tested, and they are eligible for special housing benefits and to economic subsidy for childcare institutions. State support in terms of public services and benefits therefore forms an important part of their total income.

During the last ten years of economic crises and mass unemployment, the social and economic situation of single mothers has gradually deteriotated. Mass unemployment, coupled with substantial cuts in public expenditure, have hit single mothers extremely hard. Single mothers have high unemployment rates, and the reduction of public expenditure at a time of constant or falling wages and unemployment benefits has meant that their incomes have not been able to keep up with their growing expenses. Single mothers today have growing economic problems, especially with the cost of housing and payments to childcare institutions. It is not surprising that the general problems of single mothers with low wages and part-time work has been exacerbated with mass unemployment and cuts in public expenditure, but it is alarming that the research reports point to the danger of *a growing feminization of poverty* for this group. This tendency towards a feminization of poverty as a result of long-term unemployment and decreased government spending has also been identified in countries like Britain and the USA. The tendency is, of course, most pronounced in countries with Conservative and neo-Conservative governments, where the general problems of growing poverty are most conspicuous. In both Britain and the USA the families headed by single mothers make up a large and growing number of all poor families. In Britain it has been estimated that the majority of single mothers today live around or just above the official poverty level, and in the USA two out of three poor adults are women, and 23 per cent of all children live in poverty.[23] This is the basis of a growing realization among feminist researchers that the roots of women's poverty are different from men's, because poverty for women is related to women's socially defined responsibilities as mothers and their low status in the sex segregated labour market.[24]

We find everywhere that single mothers are dependent on the state for economic support either in the form of public services like childcare institutions or in the form of means-tested social welfare benefits. The point is, however, that there is a fundamental difference between being dependent *as consumers* of public services or being dependent *as clients* on social welfare. The status as client is often associated with economic dependency, control, and social stigmatization. The crucial thing is public control over the client, which is often much more severe than the control with wage earners or consumers. We argue that the higher the level of public services and the more comprehensive the universal benefits the better are the chances for women to support themselves and the less likely that they become solely dependent on the state as clients. As a consequence we find that it is wrong to associate a large welfare sector like the Danish one *per se* with a strong dependency on the state. From a woman's point of view it is rather the other way round: *a strong public service sector seems to be one precondition for avoiding becoming solely dependent on the state as clients*. In Denmark and Sweden women have come to rely on the state primarily as workers in the public sector and as consumers of social services, and only to a smaller degree as clients. The opposite is true in Britain and the US where women have come to rely on the state primarily as clients. In this perspective we find it important that women everywhere attempt to strengthen their roles as employees and consumers and fight to diminish their role as clients.

Sex and class

We have now analysed the relation between women and the welfare state in general, but we find it important to emphasize the differences that still exist between women in different social classes. In what way has the development of the welfare state changed class differences between women, and what new kind of differences among women have become important today?

Differences in women's economic and social position are not only an expression of social class, but are also related to the educational and occupational status of women and their husbands, their family situation and to generational and geographical factors.

During the last hundred years we find that class differences between women have gradually diminished. In the beginning of the century there were important differences in the social and economic situation of upper- and middle-class women and the majority of working women in agriculture and industry. Upper- and middle-class women often paid other women to take care of their house- and care-work as servants and maids, and if they had paid work they were usually unmarried. Working-class women on the other hand (including working women in agriculture), had to take care of their own housework within a very limited budget, and often they were forced to supplement the family income by taking up different kinds of paid work. Some of these differences have disappeared, especially since the Second World War. Today paid help in households has almost vanished, and household technology has contributed to a standardization of housework. Although differences in living standards are, of course, still important, the integration of married women into the formal labour market has made the double burden of combining paid and unpaid work a common condition for women of all classes. This is the empirical basis for the argument that working women constitute a sexual class, but we find that there are still important differences among women that make the use of the term sexual class questionable.[25]

The Social Democratic welfare state has by means of a comprehensive social reform programme helped abolish some of the inequalities between the different classes, but the expansion of the welfare state has also created new differences among women. Young and well-educated women have a far better position in the welfare state than uneducated and older women. Today there are important differences in women's position in the labour market between well-educated professional women and the unskilled women at the bottom of the job hierarchy. We find that there is another important difference between professional women employed in the social, health and educational sectors, and women who are dependent on public services and welfare benefits as consumers and clients. These two groups have both conflicting and common interests as women. The conflicts are probably strongest between the group of social workers who have to administer strong social control, and the clients on social welfare who are often on very limited budgets which cannot cover their basic social needs. In Denmark the conflicts between these two groups of women have not been as profound as, for example, in Britain, because social workers often express solidarity with their clients, and many of the social workers have been or are still actively engaged in the feminist struggle. We also find examples of solidarity between professional women and women as consumers in the health sector and in relation to public childcare. In these areas women often fight together as employees and consumers against cutbacks and the deterioration of accepted standards.

During the last ten years we have seen a growing number of women experiencing and expressing common interests as women despite differences in their social and economic situation. The old and new women's organizations have worked together with women in trade unions around claims for equal pay, equal opportunities in the labour market and in the educational system and for a breakdown of the sex segregated labour market. Women have agreed upon policies on reproductive rights and on protests against the cutbacks in the welfare state, etc. It is too early to say whether the similarities or the differences that still exist in women's social and economic situations will dominate politically. It is, for instance, an open question whether well-educated professional women will become integrated into the system in order to fight for their own narrow interests as employees, or whether they will develop a broader solidarity with the majority of working women around fundamental feminist issues.

Women and political power

We have argued that women's lives have been more affected by the welfare state than men's because their roles as mothers and wage-earners placed them in a special position as consumers and clients of the welfare state. We have also shown that a growing number of women have become public employees working in the social, health, and educational sectors. When it comes to the question of political power it seems, however, that very little has changed. Politics is still basically a male affair that supports the fundamental patriarchal power of the welfare state. There has been an increase in female representation in the legislative bodies in the Scandinavian countries during the 1960s and 1970s, and today women's representation is the highest in the world. In Denmark the percentage of women in parliament (*folketinget*) has risen from 10 per cent in 1960 to 26 per cent in 1985. This increase is important for women, but it has not given them an equal increase in real power and influence on the political decisions and the actual practice of the welfare state. This is primarily a consequence of the growing corporatism during the same period which has changed the formal power structure of the state, giving huge interest organizations with very low female representation at the top level a substantial increase in power and influence on political decisions.[25]

It has been, and to some extent it still is, an assumption that women are not as politically active as men. This has probably been true in periods where the majority of women have been enclosed in the private sphere of the family, but it is not true any more. The integration of women into the public sphere of work during the last ten to twenty years has greatly affected women's political activity. Today for the first time in history, we see women voting in the same numbers as men and there has been growing political activity by women in all areas of life. Research from Denmark indicates that young women are as politically active as young men, but it is interesting that there is a significant difference in the kind of political activity men and women become engaged in. Women are more active in the new social movements and in trade unions (although not at the top level), and men are more active in political parties and at public meetings.[26] This illustrates the connection between the concept of political activity and conclusions on gender differences in political activity. A narrow concept of politics associating it primarily with the formal political system clearly tends to under-estimate women's political activity.

The different life experiences of men and women are one obvious reason for the gender differences in political activity, and these differences are likewise the basis for the differences in political attitudes of men and women which have been found in several countries during the last five to ten years. In the USA, political scientists and commentators have registered a 'gender-gap' in the voting patterns of men and women: women tend to vote more to the left, i.e. for Democratic candidates, while men to a greater extent vote for Republican candidates. This tendency has not been confirmed by Danish data, but investigations of political attitudes of men and women reveal significant differences. Danish women tend to be more negative towards military and defence expenditures than men are, and women are more critical towards cutbacks in social welfare, health and educational expenditure.[27] Women are also more negative towards nuclear power than men and more sympathetic to the peace movement. It is significant that in all these political issues women are more in accordance with the Social Democrats and the Socialists than men, whereas on moral issues women tend to be more divided between Conservative and Socialist ideas.

Investigations of differences in questions concerning public responsibility for human reproduction reveal the most distinctive gender differences in Denmark. This is an area where there have been the most dramatic changes in women's lives, and where the differences between the activities of men and women are still most pronounced. Today women have collectively become responsible for both privately and publicly organized reproductive tasks, and subsequently women suffer most under strategies aimed at undermining the welfare state both as workers and mothers or as consumers and clients. At a time where the organization of childcare has become a political issue, women's responsibilities for care-work have become a new radicalizing political force for many women. Today a larger group of women than ever before experience and express a kind of feminist consciousness having become aware of the hierarchical character of the gender division of work and male domination in society. The feminist movement has been one of the driving forces in this cultural revolution of ideas.

Feminist organizations have existed in Denmark since the 1870s and the old feminist organizations are still actively engaged in feminist issues. There have, however, been important differences between the old women's organizations and the new feminist movement from the late 1960s. The old feminist organizations were organized as traditional political organizations working for political influence from within the system, and they became one of the driving forces in the formulation of the new equality policies in the 1960s. The new feminist movement on the other hand developed as a non-hierarchical collectively organized movement, engaged primarily in extra-parliamentary activities. It has not claimed formal political power, but wanted rather to change people's minds about women's roles and the position of women in society. In the beginning of the 1970s the differences between the old and new feminist organizations were profound, but gradually the two began working together on a number of feminist issues. Today feminist ideas have spread far beyond the original organizations, and only a small number of women are still actively engaged in separate women's organizations. Feminists have instead become actively engaged in all kinds of political activity, especially in the trade unions, in the new social movements, and within state institutions as professional administrators of equality policies in the labour market, and in the educational system. This development has been interpreted rather differently. It has either been seen as an abolition of the separatist feminist strategy or as an extension of feminist ideas to established organizations and institutions. We find that women increasingly attempt to combine integration in the male-dominated institutions and organizations with a strategy of promoting women-specific groups, for example in trade unions, in political parties and within state institutions and the universities. This 'double strategy' is both a recognition of the importance of the feminist principles of organization and of feminist ideas and an acknowledgement of the real power of the formal political system.

We find that there are still important problems connected with the development of a feminist strategy towards the state. The new feminist movement has been a rather passive witness with regard to the expansion of the welfare state in the 1970s. On the one hand feminists supported the expansion of the social services in relation to human reproduction, but on the other hand the state was opposed as a patriarchal and hierarchical institution. The old feminist organizations have conversely been rather uncritical of the welfare state, and have by and large accepted the hierarchical gender division of work and power. Under the impact of the economic crisis and the different political strategies to undermine the welfare state it has become urgent for feminists to develop a more complex understanding of the welfare state. There is a growing need to combine a strong criticism of the bureaucratization, professionalization and specialization of the welfare state with a strong commitment to defend and improve the quality of the present social services.

The Scandinavian welfare state from a feminist perspective

The development of the advanced welfare state had vastly improved women's social and economic position during the 1960s and the 1970s. The parallel integration of women in the public sphere of work and politics and the changes in family patterns have changed women's lives fundamentally, and women are today no longer economically dependent solely on their husbands. The welfare state has greatly improved women's abilities to support themselves and their children, and women have increasingly come to rely on their own earnings and on the benefits and social services of the state and only to a smaller extent on their husband's income. We find that all in all women have obtained substantial gains in the advanced welfare states, but it is necessary to emphasize that the sexual division of labour and male domination have not been abolished.

We have argued that patriarchal power has changed, and there has been a shift in the locus of oppression from the private to the public sphere. This transformation of patriarchy has had important consequences for women, but it cannot be interpreted merely as a shift from private to public dependence for women. We find that the development of the advanced welfare state has had contradictory effects on women's lives. On the one hand the improvement of women's social and economic position has also given women more influence as workers and citizens, but on the other hand male domination in the public sphere has been strengthened.

What is general and what is specific for the Scandinavian welfare states and what can women from other countries learn from the Scandinavian experience? These are important questions that feminist scholars have only recently begun to address.[29] It is important to emphasize that there is no one Scandinavian model, because the historical background and the political and economic development of the welfare state has been different in the three Scandinavian countries. Although there are many similarities between Denmark and Sweden in this respect, there are rather important differences between the situation of women in Denmark and Sweden compared to Norway.

Our general conclusion is that the Social Democratic welfare strategy, in particular the partnership between the state and the family over human reproduction, has had many advantages for women. The specific character of women's integration into the labour market has been closely related to the high level of public services in relation to childcare, health care and care for the elderly. In this respect the Social Democratic welfare strategy has undoubtedly strengthened women's situation both as mothers and workers.

In spite of the advantages for women in the Scandinavian welfare strategy, we find that it cannot be used as a model for women, for several reasons. First, and most important, in none of the Scandinavian countries have women been active participants in determining the political development of the welfare state. Politics have predominantly been a male affair, especially at the top level, and there is a strong concentration of men in the administrative, economical and political power centres. Corporatism has strengthened male dominance in the public sphere, and has limited women's influence on the actual decision-making process both as workers and citizens.

Second, the expansion of the welfare economy and the increased public responsibility for human reproduction has not been motivated by concern for women's social needs or by goals of greater equality between men and women. Progress for women has rather been a by-product of a broader welfare strategy. Equality policies and social policies concerned with human reproduction have always been subsumed by other political and economic concerns, and this becomes a problem during an economic crisis, when the official strategy from all political parties is to cut down on public expenditure, especially in the social, health and educational sectors. It is a strategy that has hit women especially hard in their different roles as wage-earners, consumers, clients and mothers.

Third, there is still, as we have seen, considerable sex segregation in the labour market, which was exacerbated during the 1970s. In spite of an increasing number of women in the public sphere, their relative position has deteriorated, compared to that of men. The strong trade union movement has helped women raise their wages through a wages policy aiming to reduce differentials between men and women, but at the same time it has been hard for women to influence union policies because of strong centralization and male domination at the top levels.

To summarize, we find that the Social Democratic model has

improved women's social and economic situation as mothers and wage-earners. The state has helped to integrate women into the public sphere and enabled them to become more economically self-sufficient through its expansion of the public service sector and the institutionalization of equality policies. On the one hand, one consequence of the Social Democratic model has been to help maintain patriarchal power through the institutionalization of women's dual roles as mothers and workers. Another consequence has been to strengthen male domination in the public sphere of work and politics through growing corporatism.

What can feminists learn from the Danish experience? We would argue that the most important question for feminists has become the problem of political power in a broad sense. In the advanced welfare states it has become crucial for the further improvement of women's situation that women fight collectively for more power and influence as wage earners and citizens, and work together as consumers to increase their influence over how public services are actually designed. It is important that women today have the economic means to support themselves and their children and, although this is not the case in Britain and the United States, the Scandinavian experience tells us that it is not enough. It is necessary that women participate in the determination of what their social needs and political interests actually are. Women must develop more concrete strategies towards the state, which include policies to strengthen women's position and give women more power as mothers, workers and citizens within the framework of a more democratic welfare state.

Notes and references

1 These concepts have been developed by Zillah Eisenstein; see *The radical future of liberal feminism* (New York, Longman 1981).

2 Johs. A. Nordhooek, *Gifte kvinder i familie og erhverv. Bd. 1, Deltagelse i erhvervsilvet* ('Married women in family and work, vol. 1: Employment', with an English summary), The Danish National Institute of Social Research, Report no. 37 (Copenhagen 1969).

3 Anette Borchorst, *Krisens konsekvenser for kvinders stilling på det danske arbejdsmarked* ('The impact of the crisis of women's position on the Danish labour market) Aarhus: (Institute of Political Science, University of Aarhus 1981).

4 *Børnekommissionens Betænkning* ('Report from the Child Welfare

Commission', with an English summary), Report no. 918 (Copenhagen 1981).

5   The right to legal abortion up till twelve weeks pregnancy was introduced in 1973. Like other health services in Denmark it is free of charge.

6   Ole Bertelsen, *Den unge familie i 70'erne* ('The young family in the 1970s', with an English summary), The Danish National Institute of Social Research, Report no. 99 (Copenhagan 1980).

7   Inger Koch-Nielsen, *Skilsmisser* ('Divorces', with an English summary), The Danish National Institute of Social Research, Report no. 118 (Copenhagen 1983).

8   Johs. A, Noordhoek, Yrsa Smith, *Gifte kvinder i familie og erhverv. Bd. II, Udearbejde og familie* ('Married women in family and work, vol. II; effects on the family' with an English summary), The Danish National Institute of Social Research, Report no. 55 (Copenhagen 1972).

9   See Neils Finn Christiansen, 'Denmark: the end of the idyll', in *New Left Review*, no. 144 (March–April 1984), p. 5–32.

10 See Finn Valentin, 'Corporatism and the Danish welfare state' in *Acta Sociologica* (1978), Supplement, p. 73–97.

11 We have been inspired to analyse women and the welfare state in their roles as clients, employees and citizens by Helga Marie Hernes' 'Women and the welfare state: the transition from private to public dependence' in this volume. We do, however, see a point in making a distinction between the client and consumer role for reasons which will appear in the following.

12 For a more detailed argument about the differences between the Danish, British and American welfare states in relation to women see Birte Siim 'Women and the welfare state: between private and public dependence', Paper presented at the Centre for Research on Women, Stanford University, 1984.

13 Gitte Haslebo, *Fordeling af tid og arbejde i velfærdsstaten* ('Distribution of time and work in the welfare state'), Ministry of Environment (Copenhagen 1983).

14 *Levevilkår i Danmark: Statistisk oversigt 1976* ('Living Conditions in Denmark: compendium of statistics', with English headings) Danish National Institute of Social Research, (Copenhagen 1976) p. 70.

15 Anette Borchorst, Birte Siim, *Kvinder i velfædsstaten – mellem moderskab og lønarbejde gennem 100 år* ('Women in the welfare state – between mothering and wage work in 100 years'), (Aalborg: Aalborg University Press, 1984).

16 In speeches by the former Social Democratic Minister of Social Affairs, Ritt Bjerregård: Ritt Bjerregård, Lars Lundgård, *Til venner*

og fjender af dansk socialpolitik ('To friends and enemies of Danish social policy') (Gyldendal, Copenhagen 1976), p. 70.

17   Anette Borchorst, 'On the unemployment of women in Denmark', in *Research Newsletter no. 9*, published by Women's Research Centre in Social Science, (Copenhagen: February 1985).

18   Ministry of Labour (Economic-Statistical Advisor), *Labour market and labour market policy* (Copenhagen 1984) and Ministry of Labour, *Description of the Danish unemployment insurance system* (Copenhagen 1984).

19   Anette Borchorst, *Arbejdsmarkedets køndopdeling – patriarkalsk dominans eller kvinders valg?* (The sex-segregated labour market – patriarchal power or women's choice?) (Aalborg: Aalborg University Press 1984).

20   Marja Liisa Anttalainen, *Rapport om den könsuppdelade arbetsmarknaden* ('Report of the sex-segregated labour market'), Nordic Council of Ministers, (1983).

21   Kari Wærness, 'Caring as women's work in the welfare state' in Harriet Holter (ed.), *Patriarchy in a welfare society* (Oslo: Universitetsforlaget, 1984). pp. 67–88.

22   Søren Geckler, *Notat om enlige mødres leve – og arbejdsforhold* ('Paper on single mothers' living and working conditions'), Danish National Institute of Social Research (March 1982), and Winnie Jørgensen, *Enlige forsørgere i bistandssystemet* ('Single supporters in the system of social welfare'), Danish National Institute of Social Research (July 1985).

23   A. Walker, S. Winyard and C. Pond, 'Conservative economic policy: the social consequences' in D. Bull, P. Winding (eds.), *Thatcherism and the poor*, Poverty Pamphlet 59 (London: The Child Poverty Action Group 1983).

24   Commission of Civil Rights, *A growing crisis: disadvantaged women and their children* (May 1983). Diane Pearce, 'Women, work and welfare: the feminization of poverty' in Karen Wolk Fenstein (ed.) *Working women and families*, Sage Yearbook in Women's Policy Studies, 4 (1978), p. 103–24. Diane Pearce and Harriette McAdoo, 'Women and children: alone and in poverty', in Rosalie G. Genovese (ed.) *Families and change: social needs and public policies* (N. Y.: Praeger 1984) p. 161–78. See also *Signs* issue on Women and Poverty, *Signs: Journal of Women in Culture and Society*, **10**, no. 2, (Chicago: University of Chicago Press 1985).

25   Zillah Eisenstein, *Feminism and sexual equality: crisis in liberal America* (N. Y.: Monthly Review Press 1984) pp. 146–70.

26   Elina Havio-Mannila and others (eds.), *Unfinished democracy: women in Nordic politics* (Pergamon Press 1985).

7 Lise Togeby, *Politik – også en kvindesag* ('Politics – also a female concern'), *Politica* (Aarhus: Aarhus University 1984).

8 Jørgen Goul Andersen, *Kvinder og politik* ('Women and politics'), *Politica* (Aarhus: Aarhus University 1984).

9 Mary Ruggie, *The state and working women* (Princeton: Princeton University Press 1984). Carolyn Teich Adams and Katryn Teich Winston, *Mothers at work. Public policies in the US, Sweden and Britain*, (Princeton: Princeton University Press 1980); Birte Siim (1984).

5 Women's new social role: contradictions of the welfare state

Anne Showstack Sassoon

Any discussion of the crisis of the welfare state which is limited to a debate, however important, about the quantity of resources and their distribution between contending groups prevents us from understanding the full social and political dimensions of that crisis. Moreover, such simplification fails to reveal important aspects of the restructuring of the economy or the interrelationship between economic, social and political transformations. Today the welfare state form is decreasingly able to meet the needs of society. I use the term 'the welfare state form' to refer to the type of state which has developed in Europe and North America based on a social pact the most important clauses of which were a commitment to full employment, the development of social payments and services to provide a safety net against poverty, and an educational system based on the principle, if not the fact, of equal opportunities.[1]

Although the crisis faced by this state form has been analysed from various perspectives, the changed socio-economic role of women tends to be eclipsed.[2] Whatever the merits of some of this work, it is my argument that an analysis of the contradictions implicit in women's social role and everyday experience can reveal what is otherwise missed: the way questions are being posed for which this state form is outmoded. Confronted by the general difficulty of 'reading' this crisis and of 'knowing' reality, starting from the point of view of women allows us to understand better such phenomena as the crisis of the trade unions and left-wing political parties, the inadequacy of neo-corporatist relations,[3] the importance of the way in which the productive sphere is organized, and the impossibility of considering the private and public in isolation from one another. At the same time, by focusing on the

multifacted nature of women's role today, we will arrive at a
sense of how women's subordination is being restructured within a
situation where new opportunities are being provided by the
welfare state for women as citizens and employees. These new
opportunities have been part and parcel of contradictions which
it has produced and finds impossible to overcome. And finally, we
will come to understand how these contradictions are extremely
advanced because they raise issues which can only be resolved by
a transformation of the productive system and a new relationship
between public and private.

A central contradiction

My analysis starts with the socio-economic position of women in
Britain, which manifests a number of trends common to various
countries despite differences between them. The norm for women
in Britain today is to have a dual role: in the home and in paid
labour. The vast majority now have a permanent role in the labour
market with only a short interval when their children (probably
only one or two) are very small.[4] By the same token, very few
men have wives who stay at home full-time to service them and
their children. They are serviced but by someone with another
job.

A dual role for the vast majority of women in society is a recent
phenomenon. After remaining static for about a century at 30 to
32 per cent, the proportion of women workers began to increase
in the 1950s and, after a dramatic rise in the 1970s, women now
make up more than 40 per cent of the workforce. The most
significant aspect of this numerical increase is that unlike earlier
periods, an overwhelming majority of married women, 59.4 per
cent, now have jobs in the formal labour market. This rises to
67.1 per cent after 35 when children are most likely to have started
school, and to 71 per cent by the time the youngest child is 10
years old.[5] This means that whereas in 1921, for example, fewer
than 10 per cent of married women were in the official labour
force,[6] married women workers now outnumber unmarried
women workers by almost two to one.[7] In fact, more women
marry, and although individual women are having fewer children,
more are having at least one child. Therefore most women have
childcare and/or 'husbandcare' responsibilities[8] at the same time

as they are in the labour market. This increase in married women in the *formal* labour market represents a *qualitative* change in the relationship between women and paid work because of the nature of the domestic responsibilities they bring with them. Although many women, particularly from the working class, always made a financial contribution to households even after marriage, and during widowhood, for example, a whole series of contradictions between paid work, welfare state services and social needs are becoming clear because of the constraints which derive from the inflexible organization of formal jobs. This contrasts with the *relative* flexibility of casual jobs in the informal economy.[9]

However, although women are in the labour force on this massive scale, society as a whole has not really accepted this fact of life: the domestic sphere, the world of work, the welfare state are all organized as if women were continuing a traditional role. The institutions and practices of the welfare state are organized around the same traditional model of work and domestic life, where women remain the backbone of domestic labour, and the world of work is organized round a 'male model' which assumes one human being at work for, say, forty hours a week (plus commuting and possibly overtime) with a partner available full-time for domestic tasks.

These changes in women's lives have produced conflicts in different spheres of social life which derive from the choices women make in which the need and desire to *combine* having children and to remain in the labour force structures their lives. These conflicts run through the organization and the economy of the household, and are manifest at the level of collective reproduction of society as a whole. It is part of a long-term development, what Gramsci would have called an organic crisis. The influx into the labour force of women who have what I will call adult caring and servicing responsibilities, has taken place at a time when the biggest growth areas in the economy have been precisely in traditional 'female' areas: in the service and state or tertiary sectors, and in part-time work. That is, the influx of women into the labour force parallels a structural change in the economy and has ramifications for the whole of British society. It constitutes a central contradiction in social development.

In investigating this contradiction I have a particular starting point: a woman who seeks part-time or full-time paid work, is in domestic partnership with a man, has one or more children, and lives in a new version of the nuclear family. Most women are heterosexual, most are in and out of a more or less 'permanent' relationship with a man, most have one or more children, and the vast majority are in paid work for most of their lives. This is not a prescriptive model but rather a description of an important part of reality which also has implications for households organized differently or without children.[10] While this is my focus, I will also try to consider the role of men from a particular perspective. Men's role has remained relatively static. In order to have a greater chance of changing that role, we have to go beyond mere condemnation of the *status quo* to consider the practical dimensions of changing those concrete factors which now reinforce it.

Women's choice to have children and to go to work

In considering the implications of the changes in women's lives, I start with what is the disruptive element in the situation: the choices made by individual women. Women tread a minefield of contradictions as they attempt to fulfil what are now contradictory desires and make a series of choices about marriage, children, and work in the face of a variety of constraints. On the one hand, given the lack of childcare and other services in Britain, the costs for most people of combining two jobs with even one small child are extremely high in physical and emotional energy as well as economic terms. (In fact only 7 per cent of women with the youngest child below school age, i.e. 5 years old, work full time.)[11] On the other hand, so are the costs, economic and emotional, for women of continuing in a traditional role.

What then are the costs and benefits which women weigh up and what constraints do they face in the choices they make? Let us look first of all at the choice to have children which creates conditions which fundamentally structure a woman's life. Adequate birth control and the achievement of legal abortion has expanded our freedom enormously and allowed us to talk about a choice for the mass of women. Yet abortion and contraception are only the beginning of expanding this freedom. Not only is abortion a difficult decision and an awkward procedure for many women, but the decision to have children is also difficult. The choice to have children is taken in the context of a need and a desire by the majority of women to be active in the labour force but with little freedom of choice about childcare or general domestic arrangements. The fall in the birthrate in industrially advanced countries is undoubtedly linked to the fact that we can choose but must make this choice within these conditions.

Having children is no longer a 'natural' fact but a conscious decision. If it is taken today, it is because having a child is not simply imposed by social convention but is an experience that many women (and men) positively seek; something they consider a 'benefit'. The experience of having children involves not just demands and responsibilities, but positive, personal pleasures which are not often discussed. Women do not want to be trapped at home, but they, and many men too, want to be able to spend time with their children. So we arrive at the fact that most women choose to have children although they are choosing to have fewer of them.

A constraint on the freedom of that choice is lack of alternative childcare arrangements. This is not just another 'women's demand'. The fight for nursery, after-school and holiday facilities, which are particularly lacking in Britain, corresponds to the needs of millions of people, bringing benefits not just to women and not just to one class. Properly organized, socialized childcare not only brings great benefits to all children, but the intellectual, social and creative stimulation provided by nursery and other school provision benefits children from less privileged backgrounds proportionately *more*. A mother or any parent on her/his own simply cannot provide the range of enriching activities that a nursery can. The nursery also serves as a safety valve for the isolated, overly intense relationships that can so easily develop in a nuclear household. Thus the struggle to give people access to socialized childcare is a battle not only to expand women's freedom: it is also for the benefit of children; it is a need which extends across social groups; and to the extent that many households depend on a woman's wage, which I discuss below, it is also in the interests of most men.

Needs

When we look closely at the practicalities of expanding choice in childcare arrangements, however, we find that taking care of these needs is no easy feat because of their complexity. What is required is a flexible, sensitive response rooted in the collective experience of millions of people in the context of women's dual role. This experience tells us that providing good nursery facilities is only part of what is needed. From the point of view of the individual, the need for services changes rapidly as children get older, and, from the point of view of society as a whole, there is at any one moment an enormous variety of needs to be provided for. Once children start school they still require supervision after the school day and during holidays. Moreover, many activities, as things are now organized, require an adult to accompany them, and sick children need to be at home with an adult to look after them. Later a parent needs the time and energy to give support to a teenage daughter or son.

Yet despite inadequate services to meet these needs, women still combine having children with paid labour. How do people cope now? In fact most people depend on a network of informal relations, increasingly friends rather than family, especially in emergencies.[12] In a sense a spontaneous social response to individual needs has grown up outside the state, a response which is flexible and intimate although with its own costs for women. There is an enormous burden of organization and logistics involved which is experienced in a very isolated way – for example, when a child or baby-minder gets ill, if the school is shut for a day at short notice, during half-term break or a strike, or when something comes up at work. The problem is how to facilitate a social response in which the burden is not just on individual parents and yet at the same time fits a large variety of circumstances and needs.

A sequence of caring

Turning to the other end of the life cycle, this is nowhere truer than in regard to the care of old people. Whereas women can choose, within the constraints of socio-economic pressures, whether to have children and how many, they cannot choose whether to have parents or an elderly spouse. The demographic facts are dramatic.

In the last twenty years the number of men and women in Britain over 65 years old has increased by a third, and the number of the very old will soon increase significantly: those over 75 will increase by about 21 per cent by the end of the century with most of this increase coming imminently, while the number over 85 will increase by 50 per cent.[13] While it is taken for granted that children are a family responsibility and that this affects women's lives in particular, it is often assumed that in comparison with some 'golden age' older people are no longer looked after by family members. In fact studies have shown that every generation bemoans the family's neglect of its old. In 1832, for example, a Royal Commission observed that:

The duty of supporting parents and children in old age or infirmity is so strongly enforced by natural feelings, that it is well performed even among savages and almost always so in a nation deserving the name of civilized. We believe that England is the only European country in which it is neglected.[14]

In fact, the proportion of elderly people in state institutions has *not* increased since the beginning of the century. It is still only 5 per cent.[15] Indeed, studies have shown that in Britain and in other countries such as Sweden and Norway[16] family members are 'the major providers of personal care and help'.[17] This is also true of care of the disabled.[18] A major study has also shown that of those elderly living at home who have living relations, over 50 per cent received a visit at least once a week, and almost a third 'several times' a week.[19] What little care is provided by the welfare state has eclipsed the large amount provided by women in the private sphere.

This current dependence on family care has various implications. From the point of view of the elderly themselves, it is important to point out that one third of them have no living children at all.[20] At the same time, from the point of view of younger families, more of them have surviving parents or grandparents so that in fact a multi-generational family network is quite common.[21] If we focus more closely on who in fact provides care for the elderly it is usually *women* who care for elderly spouses or for parents.[22] Women therefore experience a *sequence* of caring responsibilities, from children to parents and then spouses. Already in 1967 it was estimated that between the ages of 35 and 64, one in two 'housewives' could expect to give help to an elderly or infirm person, while one in five of those between 35 and 49 years old had a disabled or infirm person in the household. This rose to one in four of 'housewives' aged between 50 and 64.[23]

At the same time this caring is carried out in very different circumstances to those of the past. At the turn of the century almost *one third* of the female population never married, mainly because of male emigration, differential death rates, etc.[24] There was, therefore, a pool of unmarried daughters in the population. Second, as more women marry, they are likely to have childcare responsibilities and later to have to look after an elderly spouse. Finally, with regard to the economic dependence of families on two wages and the high economic activity rates of married women which I will discuss below, women who are providing care for the elderly either do so in conditions of great stress as part of their dual role or, if they give up paid work, at considerable economic and social cost to themselves and their families. In addition to the hard work and isolation involved, one study estimated that the 'cost' of losing a wife's earnings if she gave up paid work to look after a handicapped elderly person could amount to some £4500 per annum.[25] Until a recent decision in the European Court based on an EEC directive, the benefit system in Britain has assumed that a married woman 'will be at home anyway' and therefore refused any payments. The employment consequences of the 'fact that women (and men) may be involved in a *sequence* of caring – for children, elderly relatives and frail elderly spouses – has yet to be appreciated'.[26]

Men and the male model of work

This leads to a crucial constraint of the effectiveness of reforms such as the provision of socialized childcare facilities or adequate support for those who care for the elderly. If a woman's choice to have children is taken in the context of her need and desire to have a paid job, the very form of paid work is a primary obstacle standing in the way of a change in the division of labour between men and women. The only way the full development of childcare facilities, for example, will in fact help to liberate women from their double shift and disadvantageous relation to the labour market, is to change the way work is organized.

The male model of work explicitly assumes one human being in paid work for forty hours or more a week. Implicitly, it is presumed that domestic tasks will be taken care of by someone else at home full time. Almost no one enjoys the services of a full-time housewife any longer, and most domestic tasks are in fact only taken care of because women work a second shift. Shorter working hours and built-in flexibility in the organization of work for all workers is important not only to lift the burden from women's shoulders – it is *essential* if we are to create the real premises for a domestic role for men. The male model of work does not 'fit' with children whatever the childcare arrangements. Whatever the domestic division of labour and however good the childcare facilities, a parent working full time mainly sees her/his children in the rush to get ready in the morning and the hours after work when she/he is likely to be exhausted – and the kids are rested and full of life! Manual workers tend to work most overtime when their children are small,[27] and many professional jobs (or at least certain models of career) require long hours. In fact the structure of full-time work does not fit in with private needs in general – how many people take 'holiday' time or pretend to be sick to wait at home for the gasman or to go to the dentist?

Personal needs and domestic tasks have to fit in somehow, and indeed, the demands on time and energy that they require have implications for single people living on their own as well as in a nuclear household where both adults work. We could all use a full-time 'wife' and we all need mothering sometimes. With regard to childcare and other demands and needs, a man or woman working full time, trying to perform in accordance with a male model of work, encounters difficulties. With regard to a man's or a woman's ability to fulfil what is required of them on a full-time job, it is costly for them to admit that private concerns affect their ability to work. In that sense women, whose dual role does not allow them to forget the contradictions between full-time work and domestic needs, are speaking for men as well as for women when they object to the way that work is organized. The incompatibility between social needs and paid work as it is now organized is now evident as never before because of the large number of women with adult caring and servicing responsibilities in the formal labour market.[28]

What about men then? Why can't they help out? Given goodwill and a push, plus an economic need for women to work, they can and do to a limited extent. Yet, in order for the myriad of individual battles conducted by women on the domestic front to have a greater chance of success, they must have the back-up not only of the wider ideological struggle but also of changes in the model of work which may make the transformation in the sexual division of labour more likely. At the moment, long working hours, greater male earning power, the male model of work which assumes the presence of a full-time wife (even if she doesn't exist), and the fact that there are only twenty-four hours in the day, vitiate against a big change in the way childcare and domestic responsibilities are shared, if at all, between men and women. They add up to a series of excuses, more or less valid, for men not to change.

The division of labour which exists today, in which men continue in a traditional role but women's lives have changed, oppresses women and underlies their continued inequality. Yet we must recognize that dividing tasks between people can be a rational solution to their needs. What we have to do is create the conditions for a new and different division of labour. The women's movement and the changes in millions of women's lives reinforce our determination to do battle with what often appears an immoveable object – men. One reason men resist change is because the new combination for the great majority of women of a paid job alongside caring and servicing responsibilities has had little impact on their lives. Although men's traditional role has been challenged by women and by changes in the economy and in society as a whole, it has remained relatively static. Men's experience of a highly segregated labour market and of women continuing to carry out servicing and caring work reinforces sexist assumptions that the division of labour which exists is natural and necessary. Without ignoring the effects of male unemployment, a man's period in paid work is more continuous than a woman's, and a man's relations between home and paid work have not fundamentally altered. By contrast the life cycle of most women is discontinuous, with rapid changes in the nature of domestic responsibilities as children are born, go to school and grow up, as parents become elderly, and as women move in and out of full-time or part-time work. A cultural revolution on the part of men, plus better services and changes in the world of work, are inextricably linked. At the moment, men's resistance to change is constantly reinforced by a whole series of very concrete factors.

Women's choice to enter the labour market and the economy of the household

If women's lives are still structured fundamentally by the choice to have children, that choice today is made in the context of a need and a desire for paid work. The lower birthrate is in part an attempt to limit the constraints of women participating in the paid labour force. This demand for jobs exists despite the difficulties thrown up by the lack of services and a male model of work. The choice to seek paid work is made in the context of what I will call the 'economy' of the household, defined not just in financial terms but with regard to all the resources at its command – time, energy, etc. – compared to its needs – material, social, emotional, and so on. What factors, what costs and benefits, are involved in this choice?[29]

The first benefit from the point of view of both the individual woman and the household is economic. Women today contribute substantially to the economic resources of households and to their material standard of living. It is very important to note that women make this financial contribution despite the fact that a very substantial part of the increase in women's employment is in the form of part-time work,[30] a particularly marked phenomenon in Britain at least in the official labour market.[31] It is well known that part-time work is worse paid, less secure, and less protected by legislation or trade union organization. Women seek part-time work because of the unpaid service work they must do, the prime constraint being the needs of children.[32] What might appear secondary from the point of view of the labour market is, however, enormously important from the point of view of families. In 1975 it was estimated by the Central Policy Review Staff, the Cabinet 'think tank', that as many as four times as many households would be below the official poverty line if women did not work.[33] In 56 per cent of households with married women the wife currently works, and the earnings of one third of working wives made up 30–50 per cent of family income.[34] On average, working wives contribute about one quarter of the household income.[35] If we extend the concept of poverty to that of having such limited resources as to be effectively cut off from normal social activities, and if we think of the many millions of people who are above the official poverty line but whose disposable income is more or less spoken for by fundamental necessities, we will arrive at a very large number of households in which the woman's wage is crucial. Thus women's unemployment has particularly serious consequences, and even above the poverty line the possibility for most households to fulfil aspirations to a higher standard of living, however socially, historically and ideologically defined, are intimately related to women being in the workforce.[36]

At the same time, if women decide to go out to work and are encouraged to do so for economic reasons, getting a job brings other benefits besides financial ones, such as self-esteem, pride, confidence, a feeling of achievement. Being in paid labour also structures domestic life. Relationships and activities outside the home which are legitimized socially and domestically because they are linked with a wage to some extent limit the demands that can be put on women by children, husbands, parents and institutions like schools. If men are beginning, however slowly, grudgingly or nobly to undertake some domestic responsibilities, it is in large part due to women not being able to do everything they did before – even if their solution is fetching a take-away curry. There is a limit even to the double shift.

Yet although being in the workforce gives some independence, overcomes the isolation felt by women at home, and, from a social point of view, provides the premise for trade union activities and a greater social and political awareness, there are also costs. For women who work, the vast majority of whom have domestic responsibilities (or for men who work and undertake substantial domestic tasks) little time or energy is left for leisure, let alone trade union or political activities.

Moreover, the economic factor itself is very complicated. One of the main reasons that women go out to work is that in a low wage economy in which the purchasing power of the average British male wage is one of the lowest in the EEC, men's take-home pay decreasingly covers the financial needs of households. Low wages reinforce the defence of overtime by individuals and by trade unions and therefore undercut the demand for the shortening of working hours. Yet if low wages constitute an obstacle to eliminating overtime and reducing the working week, they are also a factor in encouraging women to seek work and are part of a complicated picture from the point of view of the economy of the household. A certain standard of living is only achieved because the income of a large number of households includes a woman's wages. But we must also consider the non-financial needs and desires of a household. These include everything from childcare, to shopping and cooking, household repairs, and leisure activities. If we do this, we arrive at a picture of a huge expenditure of time and energy to achieve a certain standard of living and take care of household needs. The costs include women's double shift, young people not being kept in education, or giving up other activities.

Of course the relationship of men to household needs is very different from that of women. First of all, they have a discontinuous and unequal relation to the domestic. Although the specific weight of their economic contribution to the household is less than it used to be, their role is not 'also' economic but predominantly economic. The traditional image of a man 'bringing home the bacon' still corresponds to an important aspect of reality. It is *ideological*, however, because it only refers to one aspect.[37] Although women's wages are crucial, in a situation where the male wage still usually provides the greater part of the financial resources at the disposal of the household, the difference between men and women is that although men in most households depend for a certain standard of living on a woman's income, their lives are not structured by this element of dependence or by domestic demands. We have to think anew, then, about the structure and texture of the interdependence between men and women within which men dominate.

The fact that men fulfil domestic needs more in terms of money resources than in terms of time or physical or emotional energy has various consequences. An important one is to give credence to the notion that a man (but not a woman) should earn enough to support a family, the so-called 'family wage', which can be an element in male wage bargaining and often influences women's view of their own labour, i.e., the idea that men 'deserve' to earn more. The real situation of most households has moved beyond the family wage, and yet the idea continues to have real effects.[38] It is bolstered by the fact that a significant minority of households correspond to the family wage model: a husband supporting a wife who is not in the labour market, and two children. If this applies to only 15 per cent of all households, a very large slice of the population goes through this experience, and they tend to be amongst those in greatest poverty. Forty per cent of families where the youngest child is under 5 live near or below the official poverty line.[39] This is connected directly to the relatively low percentage of women who work before all the children are at school because the lack of services, combined with prospects of low pay, mean that the woman is unlikely to undertake paid work even if she would like to. The poverty trap is in part created by the lack of good childcare facilities. Although the ideology of the family wage corresponds to the reality of very few households, it functions because it reflects a significant aspect of reality. It will not be defeated simply by arguing against it. It will only lose its hold as the fight is successful for better services, for changes in the model of work to allow more women to seek employment, for the right to parental leave, and for a system of social payments to ensure that households with small children are not forced into poverty. Women could then make a much freer choice whether to stay at home when their children are young, and households could rely less on men's overtime. We could begin to create some of the conditions necessary to undermine the traditional division of labour between men and women, particularly in the domestic sphere, so that women do not simply assume the increased burden of a double shift.

Women's dual role and the welfare state

If we turn from individual choices about the domestic and productive realms to consider the role of the state, we arrive once more at the inevitable fact that the role of women is not simply a side issue but concerns the precise delineation of the web of relationships – public, private, state, economic and social – in Britain today. One of the parameters of the field of freedom within which women make choices about children and work, affecting the content of services to be provided within the household and changes in family roles, is constituted by the services provided by the welfare state. If we consider that at any one moment in time an array of services is required to provide for the needs of individuals, family-household units, and society as a whole, we can begin to investigate how public and private spheres are organized and what the relationship is between them.

From a social point of view, a fundamental assumption of the welfare state has been that the family/women will provide fundamental services. The welfare state will only provide what cannot be provided elsewhere. The less the welfare state does, the more is done by women and vice versa. Moreover, in order to make use of those services which do exist, whether from the welfare state, the market, or voluntary organizations, someone must link household needs to service. Women are therefore relied upon not only to supply services directly, e.g. childcare or cooking, but they must supply the links which enable services provided elsewhere to be used, for example a clinic, or food from the supermarket. In this sense when it is said that women cannot 'cope' or are in some way inadequate because they are not successfully fulfilling the role expected, the standard derives from an expectation upon which the welfare state is founded. This relates to the further assumption that a woman's role is flexible, that her participation in the labour force is marginal. The costs to her and to the household in which she lives of dropping out of the labour market in order, say, to take care of a disabled relative, have until recently remained invisible and unspoken. Put differently, two aspects of women's experience are masked: first, the amount and complexity of the service work done by women, and second, the fact that this service work is constrained by the need and desire for paid work.

To the extent that the welfare state is organized around what I have been calling the male model of work and the sexual division of labour implicit within it, the welfare state 'reflects' and helps to reproduce a particular form of production. Yet, as I have been arguing, this form has entered into a long-term crisis as the lives of women are changing. To begin to investigate the role of the welfare state and its relationship to these developments, we have, first of all, to define it rather more broadly than is usual in the Anglo-Saxon world. The cornerstone of the social pact on which the welfare state was founded was full employment. Beveridge, for example, assumed that men and only unmarried women would or should be in the labour market. The other feature of the welfare state was the provision of social services which were organized according to a male model of work, again, on the assumption that women would not be in the labour market. The welfare state has, however, produced the seeds of its own crisis. Its development, while depending on services in the home and on women's domestic role, has also been a fundamental factor which has allowed women to go beyond the home and private relations, to enter the world of work and new areas of civil society.

The imbalance within women's dual role, the proportion of effort directed at the domestic sphere and the way this structures women's lives, can be seen in large part as an effect of the partial way in which the state provides services which is a constraint on more women seeking full-time jobs. Yet, to the extent that services exist, the choice to work is facilitated. Furthermore, given the increased financial need and the desire of women to work, their influx into the labour force has been related in large part to the expansion of the state sector. The welfare state depends on the cheap labour of women, many of them living in poverty and/or whose financial needs are to some extent taken care of in a household with other income(s). Women, in turn, depend on the welfare state for services and for jobs.

A real and potential source of tension between society and the state is precisely that it is assumed that women can step in to fill gaps or supply services even when they cannot or when so doing incurs very concrete costs. To give just one example, when a school closes because of half-term or because it is used as a polling station, the assumption is that there is a woman with a flexible schedule who can step into the breach. Yet the statistics about women in the workforce warn us that neither mum nor auntie nor grandma nor friend next door is likely to be free, or at least only at the considerable cost of taking time off her job, or the opportunity cost of not having a full-time job. From the point of view of the school, a working mother is a problem. From her point of view it is the organization of the school which is the problem. If a woman gives up a job to care for an elderly relative, or looks after her mother on top of everything else she must do, the cost to her and to her household is considerable. But if she doesn't, the cost to the state increases commensurately. If a woman is made unemployed, there are economic and personal costs to her, and if she receives benefits, financial costs to the state.

As consumers of state services or suppliers of services which do not exist elsewhere, women mediate constantly between the domestic and state spheres. They are usually the concrete link between domestic needs and state services.[40] More often than not they are the ones who step into the breach: they take the children to school or the clinic, they confront the health visitor or social worker or go along to try to get a rent rebate. Although there is no questioning the isolating, privatizing effects of the domestic sphere, it is inevitably and inextricably enmeshed with public and in that sense political relations.

Some implications

The need and desire of women to combine a domestic role including children with an almost continuous role in the paid labour force is a contradictory element in British society. Neither the organization of the domestic sphere, the form of paid work, nor the welfare state have changed to take account of this fundamental social change. Despite the tensions and contradictions caused by the lack of 'fit' between traditional institutions and women's new role, the outcome is unclear. It is certainly not inevitable that these institutions will be transformed to meet the new situation.

What are the implications of these contradictions? The first concerns the question of reforms. The way the domestic sphere, the world of work, and the state are interrelated dictates a battle on all fronts, a war of position in Gramsci's terms, a strategy of reforms. This goes beyond the concept of 'priorities' which implies the possibility of ranking different demands in a long list. The effectiveness of a single reform, like socialized childcare, will be limited unless it is related to a series of fundamental changes which are structural and revolutionary. An alternative social and economic strategy, if it is to go beyond rhetoric and demagogy and have any political chance of success, must itself derive from social needs, from a vision of the new kind of social life which millions of people are already, in fact, trying to create.

This raises important questions about the welfare state. Public policy and much public debate, whether from the Thatcher–Reagan right or from most of the left, is based on a dichotomy between public and private. *Either* the state provides services *or* the family/woman or market does. In fact, the state, economy and family are interwoven in such a way that such a dichotomy is ideological and unreal and renders the traditional liberal concept of the relationship between state and individual inadequate. So, too, is a view which calls upon the state to substitute the individual. Given the differentiated needs of individuals in different kinds of households over the life cycle, there is no indication that the state could replace the servicing work now being done in society. The possibility that uniform and centralized provision could satisfy social needs is challenged by the experience of millions of women. The only way social needs can be met is if the struggle for social provision of services goes hand in hand with changes which will make private arrangements easier. Instead of relegating a problem automatically to the state, we are compelled to decide when it is more appropriate to ask the political sphere to enhance our social creativity and thus our freedom, and to help us to help each other by providing support and alternatives; and when a change in the law and universal provision are needed.

The building blocks of a coherent strategy and a new society are adequate provision for children and others who require care, support for the carers, and a transformation of the world of work. Not only does most recent debate about the welfare state omit the experience of women, more surprisingly (at least at first glance), given all the discussion about the economy, the way in which the organization of production shapes so much of social life is ignored. Ironically, this has meant that neither the traditional Marxist or social democratic analyses which give great importance to the economy are able in fact to comprehend the *way* in which the productive sphere is fundamental. However important are questions of resources, distribution of wealth, and ownership, it is the logic implanted in the organization and assumptions of wage work itself which is in growing contradiction with social needs, a contradiction which has always existed but has to a large extent been absorbed by women. Now that there has been a massive increase of women in paid labour this contradiction has heightened and is more and more evident, at least to women themselves. Moreover it is a contradiction not just under capitalism but also under socialism. The massive entry of women into the formal economy poses a series of advanced questions and, it could be argued, is a *premise* for equality and liberation. Yet it is manifestly not a sufficient condition. The experiences of both capitalist and socialist countries demonstrate that Engels' insistence on the importance of the entry of women into the production sphere is not wrong, but it misjudges its significance. The presence of women in production reveals that neither equality nor liberation is possible, whether under capitalism or socialism, unless the world of work, the domestic sphere and the relation between state and social needs are transformed. Women's new social role reveals the limits of the welfare state. The social figure of the worker is now more varied, and the very concepts of full employment or of unemployment which are now of necessity expanding quantitatively to include women who are in or seeking work must now be *sexed*, that is, changed qualitatively and made more complex. The very attempt to generalize meets new obstacles.

A very concrete reality lies behind what might appear a highly theoretical discussion. This reality has important consequences for the traditional organizations of the working-class movement, the trade unions and political parties and is an aspect of their crisis because they are called upon to tackle qualitatively new tasks which they have never faced before. Let me explain. The world of work has never been organized in the modern period around people's domestic needs. The form of full-time work has remained unchanged since major advances were made in reducing the working day. The trade unions have fought to protect people at work, but they have shared society's assumption that people should adjust their lives to the job and not the other way round. The highly differentiated needs of workers, women and men, *outside* the workplace in different periods of their life cycles are hardly accommodated. The relationship between what is demanded of a person on a job and that individual's needs outside the workplace is addressed through the wages system and the market, that is, in financial terms; or it is only admitted as the exception to the rule, 'to and from each according to the same standard of performance', for example, with maternity leave. In general the left, but not only the left, has looked to the state for social payments or services where the market or individual arrangements fail. The logic of what I have called a male model of work has not been challenged. The fact has been obscured that the inflexibility of paid work is a severe constraint on the individual fulfilling highly varied needs and responsibilities, for example, to accompany an aged parent to a clinic or look after a sick child, or, to put it differently, that these are social needs which cannot simply be consigned to the state, the market, or a social figure like a woman with an infinitely flexible schedule.

The traditional division between work and social needs has been reflected in the division of labour between the trade unions and the political party in the very demarcation between the sphere of production, the area of trade union activities, and the social and political sphere, the area of state intervention. Concrete reality, where women's experience teaches us that paid work, social needs, and state services cannot be thought of separately, challenges this division of labour. In particular the trade unions are challenged by the logic of women's experience in combining these spheres to develop a new perspective which includes the relationship between the form of paid work, above all the organization of time, and the need to fulfil tasks outside work. The trade unions, who are often wedded to old, outdated forms of work and whose strength has been in declining sectors of the economy, find it genuinely difficult to adapt to these new facts and new demands which they often do not even recognize.

This is no truer than in the question of part-time work which illustrates many of the themes I have been discussing. If we focus on the *demand* for part-time work, rather than on the supply (which has its own logic),[41] or on its current subordinate status, we can see that a change in the organization of work is not simply a utopian idea unrelated to the restructuring going on in the economy or the demands expressed by millions of people.[42] Because individual circumstances are so varied and change so rapidly, the need for flexibility in individual lives is *real*. The demand for part-time work can be viewed as reflecting a long-term need for shorter working hours and a new relationship between the world of work and social neeeds, a need expressed by *women* because of the sexual division of labour. This demand is answered; that is, there is a supply of part-time work, because of the need for a flexible workforce. Yet even this is taking on a different form in a period of a general restructuring of the economy.

Part-time work has appeared as marginal because in the traditional manufacturing sector it functioned, to an extent, as a reserve army of labour to be shed during a recession. But in the growth areas part-time work is at the core and is woven into the fabric of developments in an unprecedented way. More and more production is being done in a form which is neither organized by the trade unions[43] nor regulated by government, but which reflects the necessity felt above all by women to combine paid work with social needs. Alongside technological change and inscribed in the growth of the tertiary or service sectors, an important change is taking place in the world of work which reflects real needs but under conditions which maintain the old logic of 'from and to each according to the same standard'. The change is a *quantitative* one (the hours worked, the amount earned) not a *qualitative* one (flexibility built into work itself) leaving large sectors and the lives of most men untouched except to the extent they are unemployed.

Thus, part-time work is neither a goal, nor a solution, but a widespread phenomenon which reflects quite contradictory needs.

From the point of view of the servicing work which is required in society, the massive entry of women into fixed, formal, paid jobs has not only created qualitatively new demands on the world of work but a major contradiction in the way state services are organized. The political sphere must now take account of the fact that social provision must be much more varied and flexible because the inflexibility in the lives of half the adult population, men, imposed by paid work, is now also an aspect of the lives of more and more women. New contradictions have arisen for those working in the state sector. Another implication of women not being able to step in to fill the gaps in the way they used to is that they not only need *more* state services but demand something *different* of those which have long existed, like schools. To take this example further, from the point of view of working parents the school meets two needs: child-minding and specialized education. *In loco parentis* means first of all that a child is the school's responsibility during school hours and someone else's at other times. Statistics and personal experience indicate that child-minding is a crucial function of the school for the overwhelming majority of women. Thirty per cent of women work at least part time even before their youngest child is at school. This rises to 62 per cent when the youngest is between 5 and 9 years old and 71 per cent if she/he is over 10.[44] It is school, therefore, which makes it easier for mothers to seek a job, although most will have no choice but to organize their working lives around school hours. This child-minding function goes against the grain of the professional training of teachers whose job it is to teach. Moreover, the needs of a working parent often contradict their personal needs as workers. To fulfil their own domestic responsibilities they depend on a particular organization of the working day and year. Yet parents need schools to stay open longer and/or other facilities which do not require an adult to accompany a child.

It is still assumed implicitly or explicitly by state services that in a household one adult goes out to work full time and another stays at home to cover all other needs. An increasing number of households are headed by one parent or are made up of only one person. Where there are two they will most likely both have paid jobs as well as responsibility for a child or older person. Yet neither the world of production, nor the distribution of services, nor the assumption of the professionals who work in them, have changed to take account of the fact that while women continue to perform caring services and to provide the connecting threads between family needs and social services or the market, this service work is constrained by paid work.

The use of the term service work is deliberate. Women fulfil household tasks like cleaning, or caring functions like looking after a child; they mediate or are the links between the various needs of the household and the market, or a state service, or leisure and cultural activities or a self-help group, or friends – the very web of human relations. All of this requires intelligence, knowledge and organizational skill and is intricately inserted in social life. There is no simple description of this work, but it is clear that 'domestic labour' or 'domestic responsibilities' are only aspects of what women do, of their position in society. 'Service' or 'caring work' better approximates reality.[45] Any analysis which separates women's servicing work from their role in paid labour not only misses the complexity and richness of women's experience but will fail to see a series of contradictions and the nature of the interconnections between the different spheres of society. But even these concepts are limited. The difficulty in finding suitable labels stems from the fact that what we are discussing is the sphere of reproduction which has become increasingly complex and bound up with a web of institutions, and diverse social roles and identities. Whereas there are two dimensions which are the main structural determinants of women's lives – the world of production and the domestic sphere – the latter is so enmeshed with institutions and relations outside the home that women's role is, in fact, not dual but multifaceted. While an analytic distinction might be made between production and reproduction or between paid labour and servicing work, the concrete reality of women's lives can be compared to a patchwork quilt in which the fragments are stitched together with great skill, creativity and ingenuity.[46] The variety and richness, as well as the stresses and strains of this existence, reflect more accurately the complexity of society itself than men's lives which have fewer dimensions and have changed less dramatically.

Women's new role should also provide a new perspective in the debate on the family. Although there is no evidence that the family in its different forms[47] is disappearing, neither is it nor the relations within it static. For example, the economic role of men is being undermined or acquiring a different relative weight while a new economic and social role for women is being constituted. New, public relations of dominance and subordinance are being created as the *relative* weight of private patriarchy decreases.[48] This does not mean that women are not still subordinate to men in private relations. The 'feminization of poverty'[49] in which the poor are increasingly single mothers and their children, or elderly women, illustrates the continuing dependence, for instance, on a male wage. When that disappears, because of divorce, for example, low wages and/or inadequate social support often means living in poverty. The same phenomenon is also a good example of the increasing dependence of women on the state. The welfare state has produced new contradictions. Women's financial dependence on the state for both social payments and jobs has grown. So has their dependence on state services. Services allow women to choose to be more active in the labour market. Consequently, given (and today it is given for the vast majority of women) their presence in the labour market, women are more dependent on services than before.[50] These transformations in the nature of women's subordination and in our relative freedom, and the new contradictions which are arising, are missed by any functionalist view, with or without a Marxist label, which defines the relation between women and the state in terms of how state policy maintains the nuclear family or acts to keep women in the home.[51] Private relations of dominance and subordinance now exist in the context of these public relations. Women are at one and the same time freer *and* enmeshed in a new web of dependence.

In order to undercut the oppressive effects of an ideology based on a certain model of the family, we have to consider the problems people face in escaping this oppression and the changes which are taking place in society in order to think about what kinds of reforms will maximize the possibility of creating new types of human relations, of constructing material conditions or premises for women's liberation, of removing the excuses used by men for not giving up their privileges. We must consider, in other words, the realm of freedom we inhabit, and people's creativity in expanding that freedom, as well as the boundaries to that freedom. The struggle against sexism and women's subordination will only be successful if it is rooted in concrete changes.

Yet we should not underestimate the revolutionary nature of the changes which are needed. A process has begun in which the need to revolutionize the world of work and the relationship between production, the state and social needs is on the historical agenda; that is, it is not utopian, as women are pulled into the workforce. New questions and contradictions are appearing in both capitalist welfare states and socialist societies which are historically so advanced that they can only be fully resolved by a new mode of production and the socialization of politics, when the rule is 'from each according to her/his ability, to each according to her/his needs'; where men and women are able to combine different roles, say, paid work in the morning, fishing in the afternoon, and cooking dinner and playing with the kids in the evening, without the kind of contradictions and conflicts they now face. It is historically significant that neither welfare state capitalism nor really existing socialism of the socialist countries are able to resolve the problems which they are posing in a parallel way.[52]

Because neither the domestic sphere, nor the world of work, nor the welfare state 'fit' the changed world of women, there is a potential basis of mass consent for a fundamental change. Yet for the most part the social and political system succeeds in simply 'absorbing' the contradictions I've discussed – people and institutions just 'cope'. To the extent that women are forced simply to do more and to accept a double shift, they, and to a lesser degree their families, absorb the costs of their new role leaving institutions and the male role intact. Without an improvement in the quality of women's lives, these changes could simply provide the basis for a reaction against the women's movement and nostalgia for an idealized past. If, because of the need for women to earn wages, there is no widespread support for excluding women from work[53] (reinforced in the socialist countries both by the need for labour and by ideological considerations), a new system of passive social consent is developing around what benefits people manage to obtain from institutions as they are, within the new version of the sexual division of labour in which women have two jobs.

Yet, if the social system can reproduce itself while containing or managing these contradictions, an entirely different social logic is inscribed in the advanced problems which are being posed. Against the background of, for example, laws on sexual equality in capitalist countries or the *promise* of sexual equality in the ideologies of really existing socialism, the reality of inequality, the difference between formal and real equality – that is, the question of women's liberation – is posed more clearly in women's material circumstances than in earlier periods, even if this is not always or even usually reflected in our ideology. Two logics of equality exist simultaneously. For example, women are at a disadvantage in applying for jobs because employers usually assume that they bear the main burden of servicing work. A necessary demand is, therefore, to exclude all questions about dependants or marital status in application forms and interviews. How private needs are taken care of should be left to the individual. This implies a split between work and private life and follows the logic of formal justice: the same rule is to be applied to everyone whatever the circumstances. At the same time, a necessary demand is that in the workplace itself such 'private' or social needs are both recognized and addressed, for example with paid leave for both men and women not only for caring responsibilities but, say, to stay home for the gasman. This follows the logic of distributive justice.

While contradictory logics exist in the here and now, compared to the enormously varied needs and desires of people concrete solutions appear partial and inadequate. A comprehensive solution is difficult to imagine because we have not yet seen what might be termed a post-male model of work, which would reflect a communist (not socialist) mode of production or a form of politics adequate to social needs. The slogan 'from each according to his ability, to each according to his needs' is made meaningful, first, by a change in gender to include women and second, by a recognition of the complexity of needs which are much more than financial, which both involve and extend beyond the productive sphere and which cannot simply be consigned to the state. It is relevant to men as well as women, but is becoming more concrete because of the material conditions of most women and because of their social role in both capitalist and socialist societies.[54]

But this does not mean that we should interpret women's new social role in both socialist and capitalist countries fatalistically as the inevitable reproduction of women's subordination whatever the social system, or as suggesting that the struggle for women's liberation must wait for the never fulfilled promise of communism. Rather, this new social role reveals that this struggle is not utopian or purely ideological, unrelated to material circumstances, because the everyday experience of millions of women reflects a fundamental socio-economic change which could be the basis for their liberation. Yet the contradictions embedded in women's lives and in social development may simply be absorbed and old social relations simply reproduced in new forms, in what Gramsci referred to as a passive revolution, if a political struggle is not conducted which recognizes and addresses these new needs. The starting point for such a struggle is a critical analysis of what women's common sense tells them. The contradictions and the promise contained within historical development and social reality can only be known if the problems posed by the daily lives of millions of people are the raw material for intellectual work. Moreover, the establishment of a new perspective can only develop on the basis of recognizing that people are not mere dupes but are both active agents of obtaining what satisfaction they can within present arrangements and fight to expand their freedom of action. Women are forced to struggle by the contradictory situation of their lives. The creativity, ingenuity, and enormous talent and energy of millions of women who juggle their many roles with such great agility can serve as an inspiration in the fight to create the conditions to alleviate the burdens they bear and to eliminate men's excuses not to change.

Notes and references

1 There is a debate, of course, about how to define the welfare state. See Franco De Felice, 'Il Welfare State: questioni controverse e un'ipotesi interpretativa', *Studi Storici*, no. 3, 1984; Ramesh Mishra, *The welfare state in crisis* (Wheatsheaf Books 1984); and John Keane and John Owens, *After full employment* (Hutchinson 1986) for overviews.

2 In addition to the references listed above see, for example, Ian Gough, *The political economy of the welfare state* (Macmillan 1979); Claus Offe, *Contradictions of the welfare state* (Hutchinson 1984); Fred Hirsch, *Social limits to growth* (Routledge and Kegan Paul 1977). These are just a few examples from a vast literature which extends across the political spectrum.

3 Helga Maria Hernes discusses how neo-corporatist relations leave out women. See her piece in this volume.

4 Women are out of the workforce on average a total of about seven years or 16–19 per cent of the time between the ages of 20 and 59. Joshi and Owen, *Demographic predictors of women's work participation in postwar Britain*, Centre for Population Studies Working

Paper 81–3, August 1981. From *The fact about women is*, Statistics Unit, Equal Opportunities Commission. They also return more quickly after the birth of a child. Study Commission on the Family, *Families in the future* (Study Commission on the Family 1983), pp. 17–18.

5   Department of Employment Gazette 1981; General Household Survey Preliminary Results for 1981.

6   Study Commission, *Families in the future*, p. 17.

7   Lesley Rimmer and Jenny Popay, *Employment trends and the family* (Study Commission on the Family 1982), p. 15.

8   The Finer Report, quoted in J. Dominian, *Marriage in Britain 1945–80* (Study Commission on the Family 1980), p. 11.

9   The fact the informal sector of the economy has also been expanding in most OECD countries and is the site of economic activity for many women in addition to the formal sector must be borne in mind and furthers the argument that the overwhelming majority of women have a dual role.

10 The diversity of family forms is increasing. See Study Commission, *Families in the future*, p. 9.

11 General Household Survey Preliminary Results for 1980. The 1974 Office of Population Censuses and Surveys showed that by the time their children were 2, 72 per cent of parents wanted some form of childcare which rose to 91 per cent by the time the children were 4. Given the image of Britain as a welfare state, most people are surprised that except for incomplete and inadequate provision for 2½ hour nursery classes at state schools, a very few nursery schools, and day care for some children at risk there is *no* state and practically no private nursery provision in the UK. This contrasts with countries as diverse as Italy, Mexico, Sweden, France, or the US.

12 In some countries, for example the US, the market has responded more than in others to provide private childcare facilities, and in Britain there are agencies to supply a nanny or babysitter at short notice, but both the cost involved and the nature of emergencies mean that most people rely on informal relations.

13 Study Commission, *Families in focus*, pp. 11–12.

14 Quoted in *Values and the changing family: the Final Report from the Working Party on Values* (Study Commission on the Family 1982), p. 19.

15 *Values and the changing family*, p. 20.

16 See Gerdt Sundström, *Caring for the aged in welfare society* (Stockholm: Liber Förlag 1983).

17 Chris Rossiter and Malcolm Wicks, *Crisis or challenge? Family care, elderly people and social policy* (Study Commission on the Family 1982), p. 43.

18 Rossiter and Wicks, *Crisis or challenge?*, p. 43.
19 Lesley Rimmer, *Families in focus – marriage, divorce and family patterns* (Study Commission on the Family 1981), p. 57.
20 Rimmer, *Families in focus*, p. 55.
21 Rimmer, *Families in focus*, p. 53.
22 Rossiter and Wicks, *Crisis or challenge?*, p. 44.
23 Rimmer, *Families in focus*, p. 65.
24 Dominian, *Marriage in Britain 1945–80*, p. 11.
25 Rimmer and Popay, *Employment trends and the family*, p. 15.
26 Rimmer and Popay, *Employment trends and the family*, pp. 52–3.
27 Jean Coussins and Anna Coote, *The family in the firing line*, NCCL/CPAG 1981.
28 See Chiara Saraceno's piece in this volume. I have found her work extremely stimulating. See for example, 'Identità in transizione', in *Il Mulino*, no. 5, 1981, or 'Il tempo nella costruzione dei ruoli e identità sessuali', *Rassegna italiana di sociologia*, no. 1, 1983.
29 In what follows my argument is different from the analysis of the 'New Home Economics' of writers like Jacob Mincer and Gary Becker in which women's choice to enter the labour market is explained by differential wage rates and their impact on the allocation of time. See Daniele Del Boca for a succinct summary and very good critique of this literature. 'L'economia della famiglia', in *Quaderni di Rassegna sindacale*, no. 88, 1981.
30 Rimmer and Popay, *Employment trends and the family*, p. 17, and *Change in total GB employment 1975–1985*, Table 3, *Department of Employment Gazette*, June/July 1986.
31 Peter Manley and Derek Sawbridge, 'Women at Work', *Lloyds Bank Review*, no. 135, January 1980. See Mara Gasbarrone for an international comparison. 'Modelli di famiglia e lavoro, domanda e offerta di part-time' in 'La Forza lavoro femminile, analisi e prospettive', *Economia Istruzione e formazione professionale*, III, no. 11, July–Sept. 1980.
32 Rimmer and Popay, *Employment trends and the family*, p. 49.
33 Study Commission, *Families in the future*, p. 23.
34 *Family Finances*, an interim report from the Working Party on the Financial Circumstances of Families, London (Study Commission on the Family 1981), p. 12.
35 Marie McNay and Chris Pond, *Low pay and family poverty* (Study Commission on the Family 1980), p. 11.
36 As an illustration, at one end of the scale, single parent families, seven out of nine of which are headed by a woman who is less likely to work than other women, are in particular risk of poverty. Only 48 per cent of all lone parents have earnings as their major source of income compared to 97 per cent of two parent families. It should

be borne in mind that maintenance payments are the main source of income for only 6 per cent of all lone parents. Jenny Popay, Lesley Rimmer and Chris Rossiter, *One parent families and social policy* (Study Commission on the Family 1983), pp. 40 and 47. At the other end, Ray Pahl is struck by the relative affluence of multi-earner families and an increasing polarization and differentiation within the working class based on empirical research. 'La divisione del lavoro: nuovi problemi per il *welfare state*' in Ires Lombardia, Camera del lavoro di Milano, Funzione pubblica CGIL Milano, (Milan: Franco Angeli 1986).

37 It is so difficult to change ideas because *aspects* of reality continue to support old ideas. The concept of women's role as domestic 'works', that is, has a continuing hold, because domestic responsibilities are still a fundamental aspect of women's existence. It is interesting to note that despite most interpretations to the contrary, Antonio Gramsci actually argued that ideology always lagged behind material conditions. Antonio Gramsci, *Selections from the prison notebooks* (Lawrence and Wishart 1971), p. 168. He was very impressed by how difficult it is to change people's ideas. See his notes where he puts himself in the shoes of 'Everyman', pp. 338–40. Stuart Hall has a very useful discussion along similar lines of Marx's concept of ideology; see 'The problem of ideology – Marxism without guarantees', in Betty Matthews (ed.) (Lawrence and Wishart 1983).

38 Only 5 per cent of the 'economically active' population are men with wives who do not work and two dependent children (General Household Survey 1979). Despite this, during a strike by nurses, I once heard an interview with a woman student nurse who said she supported the strike, 'Because I don't know how a man could support a family on a nurse's wages.'

39 Sarah Curtis, 'Who really loves the family', *The Times*, 23 June 1982.

40 See Marina Bianchi, 'La condizione femminile nella crisi del "welfare state" ', in *Crituca marxista*, no. 5, 1979 and *I servizi sociali. Lavoro femminile. Lavoro familiare. Lavoro professionale* (Bari: De Donato 1981).

41 See Vicki Smith's piece in this volume.

42 It is interesting to note that when Margaret Thatcher was pressed to admit in a recent television interview that a large proportion of new jobs in Britain were only part time, she defended these as real jobs which served the needs of many women. Panorama, BBC1, 17 January 1986.

43 In a recent debate Tessa Woodcraft, Women's Rights Officer of NALGO pointed out, for example, that there is no mention of part-time work in either the 1981 TUC 'Plan for Growth', which many consider the most radical statement of the British left's alternative

economic strategy, nor in the 1982 TUC 'Programme for Recovery' which states baldly that 'a fairer society goes hand in hand with growth'.

44 General Household Survey Preliminary Results for 1981.

45 See Ilona Kickbusch, 'A hard day's night' in Margarita Rendel (ed.), *Women, power, and political systems* (Croom Helm 1981) and 'The political economy of personal services: women's paid and unpaid labour', unpublished paper, 1978. See also the work of Laura Balbo and others who are associated with the GRIFF (Gruppo di ricerca sulla famiglia e la condizione femminile) of the University of Milan which has been seminal for me. In addition to the work by Chiara Saraceno cited above, see Laura Balbo, *Stato di famiglia* (Milan: Etas Libri: 1976). Laura Balbo, 'The servicing work of women and the capitalist state', in *Political power and social theory*, 3, 1982; Laura Balbo and Renata Siebert-Zahar (eds.), *Interferenze. Lo stato, la vita familiare, la vita privata* (Milan: Feltrinelli 1979); Laura Balbo and Lorenza Zanuso (eds) 'Più facce, molte teste. La condizione della donna', *Inchiesta*, no. 55, January–March, 1982 and no. 56, April–June, 1982. Laura Balbo and Marina Bianchi (eds.), *Ricomposizioni: Il lavoro di servizio nella società della crisi* (Milan: Franco Angeli 1982). See also Chiara Saraceno, *Dalla parte della donna. La 'questione femminile' nelle società industriali avanzate* (Bari: De Donato 1979). In Italy considerable empirical work has been done on the question of how services fit or do not fit with women's multiple roles. See, for example, on Turin, Guido Martinotti (ed.), *La città difficile* (Milan: Franco Engeli 1982). Several pieces include this perspective.

46 See Laura Balbo's piece in this volume. The way woman and families combine resources, time and different spheres can be described as a strategy of woɪk, of resources, of survival. Another useful concept is 'double presence'. See Franca Bimbi and Fulvia Prestinger, *Profili sovraposti. La doppia presenza delle donne in un'area ad economia diffusa* (Milan: Franco Angeli 1985), in particular Franca Bimbi, 'La doppia presenza: diffusione di un modello e trasformazione dell'identità'.

47 Study Commission, *Families in the future*, documents the diversification of family forms.

48 Helge Hernes and Anette Borchorst and Birte Siim argue this in their pieces in this volume.

49 See Hilda Scott, *Working your way to the bottom: the feminization of poverty* (Pandora Press 1984).

50 They are also dependant on the market and/or friends. How often this reinforces the feeling, 'It would be easier just to do it myself'!

51 This is a strong element in *Women and the welfare state* by Elizabeth

Wilson (Tavistock Publications 1977); and in Mary McIntosh, 'The state and the oppression of women' in Annette Kuhn and Annmarie Wolpe (eds), *Feminism and materialism* (Routledge and Kegan Paul 1978).

52   See Claudio Fracassi, 'L'Unione Sovietica', in Balbo and Siebert-Zahar, *Interferenze*, and Maxine Molyneux, 'Family reform in socialist states: the hidden agenda', in *Feminist Review*, Winter 1985. I was also struck by the parallels in the novel, *Una settimana come un'altra* by Natalija Baranskaja (Rome: Editori Riuniti 1977). An English version appeared serialized in *Spare Rib*.

53   Ian Hargreaves, 'Women and immigrants – a blurred picture', *Financial Times*, 30 June 1982. It is significant that after a few early statements from Conservative government ministers that women should stay at home, this has not been pursued. In Germany the argument that women have the right to work has even been used by liberals and conservatives to say that social payments should be cut because they encourage women to stay at home.

54   In his notes on passive revolution, Gramsci referred to the way elements which belong to capitalism coexist with the 'need' for communism in a whole historical period, across both capitalism and socialism. He also discusses how the contradictions which ensue might simply be absorbed by reproducing old social relations in new forms. See, for example, Gramsci, p. 106.

Part Two

Inside and Outside the Home: Women's Experience and the Transformation of Public and Private

6 Division of family labour and gender identity

Chiara Saraceno

The observations in this chapter spring from a series of research projects on the organization of the family and woman's location within it, conducted between 1977 and 1978 in the city and province of Trent (a city of about 100,000 inhabitants in northern Italy). These studies, which were carried out with different methods and different populations (composed of women only, or composed of couples),[1] were designed to examine the concrete way in which family labour is organized, and to specify how the roles and reciprocal expectations of wives and husbands, mothers and fathers, are structured around this organization.

Such studies can be placed within a research approach which sees family labour (in its various modes, phases, and contents, which vary within the course of the cycle of family life and which take specific forms in different socio-cultural contexts), both as a key element in the concrete definition of the condition of women in contemporary society, and as the organizing structure of the family as such. Family labour provides the response both to family needs and to social organization, primarily the labour market.[2] Precisely for this reason, family labour largely determines the events in a woman's life cycle, at least as far as her entrances, exits, and modes of presentation on the labour market are concerned, but also in terms of her social participation. This makes its imprint on the very process of female identity formation, though in ways which must be analysed more profoundly than they have been in the past.

The objective of our research in Trent was to begin a process of reflection on this problematic,[3] albeit in a partial way. With this end in mind, we set out first, to measure the quantity of daily family labour performed, and investigate its weight in the time and commitment of the woman-wife; second, to provide a complex description of the burden and distribution of family labour with respect to its different components; and third, to specify the various types of organization of the couple which correspond to this labour. I am aware of the fact that a more precise description of family organization would itself require taking other elements, and other family members, into consideration.[4] This applies especially to children, and the network of relatives which compose the extended family, and in our research there are some traces of the presence of these different figures on the scene of family labour, since they (especially the extended family members) constitute an important source of help, particularly in the area of childcare. As a matter of fact, it is interesting to note that this is the only sphere of family labour in which there is a significant amount of help from (women) relatives, whereas it is scarce or non-existent within domestic labour in the strict sense. Only families (women-wives) which are economically more fortunate can in part delegate this latter work to paid help (again, by women).[5]

In any case, in our research we were interested in exploring the material contents of the female family role, beyond (or within) the myths which surround and exalt it, and at the same time we wanted to look at the way in which this role affects the subjective and reciprocal definition of the conjugal roles. In other words, we wanted to understand not only the organizational–material dimension of the family, but also how this was perceived, together with their own role within it, by both husband and wife: that is, to understand the way in which they construe it, both materially and cognitively. It is, in fact, true (and these studies show it explicitly), that as Jessie Bernard suggests,[6] the husband and wife live in two different families, above all in the sense that each works in a different way for the family and thereby receives a role and an identity very much differentiated from the other's: the father of the family is above all the one who works to provide an income to maintain it, while the wife is the one who (whatever else she does, even if it's a paid job) above all holds it together, creates it in her incessant daily labour of maintenance (of the house and of persons) and by her very presence. The differentiation is such that the presence of one (the wife) seems to exclude (exempt) the presence of the other (the husband), and the (necessary) absence of the man imposes, or requires, the presence of the woman. Even today one often hears young people identify the family with their mother, for better or worse. This fact leads to the impossibility of distinguishing one from the other, of giving the woman a face of her own and an autonomous identity. The labour of the husband-father, on the other hand, though carried out for the family, maintains a space of independent meanings, and furnishes an identity (and relationships), though partial and alienated, which is not reducible to the family identity. And in this space the man is both distant (excluded) and defended, able to enter and exit, to define (certainly within the small margins allowed by the great rigidity of working hours) his presences and his absences, and their forms.

It has been shown by Andrée Michel, based on the results of research carried out mostly within the United States,[7] that the married man really does have margins of freedom and possibilities which allow him to have time for himself, leisure time, time to learn and grow, to cultivate friendships, involve himself in politics, etc. This in some way compensates him for the restrictions which having a family imposes on his autonomy. In particular, one of the studies of Michel showed how a man, simply by getting married (that is, by acquiring a wife who does domestic work for him), gains an amount of time equivalent to five years of working days over that which he would have as a single man. In other words it seems that, at least in the United States (data for Italy are missing), single men do more domestic work than married men, despite the increased familial responsibilities of the latter. Even if it were the case that these men were using those extra hours to take on a second paid job (something which Michel does not consider in her book, but which, at least in Italy, is true for many men whose wives are housewives),[8] there always remains a block of time for themselves. This fact becomes particularly clear when the wife is also engaged in extra-domestic work (that is, paid work outside the house). Research done in many countries shows, in fact, that the women-wives-extra-domestic workers have less free time than either men or just housewives. For them their double job (domestic plus extra-domestic) is a more universal, more constrictive and necessary fact than the double job (normally extra-domestic) which the husbands may have, and tends to take up all their time.

These different forms of male and female presence in the family and in family labour further contribute towards differentiating, if not to dividing, the experience which each has of the 'same family'. The family that one 'comes home to', in which 'one can be oneself', with which 'one chooses to spend time'; the children one stays with when one 'has the time', whom one meets and discovers (sometimes unexpectedly) at mealtimes, with whom one talks 'from man to man', with whom one plays ball or teaches to ride a bicycle, whom one spoils with attention or chooses to ignore, for whom one feels and is held responsible only in terms of providing a paycheck and participating in exceptional events – how can this be the same family and the same children as those who are the objects of preoccupation and constant care, who demand one's time in the most impossible moments, who get sick at the most inconvenient times, who have friends and a social life which bring great moments of joy but also unhappiness, for whom dirty socks and dishes have to be washed, for whom new clothes must be bought and old ones mended, who must be fed, who are always in your sight, in your way, and in your thoughts?

Men and women, husbands and wives, thus live two different lives not only because of the different relationships they have to the world outside the family (the world of paid work, of politics, of social relations in general), but because of the different relationships they have *within* the family. This difference emerges clearly and often dramatically as a serious communication problem as the children grow up and become more autonomous: though this never absolves one from all responsibility or work in their regard (and above all from domestic duties), it does relieve one of the necessity of continuous presence and total identification. Husband and wife then find themselves at the breakfast table having to confront experiences, desires, and perceptions which, without the harrassing interruption of children's needs, are often revealed explicitly as incommunicable. The estrangement, the difficulties in communicating about experiences which one considered mutual, might have been perceived in past years, but these problems were more easily cancelled then by other needs which were more pressing and visible. Now these problems seem to manifest themselves all of a sudden, and are no longer escapable. This experience is becoming increasingly common also, or above all, because of the phenomenon of the declining birth rate, which accelerates the arrival of the moment in which the couple is constrained to confront itself once again without mediators.

Undoubtedly, behind these 'two families' which spring from

two different ways of being present and responsible, stands the rigidity of the organization of work and social structures. The rhythms of work, for example, ignore the family needs of individuals, ignore their responsibility with regard to relationships and with regard to family labour (not only of providing an income), and at the same time assume that they have a family, a woman (mother, sister, wife), who takes on these responsibilities even for the worker himself. The hours and the requirements of the social services are another example of rigidity, and they necessitate a complex labour of piecing together and integration.

It is precisely the presence of the woman–wife–mother in the sphere of paid work which immediately highlights this rigidity, showing its incompatibility with the needs and the organization of the family. Or better, showing how there is compatibility only when there is flexibility in the hours of family work which corresponds to the rigidity of the hours of paid work and social services, and vice versa. For this reason, women with children, especially small children, disappear from rigid jobs which require eight hours a day for five days a week. They prefer the more flexible schedules of the small family or artisan workshop, or do piecework at home, where the lower pay is compensated for by the possibility of organizing one's work to correspond to 'family time'. The term 'accordion day' well expresses the flexibility of the woman at home, her (necessary) capacity to adapt herself to all the external schedules (of the school the children attend, of the husband's job, of everybody's free time, of health services, of the county offices, etc.). And this same term, 'accordion day', also expresses the near impossibility of defining precisely the length of time family labour lasts, or of distinguishing the time spent in work from the time the woman has for herself.

While the demands of paid work limit the presence of the woman in the family, and thus limit her time for family labour, what emerges is an incredibly long working day (only alleviated minimally by the husband's help): from ten to fourteen hours long, if one considers both the time spent working for pay and the time spent in family labour. This means social isolation for these women, especially in the crucial phases of formation of the family, and also means they are deprived of spaces for reflection (let alone rest or relaxation). A kind of compression appears, an intensification of family demands, especially in the area of relationships. This above all hits the lower economic strata. In this case one could speak of a real relative deprivation or of a 'new poverty', which affects the quality of life not only or not so much at the level of consumption, as at the level of relationships, both extra-familial and, above all, familial.

In the middle classes, and above all in the upper middle classes, there is greater flexibility or shorter working hours (for both women and men), and a culture which is more greatly influenced by ideals of equality and the virtues of domesticity even for men, at least at an ideological level. These combine to have the effect of pushing the men to join their presence to that of their wives, both in domestic labour and, above all, in the caring for and relating to their children.[9] Conversely, the greater rigidity and especially the psychological–physical heaviness of the working hours and conditions of working-class jobs not only make the working-class mother more exhausted than, for example, the mother-teacher, but do not facilitate a willingness on the part of the father to get involved in family labour and the care of the children.

Material problems combine with the psychological–cultural ones (male prestige within these strata is more often tied, for lack of alternatives, to the visible distinction of roles, abilities and tasks) in bringing about a rigidity to the familial scene. This above all affects relations with the children, both in terms of time and in terms of quality. At the level of social organization, and in particular at the level of the functioning of social services, it is understood that babies and children always have a family (a mother, in other words), to back them up, to take care of them, help them with homework, listen to their problems when they are sad, supervise their games, etc. Knowing this, it is easy to understand why children on their own can't come up with anything but clandestine and interstitial alternatives, among the wrinkles of the organization of space and time of adults: experiences often full of fascination, adventurous and freer (especially in the small cities and the countryside) than those offered to the supervised and cared-for children of the more privileged classes; and although sometimes reaching the level of minor gang deviance, they are more often limited to long afternoons in front of the television set and the vicarious adventures that this allows.

Getting away from the traditional and stale attitude of blaming the working mother, we see how the incompatibility mentioned earlier exposes the social reasons for the distribution of tasks and responsibilities according to sex: behind the veil of the vocation and the 'naturalness' of desires and dispositions, there are in reality precise requirements for the functioning of the system – above all the rigidity of how time is organized.

This attribution of responsibility to women has produced, if not a specific 'female social character', as Prokop[11] suggests, at least an attitude of attention to needs, a sensitivity to the daily requirements of relationships. This can become suffocating at times, both for the women themselves and for the others, especially when an over-identification with the role reveals all of its grotesque one-sidedness and compulsion (all of us can bring to mind the caricature of the frenetic housewife, or the anxious mother, or the chiding wife). One of the problems in the female family role (as a multiple set of tasks and obligations) is, in fact, precisely that of 'maintaining equilibrium'. This is often affected more by social expectations, and in particular by those of one's own reference groups, which are not always in agreement among themselves (the expectations of one's own family of origin can be different from those of one's peer group, for example), than by personal disposition. Who can predict upon which element out of the whole complex a woman might choose to stake her social respectability, if not her identity, once she fails to maintain the equilibrium between role demands which are not only different, but sometimes conflicting among themselves? And yet this ability to adjust to multiple demands, this attention to both essential needs and to the trivial details of relationships, is what guarantees not only daily survival but also humanity within the relationships themselves, personalization in the satisfaction of needs.

It is certainly not the fault of the family, or of the woman, if these needs are only satisfied on a family scale. In fact, a large part of the current demand for humanization of social services does not manage to go beyond a re-attribution of tasks to the family, to the woman (a telling lack of fantasy and social creativity!), after they had been more or less consensually taken away from her (the care for the sick, the aged, the handicapped, for example). For the woman this represents a kind of mockery or derision, in which she is blamed for letting herself be deprived of one of her prerogatives (thereby emptying herself of value), or for having wanted to 'unload' one of her obligations on to someone else (on to social services), with dehumanizing consequences for the persons involved (children, the aged, the sick).

The theoretically false but empirically true alternative – family/women *vs.* social services, sometimes formulated in terms of individual care *vs.* standardization – eludes (denies, represses, censures) in its apparent exclusiveness other possible formulations of the terms of the issue. One obvious possibility would be the involvement of men-husbands in the attention to others' needs and in the incessant labour of reconstitution required by the demands of daily life. This, however, would imply a radical revision of the rhythms of work, on the one hand, and an equally radical revision of male and female roles on the other. And it would probably involve, at least in the long run, transformations of male and female identities, of the relations of power between them, including that of defining both the time and the content of relations and needs.

The empirical truth of that alternative (family/women *vs.* services, or individual care *vs* standardization) exists, however. It is based on the fact that the obligation/privilege of reconstituting humanity and of recognizing the value of the individual is assigned to the family and to the female role in the attempt to provide a priori, at least within that space or relationship, a connecting theme running through the life of the individual and holding together an identity which has become more and more fragmented in the diverse roles, experiences, and modes of functioning and feeling which characterize the daily existence and biography of each person in developed industrial societies.[11] It is undoubtedly an attempt beset with failures, as shown by everyday, often dramatic, family conflicts – not to mention the personal costs involved (not only for the woman). But the hope that this attempt will succeed, and above all the empirical impossibility of this taking place elsewhere, combine to continually re-propose it as a value, whose significance furnishes possibly the only acceptable motivation – for the woman – to continue to take on family tasks and responsibilities without reciprocity or recognition.[12]

The process of construction of 'two families' (that is, that of the wife and that of the husband) is deep-rooted and derives only in part from the rigidity of working hours and social organization (although, as we have said, this is its most immediate and evident cause for the majority of persons). This has been shown by the numerous studies of so-called dual-career families. Despite all the flexibility, the ability to invent and adapt which these (very privileged) couples manifest, they still indicate how it is much easier (so to speak) for the woman to enter the sphere of male prestige than for the man to enter that of female duty. Though none of the dual-career couples studied seriously doubt the right of the woman to have a career and to respect its exigencies, and though the husbands seem to have overcome, with greater or lesser difficulty, any fear of losing their role (if not identity) for this reason, it seems that the insurmountable threshold for not losing psychological security and privileges is precisely that of reciprocity. For all the willingness to 'service' and collaborate which these husbands might exhibit, for all the enthusiasm they might show in the discovery of the pleasures of domesticity and especially in a more intense relationship with their children, the ultimate responsibility for family labour remains with the wife.[13]

This is a fact which is confirmed in other ways by the experience of many couples who have, for idealistic or ideological reasons, searched for a way of developing relationships and a division of labour which is more equal within the home, at times even leading to a reorganization of paid work.[14] Even these couples – that is, those who have come to understand that it is precisely the division of labour within the home, and not just that outside it, which constitutes a crucial element for the female condition and the inequality of power between the sexes, and who have actively tried to change it – have problems in completely overcoming the barrier of the attribution of final responsibility. And, even more subtly, there remains the distinction between the man, who can (who has the psychological and material resources to) choose to be present; and the woman who, on the other hand, still has a much too strong, though conflictual, base of identity in her presence on the family scene, combined with a much too heavy social attribution of responsibility, to be able to perceive it as, and make it, a question of choice (a choice which, as such, implies a character of non-necessity, of exterior and interior liberty). It is the woman who, above all, knows and experiences the dimension of inescapable necessity which structures family relations, especially as far as intergenerational relations (and most specifically relations with the youngest children) are concerned. Can one really choose absences, or non-relating, or is that only possible because someone else guarantees a priori, before any choice is made (other than that to procreate) precisely this presence and recognition? Choice and necessity present themselves in an inextricable way in family relations, at least in a woman's experience.

It is only because they come from centuries-old and legitimated absences (from everyday relating, not from social responsibility and responsibility for survival) that fathers can experience relationships with their children as a completely voluntary and (abstractly) free activity.

The Rapoports have shown the tensions implicit in the organization of the family for dual-career couples. These tensions derive not only from the material problems provoked by the effort to hold together and make compatible two professional careers and a family, but also from the difficulty in finding support in the prevailing cultural models and in one's own reference groups, despite the undoubted prestige associated with highly qualified and well-paid professional positions. These tensions seem all the more powerful in the case where it is not only the woman who enters the male sphere of paid work, but the man who enters the female sphere of family work and care. The experience of paid work in the formal labour market is, in fact, no longer (and for many categories of women never has been) an exceptional experience, though it is usually marginal with respect to the priority given to family responsibilities and discontinuous along a woman's life cycle. Much more exceptional is the experience of daily responsibility for family administration on the part of the man. This experience translates most visibly and immediately into a loss of male privilege on one hand (the privilege of being uninvolved, which is even more important than the privilege of being served), and the loss of female monopoly on the other. If the latter can undoubtedly represent a relief and an aid, it can also constitute a psychological threat, above all in so far as no realistic alternative exists, no immediately acceptable and handy compensation. Gratifying and prestigious jobs are scarce, especially for women, and work in itself is increasingly less sought after as a source of identity, even for men. Other possible, though partial, sources of identity are even more provisional and precarious. Above all the woman may experience as a loss that which is an enrichment for her companion. It may be difficult for her to accept a criterion other than her own in the handling of family relations and family work, especially when the sphere of relations with the children (particularly small children) is touched. The 'helping husband', held at a distance and directed, can be more easily integrated into a system of monopoly of family administration than a co-participating husband. Processes of communication about the family have to be set in motion; a common family experience at both a perceptive and cognitive level has to be sought. Yet for this task there is neither a tradition nor even a language between the sexes,[15] as we mentioned earlier. Co-presence and co-responsibility in the family arena therefore imply the acceptance of a dose of unforeseen and unforeseeable conflict, at least at first. This is especially true when it is not necessity imposed by circumstances (the woman-mother's paid job, lack of social services, etc.), but a precise value choice, which implies an intentional redefinition of the attributes of the sexual roles and of one's own identity.[16]

The situation is further complicated by the fact that, as we were saying, this co-presence and co-responsibility in reality continues to be partial. Thus on one hand the woman feels that interference in decision-making (from how to organize and do chores to how to treat the children) is unacceptable, unless there is complete co-responsibility; and on the other hand the man feels himself unjustly excluded.

But this also produces the phenomenon which I would call rising expectations. Once the equilibrium of role attributes is broken, especially if this rupture comes about through specific value choices, every step forward also shows how much ground there is left to cover, thereby generating not only confirmation and satisfaction, but a sense of impotence and dissatisfaction as well. Here too it is necessary to invent, to elaborate new modes of mediation, negotiation, and communication within the couple, modes which facilitate the process underway, which are sensitive to the reciprocal expectations and the reciprocal thresholds of tolerance. Besides this, spheres of verification and confirmation outside the couple are necessary to sustain this complex process of redefinition.

But the fact that co-responsibility and co-presence are still only partial brings about yet another phenomenon, at least at the present moment (and our data demonstrate this very clearly, confirming research carried out in other contexts). Not only is it true that the ultimate and major responsibility for family work and family relations is left to the woman-wife, with the husband assuming 10 to 30 per cent of the load, but what happens, it seems (especially when it is a conscious and intentional process), is that the man makes a definite selection among family tasks, skimming off the cream, so to speak. All the most routine and servile jobs, those least immediately tied to some gratification or relationship (cleaning, washing, ironing, etc.), are rejected in favour of precisely those tasks richest in symbolic meaning, having the greater relationship content, and characterized by being freely-given or spontaneous (cooking, giving the baby its baths, going for a walk with the children, playing with them).

In other words, the men seem to be re-enacting the history of the birth of the modern family, mediated by the centrality of children and affectivity, as Philippe Ariès and other social historians have reconstructed it.[17] But the aristocratic and bourgeois women (for it was in this class that the phenomenon first developed) had servants to take care of the material (and tiring) dimensions of family organization and infant care while they developed the affective and pedagogical dimensions of their relations with their children. Today's men do not have servants to enable them to do this; they have only their wives. That is, men make this important discovery and carry out this appropriation of a previously prohibited dimension, but again, at the expense of their companions. It is no wonder then that women often feel themselves once again the losers in the operation, seeing their monopoly on affectivity taken from them. This monopoly constituted (and to a large extent still constitutes) the cause of their subordination, but was none the less also the only secure base for social and family recognition they had. Now they are left almost entirely with the monopoly of domestic toil, material problems, boring and non-gratifying routine work, including the work involved in using services external to the family. Furthermore, women discover that the playful and joyous dimensions of maternity, too often denied them because of domestic and professional necessities, emerge triumphantly in these new paternities – freely chosen, freely given, free from domestic schedules. It is, of course, limited by working hours, but is thereby also limited in the defensive sense of being protected against invasions and risky identifications.

It is difficult to say whether this is only a phase of the process towards a more complete responsibility-sharing within the family, and a more general taking of responsibility for those to whom one is tied (by membership or by solidarity); or if it instead indicates a new dislocation in the relations between the sexes, one in which power and prestige are no longer simply tied to control of financial means and to activity in the public sphere, but also to pleasure, and to the possibility of choosing what for others (for women) is an obligation or even a vocation. Even conceptualizing it as a problem is difficult, given that it is still a very new phenomenon, about which we know much too little to be able to advance more than simple hypotheses. Above all it is difficult to say, without, among other reasons, in-depth analysis, how these processes affect male and female identities.

There are many elements involved, in any case. They range from the degree of flexibility which can be introduced into work schedules, in order to allow everyone to be more present in the other spheres of experience and relationships, to the forms of consciousness which develop within these processes, and to the meanings and values they produce. Thus they also involve the forms of aggregation and intersubjective communication (also at the group level) that will be possible and/or positively sought, and within which the above can be elaborated and experimented. Moreover, the story of the women's movement in these years can also be read as the story of successive projects of identity-creation and of relationship model-building, certainly only partial and provisional, but no less necessary as phases of clarification and passage. In a less explicit way this is taking place for all individuals, couples, and groups who must daily invent models of behaviour and reciprocal expectations, because those acquired from the past for various reasons no longer function. It is inevitable that this takes place above all within the family, structurally the sphere of continual redefinition of oneself throughout one's life.

Only those who think that a perfect model of identity (or even of society), exists, or should exist, which needs only be realized, can be shocked by this partiality. But this is an age in which people are beginning to understand that identity can be gained only through conscious reflection and that meaning (both collective and individual) is not given a priori, but constructed collectively in a perpetual 'work in progress'.[18] And in this age, despite the costs and risks involved, this trial-by-error process, this innovating (which does not, however, intend to throw away anything that has been learned or that is loved), is the only method that makes any sense.

Notes and references

1 I am referring to three research projects: one carried out with a sample of 503 married women living in the province of Trent, the

object of which was to determine the total workload (family labour plus eventual extra-domestic work); another dealing with the domestic workload and the perception of the role of wife and house-wife in a group of 60 women of Trent; and finally, a study of 148 married couples with children, living in Trent, the purpose of which was to investigate the division of family labour. These studies have been collected and published in C. Saraceno, (ed.), *Il Lavoro Maldi-viso* (Bari: De Donato 1980). The pages which follow are a re-elaboration of the introduction to that book.

2   For an Italian development of this approach see L. Balbo and R. Siebert Zahar (eds.) *Interferenze* (Milan: Feltrinelli 1979) where the organization of the family in different welfare states is analysed in this perspective.

3   Although they are the work of different people and different groups, these studies all in fact originate within a systematic discussion of these themes which is now under way in the Department of Sociology of the University of Trent, among a group of professors and researchers. The continuity of these studies goes well beyond the simple link provided by my presence, which has a different role in each. They are therefore in different ways the result of collective work of hypotheses-clarification and research.

4   I would like to emphasize precisely for this reason the fact that in the third study both the husband and the wife were interviewed, in an attempt to get away from what C. Safilos Rothschild once aptly defined 'the wives' family sociology'. Although this is a way of undertaking research which is widely diffused, especially in the United States and Britain (and is now being debated in terms of enlarging the range of interlocutors to the entire family), in Italy it is still a new approach.

5   Other investigations, with another focus, would probably have demonstrated the relevance of the extended family network as an economic resource: as a source of help in the form of providing labour power (to build a house, for example), or by furnishing agricultural products, or even in terms of lending money or goods. For instance, a survey conducted in Rome in 1979 showed that 53.5 per cent of newly-married couples were helped to pay for an apartment by their families of origin. See CENSIS, *Sondaggio sulla povertà* (II Rome 1979), pp. 24–5.

6   See J. Bernard, *Women and the public interest* (Chicago: Aldine 1971); and J. Bernard, *Women, wives, mothers* (Chicago: Aldine 1975).

7   See A. Michel (ed.), 'Introduction', *Les femmes dans la société marchande* (Paris: PUF 1978), pp. 16–17.

8 See, for example, L. Gallino (ed.), *Lavorare due volte* (Torino: Bookstore 1979).

9 Young and Wilmott, with their now famous study on *The symmetrical family* (Routledge and Kegan Paul, 1973), are mainly responsible for having pointed out this phenomenon. Although the concept of middle class is rather controversial (and especially in this case, since the English and Italian middle classes are grounded in very different cultures and experiences), and although Trent is not London, our data on couples in Trent seem to confirm this tendency.

10 See U. Prokop, *Ambivalenza e realtà femminile* (Milan: Feltrinelli 1977).

11 P. L. Berger, B. Berger and H. Keller discuss the forms of consciousness which appear in this type of society in their book, *The homeless mind* (Penguin Books 1977), in particular chapter 1, 2, and 3.

12 For a discussion of the lack of reciprocity in contemporary family relations, in particular as far as the man–woman relationship is concerned, in as much as that which is exchanged by the woman (family work) is never in any way recognized, even at a symbolic level (actually, at that level it is denied by the myth of love and motherhood), see the book by Andrée Michel, *Les femmes dans la société marchande* (Paris: PUF 1978), especially pp. 18–19, and the essay by E. K. Boulding, 'Reciprocité et echange: l'individue et la famille dans la société', Michel, pp. 22–37. The latter suggests that a tribute economy (which is precisely what the familial relation is) cannot last very long if the flow of gifts is always in one direction. See also A. Oakley, *The sociology of housework* (Martin Robertson 1974), for a discussion of the function of family myths.

13 See, for instance, R. Rapoport and V. R. Rapoport, *Dual career families revisited* (Martin Robertson, 1976); J. B. Bryson and R. Bryson (eds.), *Dual career couples* (NY: Human Science Press 1978); and J. Scanzoni, *Sex roles, women's work and marital conflict* (Lexington, Mass: Lexington Books, 1978).

14 Data concerning these phenomena have not yet been collected in a systematic way that would allow comparison. For the most part we only have evidence collected in small groups. Purely indicative of these phenomena would be the following works: E. Gronseth, 'Work-sharing families: adaptations of pioneering families with husband and wife in part-time employment', in *Acta Sociologica*, 18, nos. 2–3, pp. 202–21;and D. Ehrensaft, 'When women and men mother', in *Socialist Review*, no. 49 (January-February 1980) pp. 37–73.

15 In modern culture, the only communication which has developed between the sexes concerning family relations seems to be the asymmetrical one between expert – priest, doctor, psychologist, or teacher

– and mother (each in its own specific code). See J. Donzelot, *La police des familles* (Paris: Edition de Minuit 1977).

16   Goode has emphasized that conflicts regarding family responsibilities of the spouses take different forms in different cultures and different class situations. Many husbands of the working class help out a lot in the home, relatively speaking, out of necessity rather than from a value choice. However, many husbands of the middle and upper classes *say* that it would be fairer if there were a sharing of responsibilities (just as they claim that women are equal to men), but in fact their behaviour does not live up to their values. Thus the former feel themselves less excluded than the latter by a wife who refuses to allow them to intervene in decision-making or substantial matters, but permits them to 'give a hand' as far as the work is concerned. And similarly, the former feels less confident of their behaviour, which they duly try to minimize. The latter, to the contrary, will praise even the smallest act of collaboration. See W. Goode, *World revolution and family patterns* (Glencoe: Free Press 1971).

Although behaviour patterns have probably changed since Goode carried out his comparative research (at the end of the 1950s) his suggestion is still valid that attention should be paid to the various levels of values, of attitudes and of behaviour patterns as they interact in the various specific cultures and subcultures.

17   See, for example, P. Ariès, *Centuries of childhood* (Penguin 1973); J-L Flandrin *Families in former times* (Cambridge University Press 1980); E. Shorter, *The making of the modern family* (Fontana 1977).

18   Both the analysis of the Bergers, developed on the basis of the phenomenology of A. Schutz, and that of Habermas, based on a complex re-elaboration of Weberian categories and of the evolutive psychology of Piaget and Kohlberg, seem to converge in this conception. See J. Habermas, *Zur Rekonstruktion des Historisches Materialismus* (Frankfurt am Main: Suhrkamp Veria, 1976), in particular the first three chapters.

7   On the rationality of caring

Kari Waerness

Introduction

While rationality has always been a central issue in the social
sciences since the time of the founding fathers, caring is a concept
that until recent years has scarcely received any attention in sociological literature. What it means to care for others and how caregiving services are to be carried out in the welfare states of the
western world today, is now attracting the interest of social scientists; in part, because of the challenges emerging from feminism
and the search for a women's perspective in social theory; and,
in part, because of the more recent shift in social policy debate
dealing with the public services. In Scandinavian countries, for
example, public opinion shows a declining confidence in
professionalization and increased socialization, once considered
to be the cornerstones in the development of the welfare state.
Instead, a belief in so-called 'community care' is spreading rapidly
because it is supposed to be cheaper and morally preferable to
the public caregiving services.

The feminist critique of sociological conceptualizations and
theories that do not adequately reflect the position of women in
society is highly relevant for understanding this shift or change of
direction in social policy thinking. The enthusiasm with which
'care by the community' or 'informal caring networks' has been
discussed in public debate is rarely matched by a clear analysis of
either the conditions for or the consequences of methods and
measures for its implementation. In fact, the knowledge that can
be applied to this new policy option is very limited because there
are few systematic theories in sociology on the study of reproduction and the social order. There is no conceptual framework

that can be applied in analysing experiences and activities transcending our traditional sociological dichotomies like public/private, home/work, labour/leisure. This makes it difficult to formulate a theory of caregiving work.

Lacking a ready-made conceptual framework, I will use some empirical facts as a starting point to suggest a basis for a more thorough understanding of the factual changes going on in the organization of caregiving work and of the changes in beliefs concerning optimal caregiving.

One fundamental fact, of course, is that the responsibility for caring is still ascribed on the basis of gender – as a part of the formation of 'femininity'. What this means for women today is that they are faced both with the task of caring for children, the ill, the disabled, and the elderly in the private sphere, while at the same time trying to achieve more command over their own lives and a greater measure of economic independence. The new ideology that informal care is better than public care contributes to reinforce these problems.[1]

However, the increasing transfer of caring responsibilities from the private sphere has meant that the public services have become a very important part of the female labour market. Even if the high-ranking professional and administrative positions in this sector are mostly filled by men, and a great number of the newly created jobs for women are unskilled and low-paid, the importance of the public services for the welfare of working women has to be carefully evaluated.

Such an evaluation seems especially important in a situation where we are confronted with the idea that it would be better to replace these services with different kinds of informal caring. From a woman's perspective the sociological description of the growth of the public caregiving services as 'an emptying of the functions of the family' or as 'deprivatization of social reproduction', is very inadequate and needs to be re-examined and qualified. In addition to the fact that a lot of research has documented that most of the caregiving work is still performed on a family or private basis,[2] informal resources very often have to be mobilized both to make use of existing social services and to substitute for its shortages. Most often women are the ones who have to cope with the deficiencies of the welfare state services. Besides, many of these services have not first and foremost replaced informal caring, but have instead gradually changed its content, as an increasing number of professional educators, advisors and consultants have invaded the private sphere.[3]

I think the most educated guess social scientists can offer to the question of community care is the following: any idea of a massive replacement of public services by unpaid and informal caring arrangements is unlikely to be realized in the foreseeable future.[4] More probably, in societies like ours, the demand for public care will continue to increase, both as a result of the changes in the age distribution of the population, changes in family behaviour and women's increasing demand for paid employment. Unless more stigma becomes attached to the use of public services, it also seems reasonable to expect that the number of people who consider public caregiving services to be among the social rights connected with their status as citizens in the welfare state, will steadily increase.[5]

As a result of the development of the welfare state, informal care in the private sphere can more adequately be viewed today as a supplement rather than as an alternative to public care. Suggested policy alternatives which aim at transferring more caregiving work from the public to the private sphere already exist and simply need to be activated. This assumption is, however, unrealistic. Social scientists should therefore, first and foremost, concentrate their research and analysis on the possibilities for a more rational use of currently available resources for public care. By 'rational' in this context, I mean rational in relation to what most of us in our everyday life perceive as the essential values in a 'caring relationship'.

The recent trend in favour of more community care is at least in part a consequence of many people feeling that the public care system lacks the very qualities necessary to transform 'services' into 'caring'. Both in view of today's economic recession and in view of the challenge posed by those who for other reasons than economic ones, question the legitimacy of many welfare state services,[6] there is a great need to find better models for organizing caregiving work. To develop such models, it seems necessary to study not only the exploitative nature of women's traditional caregiving work, but also the positive qualities inherent in it[7] as well as why they seem to get lost when professionalized and socialized. To be able to carry this analysis further, however, more theoretical attention must first be given to the concept of 'caring'.

Caring: both labour and feelings

The conceptual and theoretical tools from our sociological tradition are inadequate to analyse a phenomenon like caring. Thus it seems reasonable to use the definition in a well-known dictionary as a starting point. In broad terms, caring is a concept encompassing that range of human experiences which has to do with feeling concern for and taking charge of the well-being of others. This definition tells us that caring is both about activities and feelings. 'Feeling concern' and 'taking charge' have both practical and psychological implications. We often choose the words 'to care for' to convey a sense of the bonds which tie us to other people in a wide variety of social relationships. We 'care for' our friends, our lovers, our children, our parents, our clients, our patients and sometimes for our neighbours, and even sometimes for people we come into contact with at chance meeting places.

Caring is about relations between (at least two) people.[8] One of them (the carer) shows concern, consideration, affection, devotion, towards the other (the cared for). The one needing care is invaluable to the one providing care, and when the former is suffering pain or discomfort, the latter identifies with her/him and attends to alleviating it. Adult, healthy people feel a need to be cared for by others in many different situations. Worn out, dejected, tired, depressed – there are many adjectives to describe states in which what we need or desire is for others 'to care for us'. In such situations we may feel that we have a *right* to our need for care being met. This means there must be others who feel that it is their duty or desire to honour this right. Persons to whom we are attached through the ties of family, love or friendship, most often are the ones we expect to feel this obligation.

In *principle* caring for healthy adults might be based on equal give-and-take relationships between people who have personal ties to each other. This kind of informal care can be based on *norms of balanced reciprocity* in personal relations, i.e. help, support and favours can be exchanged between people in symmetrical relations. When we say that people 'care for each other', we have this kind of reciprocity in mind. However, as caring first and foremost tends to be associated with women, *much* of the caring that women do for their husbands, older children and for other adult members of the family, does not imply this kind of reciprocity and should therefore, in terms of activities, be defined rather as *personal services*. When women provide these services, it is often something they feel 'forced' to do, not as a result of their concern for the well-being of others, but as a result of their subordinate position in the family. When providing help and services to persons who cannot perform these activities themselves – children, the ill, the disabled, the frail elderly – the situation is different. In such relations, the receiver of the care is the subordinate in relation to the caregiver. These groups are dependent on those who feel an obligation or desire to *care for others*.

To provide good care in such relations means that the caregiver at all times performs the activities necessary to satisfy the immediate needs of the cared for. At the same time, most dependents have to meet certain demands and challenges in order to prevent lapses in their development or recovery. Therefore, good caring should be performed in such a way that it, as far as possible, reinforces the self-sufficiency and independence of the receiver. The dependent is to be neither overprotected nor neglected.

Whether we analyse caring as 'labour' or as 'love', it seems highly important to make a theoretical distinction between caring for dependents; caring for superiors; and caring in symmetrical relations. Both in emotional and practical terms, it can be assumed that these different categories of caring relations give rise to different problems for women in their struggle for greater independence and autonomy.

These distinctions also make us attentive to problematic situations where women have to choose for whom to care – the weaker or the stronger. Both in women's family roles and in many of the traditional female occupational roles, there is a great risk of confrontations with such dilemmas.[9]

Caring for dependents, i.e. those members of society who by normal social standards are unable to take care of themselves, is the field of caring which most clearly is a concern both for social policy and for feminists. In the rest of this chapter I therefore delimit most of the discussion to problems connected with the caring for dependents, involving people who take on active caring on a consistent and reliable basis. This kind of caring I define as caregiving work, whether it is paid or unpaid, no matter whether it takes place in the public or in the private sphere.

Reproduction becomes a science: a new kind of male control over women's caregiving work

The traditional arguments for ascribing caring functions to women, in addition to the unquestionable fact that only women give birth to children, is also founded on a perception of women as more intuitive and emotional than men. With the modernization of society, however, this ascribed 'natural inclination' was no longer assumed to be sufficient for women to become 'good' carers either in the private or in the public sphere. In addition, they needed to acquire *some* formal knowledge based on science. Scientific work, however, was not for women. Either they were considered to be intellectually incapable of doing research, or scientific work was assumed to be detrimental to their biological function. (It is interesting to note that no one seems to have argued that it is 'illogical' that only members of the gender not qualified for practising care should be capable of giving expert advice on how it should be carried out.) We also find explicitly stated, if not so often, that the defining criterion of scientific knowledge, objectivity, is essentially masculine. For example, George Simmel writes:

The requirement – of correctness in practical judgement and objectivity in theoretical knowledge – belong as it were in their form and their claims to humanity in general, but in their actual historical configuration they are masculine throughout. Supposing that we describe these things, viewed as absolute ideas, by the single word 'objective', we then find that in the history of our race the equation objective = masculine is a valid one.[10]

The scientification of reproductive work, which in the Scandinavian countries started in the second part of the nineteenth century, meant that women became subordinated to a new kind of male authority – the authority of scientific knowledge. On the one hand the emergence of this new kind of authority meant a substitution or a decline of other kinds of authority – the authority of the husband/father and of the clerical profession. On the other hand, this scientification also implied that women lost positions of authority and control. The increasing power of the medical profession, still the most authoritative in the field of reproduction, is the most important case in this respect. The traditional lay healthcare system consisted of autonomous healers of both sexes, and the whole field of pregnancy and childbirth belonged to the female sphere. The history of midwifery, which is somewhat different in various western countries, tells us that the increasing influence of doctors everywhere led to the midwives losing status and autonomy.[11] At the same time, the medical profession's control over healthcare created new subordinate roles for women. Both mothers and nurses became medical auxiliaries, executing what the doctors prescribed.[12]

Much research has documented how this increasing scientific control over reproduction should not be described as an unambiguous development of progress and humanization. In the fields of obstetrics, childcare, health, psychiatry and care for the mentally retarded etc. – everywhere we find examples of professionals at times confounding traditional practices which the experts of later times evaluate as better than the new ones their predecessors prescribed on the basis of 'what we know from science'.[13] The same has been true for domestic activities such as keeping house, cooking and cleaning. Textbooks on domestic science and infant care written by male doctors and published in Norway during the last hundred years clearly give the impression of a belief in the omnipotence of science and the impotence of women, even if the latter belief is not explicitly stated in the more recent books. An illustrative example of this can be found in Norwegian history at the time when the first attempt to make housewifery into domestic science was made.

The first two textbooks on housewifery based on scientific knowledge, published in Norway about 1860, were followed by a great public debate among members of the male elite about the quality of women's work in the household. Some years earlier a woman, Hanna Winsnes, had started to write such textbooks, based not on scientific knowledge but on her practical experiences as a housewife in a large bourgeois family household for more than forty years. Comparing her books with the 'scientific' ones, the modesty of Hanna Winsnes sharply contrasts with the arrogance of the male authors. Only in the textbook intended to be of special help to the poorest housewives does she moralize in an authoritarian manner. On the basis of today's accepted standards for good practices, however, Hanna Winsnes' books still excel over those written by male 'scientists'. Many of her recipes, for instance, even if too bothersome for modern housewives, *could* still be used with relatively good results for a healthy and palatable diet.

The same does not hold for the 'scientific' books. Their recipes are mostly too inaccurate to be of much help to the inexperienced cook, and many of their general recommendations are the reverse of what is considered to be correct according to current standards. The male authors use much space to argue, in a very arrogant style, why women's traditional practices (including Hanna Winsnes') are basically wrong, suggesting that women therefore need some formal knowledge in order to be better housewives. Notwithstanding the praise they received from their contemporary critics, these scientific textbooks were soon forgotten. Hanna Winsnes' books, on the other hand, in spite of much criticism from the male elite, sold thousands of copies over a period of more than fifty years.

The recommendations of experts in the field of childcare, on subjects ranging from breast- and bottle-feeding, toilet-training, weaning, eating, sleeping, to more general problems of discipline and punishment, have also changed very much over time. To a certain extent it has also been found that what experts considered the only right thing to do at one time, they later consider to be totally wrong. Whatever the content of the advice, however, it has often been expressed in such an authoritative manner that a mother who does not manage to follow it may get the impression that this will permanently harm her children.

Evaluating the present state of knowledge on this subject the Newsons admit that

there is not a sufficient body of well-substantiated evidence about the facts and consequences of child rearing on which to base sound practical advice to parents. There is no lack of theoretical speculation, but so far very few theories of child rearing have been subjected to the inconvenience of being reconciled with the empirical evidence. Whatever the reason may be for this unfortunate state of affairs, the situation can hardly have arisen simply because the subject has no importance: indeed, it is probably because it has such immense importance that the professional advisers and pseudo-experts have flourished in such profusion.[14]

As some professionals in recent years have become more modest in their roles as advisers, the arguments for the necessity of 'parents' education' have shifted. As science has documented the importance and value of some of the traditional practices which earlier were denounced, 'parents' education' is now seen as necessary because of the assumed decline of the extended family and the increasing lack of informal caring networks.[15] In addition to the more modest experts, we still have professionals believing in the omnipotence of science. Schaffer seems to be one of them:

There is, in fact, no reason why bringing up the under-fives should not also be guided by firm knowledge scientifically established rather than depend, as happens at present, on fashion, prejudice and what grand-mother says. The parent–child relationship need be no more immune from properly conducted objective inquiry than the movements of the planets or the structure of DNA – even if its analysis presents problems of far greater complexity.[16]

We have very little factual information on how mothers react to the experts' different and often contradictory recommendations. However, the number of experts invading the private sphere has steadily increased, and women's formal training in school and employment teach them to act according to the dominant kinds of rationality in the public sphere. The question of whether this is counter-productive to their developing the skills and attitudes necessary for 'rational caregiving', therefore becomes important. Most mothers, today, probably agree with the scientific experts that 'natural inclination' is not sufficient to handle the problems they face in caring for their children. How much help they receive from formal knowledge and professional advice, however, is an unanswered question. The studies of Oakley and Holter *et al.*[17] support the assumption that Lopata's conclusions, based on a study of American metropolitan housewives, holds for western women in general.

The social role of mother does not produce many women who express full confidence in their ability to perform it at desired levels. In fact, the more educated the American metropolitan woman, the more conscious she is of the complexity of this role and of the difficulties involved in competent child-rearing. The relational emphasis of this type of mother, combined with a societal focusing of responsibility on her and awareness of the importance of the home for child development, make for worry over actions designed to best meet the goals of the relation. The physical care of an offspring is no longer a major source of concern, as it was for the lower-class antecedents of the modern woman; she quite competently handles preventative and curative situations of child health. It is her desire to provide the offspring with the best available resources for the development of their personality and potentials, coupled with the inadequacy of the sources of knowledge which she can utilize, which creates the greatest degree of concern for the new American woman.[18]

That more theoretical knowledge does not always improve the quality of caregiving work should not lead us to the conclusion that less knowledge would be better. Instead we have to ask *what kind* of knowledge is relevant in order to deal with problems that cannot be mastered by finding the perfect techniques or by acting according to bureaucratic rules, but where the quality of the work still depends on the actors' training and skills.

Wittgenstein, when discussing a somewhat different problem in *Philosophical Investigations*, illuminates what also seems to be a crucial problem when discussing notions of learning and teaching in the context of caregiving.

Is there such a thing as 'expert judgement' about the genuineness of expressions of feeling? . . . Even here, there are those whose judgement is 'better' and those whose judgement is 'worse'.

Correcter prognoses will generally issue from the judgements of those with better knowledge of mankind.

Can one learn this knowledge? Yes: some can. *Not, however, by taking a course in it, but through 'experience'* . . . Can someone else be a man's teacher in this? Certainly. From time to time he gives him the right tip. This is what 'learning' and 'teaching' are like here . . . *What one acquires is not a technique; one learns correct judgements*. There are also rules, but they do not form a system, and *only experienced people can apply them right. Unlike calculating rules.*

What is most difficult here is to put this indefiniteness, correctly and unfalsified, into words.[19] (Emphases added)

To the extent that scientific knowledge becomes an absolute gauge of what counts as knowledge, Wittgenstein reminds us that this can be detrimental to practices which earlier belonged to the non-scientific sphere. In the realm of caregiving, where we have a long tradition of male scientific arrogance in evaluating women's practices, this problem today seems to be highly relevant.

The ambivalence with which women writers confront the phenomenon 'science', is probably not only a result of the continuing exclusion of women from the business of science. I agree with List that the roots of this ambivalence go deeper. It is also because of personal experience that until recently, a feminist critique of the social sciences was seldom clearly articulated. Science's rationalist culture, and the models of behaviour which it propagates, are contradictory, if not hostile, to the feelings which women see as their own. A central task of feminist research, in my opinion, then, is to look at the context of caregiving work and evaluate the use of conventional scientific concepts and models which may well account for the fact that important problems remain overlooked. Furthermore, in this field, female social scientists can use their personal experience from everyday life to suggest alternative models. These alternatives can contribute then to a change in social theory and research which will better reflect the realities and interests of both women and the weakest members of society. A new image of the social actor and a reconceptualization of 'rationality' emerging from women's studies seems to be a promising starting point.

The sentient actor and the rationality of caring

Both on the basis of my personal experiences of caregiving in the private sphere and from my empirical research on caregiving work, I find it reasonable to argue the following: there exists something that should be called 'the rationality of caring', of fundamental importance for the welfare of dependents, and at the same time different from and to some degree contradictory to the scientific rationality on which professional authority and control in the field of reproduction is legitimated. Titmuss verges on this problem when he writes the following about the patients' situation in the modern hospital:

Why is it not understood that courtesy and sociability have a therapeutic value? *Most of us in our home know this instinctively, but somehow or other it gets lost in the hospital.*[20] (Emphasis added)

Apart from the fact that courtesy and sociability are probably of greater importance in situations where therapy no longer has any effect, one important reason that this knowledge is forgotten could be that the value of kindness and politeness cannot be calculated. I further disagree with Titmuss that we know anything about caring *by instinct*. In some way or another it has to be learned. Even if emotions are important for our caring for others in the private sphere, it seems evident that the ability to care in a 'proper' way, depends on something which can be learned and for which there are rules for proceeding, and that therefore some kind of rationality is involved.

To accept a conceptualization like 'the rationality of caring' is to go against the mainstream of western philosophy and sociology, which deals with rationality and emotionality (or instrumentality and expressiveness) as two mutually exclusive qualities of human action – a mainstream which traditionally has defined women as less rational human beings than men. Weber, for instance, even if arguing that emotions are important, still posits a model of social action that defines action based on emotion, like action based on ignorance and tradition, as nonrational.[21] This raises two problems: a confusion between rationality and lack of emotion, and the implication that emotions and feelings are not positively required by the rational action of individuals or by the smooth functioning of institutions.[22]

In the normal discourse of everyday reasoning, however, this dualistic image of rationality and emotionality is not always self-evident. Most people probably experience emotions and feelings as active and legitimate ingredients in behaviour that they at the same time define as rational. A renowned dictionary does not support the assumption of the mutual exclusiveness of emotionality and rationality, in showing that it has not been totally accepted in our everyday language.

According to Webster's New World Dictionary,[23] one definition of 'rational' is the following: 'The ability to reason logically as by drawing conclusions from inferences and *often* connotes the absence of emotionalism.' To assume that some kind of rationality is also operating in activities and relations where emotions are of crucial importance, therefore, does not seem idiosyncratic according to how rationality *can* be interpreted in everyday life, even in a rationalized culture like ours.

Russell Hochschild[24] argues that we need a new image of the social actor in addition to the two images which hitherto have dominated much of the social sciences. The first image is that of the *conscious, cognitive actor*. This image portrays people as consciously wanting something (e.g. money and status) and consciously calculating the merit of various means to reach this end. The second image, indebted to Freud, is that of the *unconscious, emotional actor*. Here the actor is guided by unconscious motivations and does and thinks things whose meanings are better understood by the social scientist than by the actor. As Russell Hochschild points out, these two images do not *deny* affective consciousness; images deny nothing.

However, it is a commonplace insight of the sociology of knowledge that we collectively construct social reality, that what we define as real is real. Because of the authority, prestige and influence of scientific institutions in modern society, science not only describes, but also prescribes social situations and forms of social actions. So, if we believe that, for instance, the scientific understanding that head and heart, or emotions and rationality, are antithetical, we act on the basis of this definition and organize our lives so as to confirm this belief. Our experience then provides further evidence that our definition is correct and the duality goes on and on. It therefore seems important to include in the social sciences an image of a social actor who is *both* conscious and feeling. Russell Hochschild suggests *the sentient actor* as a third image necessary to remind social scientists that human actors must be seen as more than bloodless calculators or blind expressers of uncontrolled emotions. In order to analyse phenomena like caring and caregiving, which seem to fall in a no-man's land when we focus either on the conscious cognitive actor or the unconscious emotional actor, this image of the sentient actor seems adequate.[25] Further, this image gives meaning to a conceptualization like 'the rationality of caring'.

To arrive at a better understanding of how the rationality of caring differs from scientific rationality, we can analyse how 'learning' in the context of motherly care, as an ideal type in the Weberian sense, differs from 'learning' in the context of science. In the context of science, one understands from the position of an outsider, and learning means to develop the ability to formulate a body of principles based on what is common to many phenomena and therefore independent of the peculiar and individual. One learns from books and theories and shows that one knows something by being able to subsume the important points in a neat system of laws. In science, one searches for predictability and control, the dominant criteria according to which scientific success is measured.

In the context of motherly care one has to think and act on the level of the particular and individual. This means one has to understand from the position of an insider, and the kind of generalized scientific knowledge one may have, at best, seems very insufficient in guiding one's practices. Moreover, 'as the child grows it requires different things from its mother and this means that she can never perfect her techniques, but must remain flexible and capable of adapting to a changed situation.'[26] Or in the words of McMillan:

It is vital for mothers to be aware that there are many things in life which can neither be learned from books nor understood from the position of an outsider. It is only because we realise that acting with rigid consistency is not always a sign of reasonable and appropriate behaviour that we do not think a mother is stupid when for example, we see her from one day to the next, making delicate adjustments in the care of her infant which other people would not think worthwhile.[27]

The point which all of those who advocate standardizing and making scientific our methods of childrearing seem to miss is the following: in the context of everyday life, it is foolish to seek 'certainty' in one's personal relations. The aim to provide women with scientific certainty that their method of childrearing will be successful is pseudo-science, because the relation between individuals is, by definition, something that cannot be subsumed under any kind of statistical generalization. Once that is done, the aspect of individuality vanishes.

It is therefore not surprising that mothers seem to be extremely hesitant about concocting theories about how other people should bring up their children, and that many of them are still sceptical about the advice thrust upon them by 'experts'.

Expertise in childrearing, according to the rationality of caring, is dependent both on practical experience in caregiving work and on personal knowledge of the individual child in question. When mothers exchange advice and support concerning problems of childcare, they can therefore at the same time insist that it is easier to bring up the second child than the first, and still say that each child has to be treated quite differently. To search for the kind of precision inherent in scientific rationality therefore seems foolish or wrong in the context of caregiving.

To illustrate the point of how working according to the rules of scientific rationality in some contexts can be counter-productive to what could be defined as rational behaviour, the work of a cook can be compared with the work of a chemist:

The use of a chemical balance in her kitchen would not make an inferior cook a better one because in the kitchen the role that the accuracy of measurements plays is not comparable with its importance in a chemistry experiment. For example, while it is obviously important to mix the ingredients in the right proportion if a good cake is to be made, it is possible to juggle with them in order to obtain a certain effect in a way that would be quite unacceptable in an experiment. Moreover, the reasons why someone may be a bad cook, in contradistinction to being a bad chemist, may have nothing to do with inaccurate measurements. *In some cases it may actually result from following a recipe rigidly and not knowing how to adapt it to suit one's own particular tastes and circumstances. Such knowledge, however, depends on practice and on the help of those who are experienced cooks.*[28] (Emphasis added.)

These arguments about concrete activities like cooking, may seem trivial or obvious at least on the level of everyday reasoning.[29] In planning public caregiving services, a similar attitude to the importance of personal knowledge and a lack of rigidity should be considered reasonable, or rational. To the extent that such evaluations should be taken into account, it follows that professional and bureaucratic control has to be diminished. As the professionalization and bureaucratization of the public care system still seems to be increasing this tells us that such evaluations may be contradictory to the principles upon which the whole ideology of public planning is based, and therefore not so easy to implement.

From various empirical studies of different public caregiving services, however, it seems that the image of the sentient actor is a perfectly adequate one in order to understand the behaviour and attitudes of the caregivers in the lower positions in organizational hierarchies.[30] The same image emerges from my own study of home helps.[31] The work of these home helps was organized in such a way that the individual employee provided flexible and versatile services and help to a few clients over longer periods of time. The most satisfying feature of these home help jobs was said to be their personal attachment to the clients. In fact, this aspect seemed to be the main reason why they felt happy about their job and wanted to stick to it. These middle-aged and elderly women argued that their experiences as housewives in their own families for many years was the most important training for being able to do a good job as a home help. Even those who had special formal training for this occupation doubted it had any value, apart from heightening the status of their job.[32] Working on the basis of their competence as housewives, however, often meant they had to break the official job instructions. Often they had to work for more hours than they were paid, and sometimes they even had to do things which were directly forbidden according to the rules. They also expressed a very clear opinion about the negative aspects of their job. The isolated working situation, which meant they had no colleagues to share problems and experiences with, and the lack of influence compared to the more professionalized working groups in the social services, were regarded as very negative features of their work-role. They also had a very clear understanding that their conduct as employees in many ways could be evaluated as foolish according to the general norms for rational behaviour on the labour market. Still, they gave priority to doing what seemed right according to the rationality of caring.

Public authorities feel compelled today to change the current organization of the home help service; in part, to secure the individual home help the same rights as other employees on the labour market; and, in part, because of the diminishing supply of middle-aged housewives who are both willing and feel competent to work under the same conditions as in the past. The authorities admit that it may be difficult to find measures to change the organization without changing the service in such a way that it becomes less personal and comprehensive.

In their study about wards in institutions for the mentally retarded, Abrahamsson and Söder used flexibility in work as an indicator of 'good caring'.[33] The work was said to be flexible to the extent that the behaviour of the staff varied over time and in relation to the individualized needs of the mentally retarded person involved.[34] To be capable of working in this way, I assume the individual caregiver had to be both conscious and feeling, i.e. *a sentient actor*. In investigating the relationships between flexibility in work and different organizational characteristics of the institutions, this study shows that decentralization of power was the factor most strongly correlated with flexibility in work. Wards where the staff had influence over decisions relevant to their work functioned with greater flexibility than wards where decision-making powers were centralized. The way work was co-ordinated was also found to be of importance. Wards where work was co-ordinated by formal planning and detailed instructions were often working in a routinized, non-flexible way. More access

to experts of any kind, a remedy which planning authorities generally believe is for the better, showed no direct correlation with
the degree of flexibility in work. Still more important, it could be
shown that a more professionally trained staff did not result in
more flexibility. On the contrary, formal training seemed to
promote a tendency to more routinization, a finding so surprising
in relation to accepted truths that it needed further comment:

It must be reasonable to assume that increased knowledge on the part
of the staff should lead to more flexibility at the workplace. When we
still do not find more flexibility on wards with a high proportion of
educated personnel, we have to question the content of the education.
Only to insist that education is for the good, seems meaningless as long
as one does not specify what kind of knowledge the caregivers need.[35]

One explanation for the fact that professional training did not
further flexibility could be that this kind of learning socializes
individuals to think and act according to the values inherent in
scientific rationality and in such a way that the values inherent in
the rationality of caring become degraded or suppressed. In other
words, the conscious cognitive actor becomes more of an ideal
than the sentient actor. Because the head–heart duality is accepted
in all sciences, it seems probable that any kind of formal education
based on scientific knowledge will to some degree promote a
more instrumental attitude towards work, at the expense of the
expressive.

What studies of medical education say about this problem probably has some relevance for most formal education in the field of
caregiving. Merton and Barber describe the doctor's role as one
of 'detached concern'.[36] They refer to the combination of detachment (an instrumental trait) and concern (an expressive trait) as
a perfect example of sociological ambivalence in that it involves
an oscillation between conflicting norms:

. . . the therapist role of the physician . . . calls for *both* a degree of
affective detachment for the patient and a degree of compassionate
concern for him . . . Since these norms cannot be *simultaneously*
expressed in behaviour, they come to be expressed in an *oscillation* of
behaviours: of detachment and compassion, of discipline and permissive-
ness, of personal and impersonal treatment.[37] (Emphases added.)

To the degree that formal education for caregivers in subordinate
positions also leads to a strengthening of the belief in the duality

of rationality and emotion, this can explain why the educated caregivers become less able or willing to give individualized care than the ones with no formal training at all.[38] Changes in the work roles of nurses support this view. In trying to achieve professional and academic status, leading nurses everywhere tend to favour the development of formally acquired knowledge. This one-sidedness has led to a devaluation of the informally acquired and intuitive kind of knowledge and skills which are learned through practising bedside care.[39] More 'nursing science' is therefore not a solution to the problem of strengthening the values inherent in the rationality of caring, at least as long as this science is based on the generally accepted notions of scientific knowledge and learning.

Schumacher argues that there are many problems in human life which cannot be solved through scientitic reasoning, but where such reasoning instead leads to different answers which appear to be the exact opposites.[40] These types of problems he proposes to call *divergent* problems in contrast to *convergent* problems to which the scientific methodology of problem-solving is adequate. Most of the examples of divergent problems he mentions belong to the realm of caregiving. What he argues about divergent problems in general therefore seem to have great relevance for the problems emerging from the increasing professionalization of caregiving work.

Divergent problems offend the logical mind which wishes to remove tension by coming down on one side or the other; but they provoke, stimulate and sharpen the higher human faculties without which man is nothing but a clever animal. A refusal to accept the divergency of divergent problems causes these higher faculties to remain dormant and to wither away, and when this happens the 'clever animal' is more likely than not to destroy itself.

Man's life can thus be seen and understood as a succession of divergent problems which are inevitably encountered and have to be coped with in some way. They are refractory to mere logic and discursive reason, and constitute, as it were, a strain-and-stretch apparatus to develop the Whole Man, and that means to develop man's supra-logical faculties. All traditional cultures have seen life as a school and have recognised, in one way or another, the essentiality of this teaching force.[41]

Better caregiving: a question of the possibilities to delimit professional and bureaucratic power

Scientific rationality is related to people's fundamental need for autonomy and control and has constantly celebrated new victories as more and more spheres of life in modern society have become rationalized. At the same time this rationalization has meant that other fundamental human needs, above all the need for care and closeness, needs we have learned to label 'feminine', have become devalued. In order to be real persons, with self-respect and worthy of the esteem of others, modern men have to define themselves as 'independent'. That 'there is an element of dependence in every relationship, even with a dog' as Freud expressed it, and the fact that helplessness and dependency are part of life itself for all of us – in childhood, illness and old age – may in part be hidden and repressed as long as the caring function is left to an invisible, oppressed women's culture. Still, women provide most of the caregiving work as unpaid family work and the bulk of the helping that in western societies is reported as community care turns out on closer scrutiny to be care by close female relatives, a point which is seldom clearly stated.[42]

As women to an increasing degree have become socialized to the dominant values in a rationalized society, their 'dual-life' in the 'welfare-service society' not only implies a heavy daily workload; it also means that they have to cope with the antithetical expectations of instrumentalism and expressiveness.[43] This coping is the more difficult as these dual expectations are present *both* in women's family roles and most of their paid work roles.

It seems reasonable to assume that the scientification of reproduction has had an independent effect on most women's feelings of insecurity and lack of competence in all kinds of caregiving in the private sphere, whether they are well integrated in an informal female network or not. This is a point which many advocates for more community care as a solution to the crisis in the public care system seem to miss. As Stacey and Price have pointed out, the autonomy of women in the domestic sphere has gradually been so reduced that younger women today scarcely have a private domain in which they feel able and competent.[44] Today's emphasis on more community care as a basis for a hierarchical and professionalized public care system, to the extent that it could at all be realized, would therefore most probably lead to professional caregivers working as advisers and consultants being strengthened and still more of the practical tasks being left to subordinate and unpaid female members of the family. Furthermore, the development of non-stigmatizing public services in the welfare state has been shown to be important for dependent people in order for them to maintain a kind of balanced reciprocity in their family relations. When they have access to such services, the chances are greater that they can be on good, affectionate terms with their family members and receive help and support from them which they value very positively, because they are not totally dependent on them.[45]

Research from different countries shows that the wish to maintain what Rosenmayr and Köckeis[46] call 'intimacy – but at a distance', describes the kind of relation a growing number of aged people prefer to have with their children.[47] A wish to maintain 'intimacy – but at a distance', seems to be a typical attitude among the aged and disabled, not only in the area of family relations, but in relation to the public care system as well. The popularity of the home help system, i.e. a caregiving service that moves on the borderline between the domestic and the public sphere and is very little professionalized, may be an indication of this development.

Studies of women's self-organized caregiving work on 'the hidden market', also show that caregiving work can be paid. At the same time much importance can be attached to ensuring that the relation between provider and receiver is to be comprehensive, personal and characterized by equality.[48] We also know that clients can prefer to have their daughters or daughters-in-law as home helps, paid by the social services. On the other hand, non-related home helps can be regarded as 'daughters' or 'friends'.[49] Such attitudes towards combining personal attachment and payment in a relation are mainly found among working-class women.[50] Middle-class women are more likely to regard the paid caregiving relations also on the hidden market more in terms of a contractual employer–employee relation.[51]

When people therefore deplore payment of informal caregiving on the grounds that the introduction of market values damages the quality of care, this is a typical middle-class evaluation. Both in the private and the public sphere, much of the paid caregiving of working-class women, both today and in earlier times, contradicts this evaluation. On the other hand, not all kinds of private and unpaid care are of 'good quality'. When focusing on the problems of today's public services as being too impersonal, rigid and insensitive, it is easy to forget the problems of oppression, injustice, violence, abuse and moralizing which can arise in more private and personalized caring relations. When public authorities today appear to accept the idea that the care for those who mainly need human consideration, warmth and a bit more time[52] is better left to voluntary organizations than to the public care system, they seem to have forgotten the working-class historical experiences with voluntary work in the form of charity.

However, the greatest problem within the public care system today is that there is too much detachment, not that there is too much concern. From the little evidence that exists, 'more concern' in fact, is not primarily a question of whether caregiving is being paid for or not.

Strengthening the values inherent in the rationality of caring is, therefore, in today's welfare state, not a question of replacing public *paid* care with informal *unpaid* family care or voluntary work. Rather, it seems to be a question of what possibilities there are to reorganize the public care system in such a way that practical experience in caregiving work and personal knowledge of the individual client can be an independent basis for greater influence, at the expense of professional and bureaucratic control and authority.

As virtually all prophets – or as they are now called, futurologists – seem to agree that the future will see an ever increasing reliance on specialized knowledge and skill and on applying that knowledge to the solution of practical problems by specially trained men,[53] such a change may seem rather utopian. Freidson, as late as in 1973, argues that the tendency towards the work of many other occupations in the different organizations to be co-ordinated around a professionalized service, would increase in the future.[54] Post-industrial society, in his opinion, will be the professional society.

However, the growing scepticism in recent years about further professionalization as a means of solving the ills of the capitalistic welfare state may imply that there is a chance that this trend could be counteracted.

As now some representatives of the prestigious medical profession also admit that 'the time has come for a major conceptual shift in the health care policy debate, from viewing lay people as consumers of health care to seeing them as they really are: its primary providers',[55] there may be reason to be optimistic. Further, in the face of the substantial shift in the pattern of diseases in the western world over the past forty years from approximately 30 per cent of all diseases being chronic to the present 80 per cent,[56] a shift which the medical delivery system has been unable to adjust to adequately,the need for a change seems urgent.

For a greater limitation or diminution of professional and bureaucratic control in the public services to be possible, there is a need for a fundamental change in the values of the interpretational frameworks of the public administration and the political bodies; an acknowledgement that many of the problems in the public care system today are *divergent* problems which cannot be *solved* with any kind of scientific methodology, but which still must be *coped with* on the basis of human actors' knowledge and skills.

More decision-making power to women on the basis of their personal experiences from practical caregiving work in the private sphere and from working-class jobs in the public caregiving services seems at least to be a necessary condition for this to be realized.

Using Dawe's metaphor of sociology as a conversation in which the prime imperative is that 'we ceaselessly listen to and converse with the voices from everyday life . . . including our own',[57] a feminist sociology could be a tool to visualize how concrete reforms in the public care system could further such changes, and thereby strengthen the values inherent in the rationality of caring.

From what we already know, the organizational principle on which we should insist, in order to improve the situation both for dependents and caregivers today, could be worded like this: 'Small, but not too small, is beautiful'. This means that neither the small, private and intimate family, nor the highly professionalized and specialized public care sytem, provide the kind of flexible and comprehensive care which seems optimal in relation to both dependents' and caregivers' contradictory needs for both autonomy and closeness.

Notes and references

The need for reconceptualizations of the notions of rationality has become a central concern for feminist sociology in Norway in recent years. The works of Marit Hoel, Bjørg Aase Sørensen, Kristin Tornes and Hildur Ve have given me great inspiration in my own work on the rationality of caring. I am also very greatful to Ritva Gough at the Swedish Center for Working Life, Stockholm, for her insight into the problems of caregiving which she has shared with me during our many informal discussions.

1 Janet Finch and Dulcie Groves, 'Community care and the family: a case for equal opportunities?', *Journal of Social Policy*, 9, no. 4.

2 See R. M. Moroney, *The family and state considerations for social policy* (Longman 1976); Kari Waerness, 'The invisible welfare state: women's work at home', in *Acta Sociologica* Supplement (1978); Gerdt Sundström, 'The elderly, women's work and social security costs', *Acta Sociologica*, 25, no. 1 (1980).

3 Margaret Stacey, 'The division of labour revisited or overcoming the two Adams', in Philip Abrams, *et al.* (eds.), *Practice and progress: British sociology 1950–1980* (George Allen and Unwin 1981), pp. 174–5.

4 On the basis of the evidence from social policy research it seems unlikely that such a change will take place in the Scandinavian countries, at least in the short run.

5 Two surveys based on random samples of old people (70+) in the same Norwegian municipality in 1969 and 1981 show this to be the case for care in old age. In 1969 16 per cent of the aged preferred public to family care, while this proportion had increased to 58 per cent in 1981. Sven Olav Daatland, 'Eldrecomsorgeni en småby de offentlige hjelpetjenester og familiens rolle', in *Tidsskrift för samfunnsforskning*, no. 2 (1983), pp. 155–73.

6 Ivan Illich, *Medical nemesis* (New York: Random House 1976).

7 The most well-known feminist analyses on the first phase of the new women's movement focused mainly on the exploitative nature of women's traditional roles. Simone de Beauvoir, *The second sex* (New York: Bantam Books 1953); Betty Friedan, *The feminine mystique* (New York: Dell 1963); Shulamit Firestone, *The dialectics of sex* (New York: Bantam Books 1971); Kate Millett, *Sexual politics* (New York: Avon Books 1971); Juliet Mitchell, *Women's estate* (Penguin 1971). More recently, however, feminist writers working from their experiences in this new movement have struggled to redefine the possible grounds of feminist theory. This has also led to refocusing on positive experiences of traditional care giving in the private sphere, especially on the experiences of motherhood. Betty Friedan, *The second stage* (New York: Summit Books 1981); Dorothy I. Smith, 'A sociology for women' in J. A. Sherman and E. J. Beck (eds.), *The prism of sex* (Madison: University of Wisconsin Press 1979); Mary O'Brien, *The politics of reproduction* (Routledge and Kegan

Paul 1981). One reason for the need for these new kind of analyses could be that analyses like de Beauvoir's and Firestone's create visions of a future society which most women probably do not want to see realized. For a woman to be liberated, she must not, according to de Beauvoir, give birth. Firestone has the vision of a society where biological reproduction no longer takes place, but has been substituted by technological means for totally mechanistic reproduction.

8   In the social policy debate on more 'informal care', most often no clear distinction is made between 'self-care' and 'caring for others'. These two concepts are, however, related to the contradictory values of independence and self-sufficiency on the one hand, and the values of responsibility and consideration for *others'* well-being, on the other. A clear distinction between them is necessary to make visible that these values often give rise to quite opposite priorities, both in everyday life and in the distribution of scarce resources for public care.

9   In the guidance literature for both wives and nurses, published around the turn of the century, we find explicit advice on how they should behave in such situations. Most often women are strongly recommended to obey the husband or the doctor.

10   Quoted in Elizabeth List, 'The science of the fathers and the science of the sons: reflection on a feminist critique of science' (Graz: Institut für philosophie 1983), working paper, p. 6.

11   Barbara Ehrenreich and Deidre English, *Witches, midwives and nurses: a history of women healers* (New York: Feminist Press 1973); Ann Oakley, 'Wisewoman and medicine man: changes in the management of childbirth', in Juliet Mitchell and Ann Oakley (eds.), *The rights and wrongs of women* (Penguin 1976).

12   Jacques Donzelot, *The policing of families* (Hutchinson 1979), pp. 7–49.

13   As we do not know to what extent women's practices have changed according to the changes in the experts' advice, historical studies tell most about changes in ideology. In the field of obstetrics, however, we have hard data on deaths attributed to puerperal fever and on infant mortality rates, which clearly show that the conversion from midwife to doctor at various points in time heightened the risk of death both for mothers and children. See, for instance, Patricia Branca, *Silent sisterhood: middle-class women in the Victorian home* (Croom Helm 1975), pp. 74–112.

14   John and Elizabeth Newson, *Patterns of infant care in an urban community* (Pelican, 1976), p. 14.

15   The public discussion about the need for parents' education is not today, as in former times, related to problems of physical care, but

to problems of bettering the psycho-social conditions for children's development. How to organize such education without professionalizing the socialization process, and without disabling the parents in the attempt to support them, is admitted to be a problem. See, for instance, 'Psychosocial conditions for development in early childhood', Fifth International Seminar on Health Education Schmallenberg 25–29 June 1973, International Journal of Health Education.

16 Rudolf Schaffer, *Mothering* (Fontana 1977), p. 11.

17 Holter *et al.* found that housewives' actual need for information was greatest on topics related to children's development. In general, the expressed need for information was highest among the most educated housewives and in the most urbanized districts. Harriet Holter, Willy Martinussen, and Bjørg Grønseth, *Hjemmet som arbeidsplass. Studier av husmorens arbeids – situasjon, av veiledningsbehov og veiledningstilbud* (Oslo: Universitets forlaget, 1967). Oakley finds the social context in which the role of the mother is carried out today very dissatisfactory as social isolation and constant responsibility are general problems for modern mothers of all classes in urban communities. *The sociology of housework* (New York: Pantheon Books 1974).

18 Helena Znaniecki Lopata, *Occupation: housewife* (Oxford University Press 1971), pp. 375–6.

19 Quoted in Carol McMillan, *Women, reason and nature: some philosophical problems with feminism* (Oxford: Basil Blackwell 1982), pp. 41–2.

20 Richard M. Titmuss, *Essays on the welfare state* (Boston: Beacon Press 1963), p. 126.

21 Max Weber, *The theory of social and economic organization* (New York: The Free Press 1966). Dawe argues that one important reason that Weber gave analytic primacy to the instrumentally rational action was the scientific aspiration he brought to sociology. As such action was crucially concerned with the scientifically accurate relationship between means and ends, it was the most easily understandable and explicable type in the rigorous and exact terms scientific analysis demanded. Thus, even if Weber acknowledges that actual social actions and relationships manifest various combinations of elements of all his types of actions and orientations, he does not analyse them in this way; i.e. for the various ways in which they manifest such combinations. Instead, the instrumentally rational action became the yardstick for analyses of actual courses of action, which were viewed in terms of their approximation to or deviation from it. Dawe argues that for sociological analysis in general, the resort to science leads to a denial of human agency. To respect and grasp and articulate the essential autonomy, contingency and

creativity of human agency, sociology, in Dawe's opinion, must abandon its obsolete and imperious scientific pretension, 'which cuts us off from the world of which we also are members'. Alan Dawe, 'Theories of social action' in T. Bottomore and Robert Nisbet (eds.), *A history of sociological analysis* (New York: Basic Books 1978), p. 409. Instead Dawe suggests another metaphor for sociology than science: the metaphor of conversation.

22 Arlie Russell Hochschild, 'The sociology of feelings and emotion: selected possibilities' in M. Millman and R. M. Kanter (eds.), *Another voice* (New York: Anchor Books 1975), p. 284.

23 *Webster's New World Dictionary of the American Language* (Cleveland, Ohio: The World Publishing Company 1976).

24 Russell Hochschild, 'The sociology of feelings'.

25 Russell Hochschild argues that the image of the sentient actor makes us attentive to the fact that the 'social' goes deeper than our current images of the social actor have led us to suppose. Roles and relations are surely not social patterns that apply only to thought and action, leaving feeling an untouched, timeless and universal constant. We therefore should integrate the sociology of the head with the sociology of the heart. pp. 299–300.

26 Sheila Kitzinger, *Women as mothers* (Fontana 1978) p. 34.

27 McMillan, *Women, reason and nature*, p. 54.

28 McMillan, *Women, reason and nature*, p. 49.

29 For someone who has not learned to cook, however, this is not obvious, and in general most of us very often forget how much learning is required even for what may seem to be the simplest tasks.

30 Bengt Abrahamsson and Mårten Söder, *Makten och verksamheten. Om villkor och versamhet vid vårdhemsavdelningar* (Uppsala: Acta Universitas Upsaliensis 1977); Rita Liljeström and Elizabeth Özgalda, *Kommunals kvinnor på livets trappa* (Stockholm: Svenska kommunalarbetareforbundet 1980); Ulla Ressner, *Vårdarbetar kollektivet och facket* (Stockholm: The Swedish Centre for Working Life 1981); Rune Viklund, *Att arbela i omsorg* (Stockholm: The Centre for Working Life 1981).

31 Kari Waerness, *Kvinneperspektiver på sosialpolitikken* (Oslo: Universitetsforlaget 1982), pp. 136–80.

32 In Sweden, a special formal training for home helps has been organized by many municipalities in order to increase the supply of home helps. So far, these training programmes have not been very successful. A very high proportion of the women who have done this training say that the actual content in the job does not correspond very well to the expectations they got from training, and that they therefore want other types of jobs (*Pensionärundersökningens*

rapporter om social hemhjalp m.m.:) (Stockholm: Sosialdepartmentet Ds S 1979:5), pp. 47–51.

33 Abrahamsson and Söder, *Makten och versamheten.*

34 Mårten Söder, *Vårdintegration, vårdideologi och integrering* (Uppsala: Acta Universitas Upsaliensis, 1981), Abstracts of Uppsala Dissertations from the Faculty of Social Sciences, **25**, p. 48.

35 Abrahamsson and Söder, p. 80.

36 Robert K. Merton and Elinor Barber, 'Sociological ambivalence', E. A. Tiryakian (ed.), *Sociological theory, values and sociocultural change* (New York: Harper Torchbooks 1967).

37 Merton and Barber, 'Sociological ambivalence', p. 96.

38 Ve shows how 'the hidden curiculum' in the whole educational system furthers instrumentalism at the sacrifice of the expressive. Apart from the first years in school, where there is some room for the giving of care to each other according to his/her personal needs, the school mainly conveys values connected to instrumentalism. As it is not made visible how this value-orientation conflicts with the rationality of caring, this created special problems for girls, especially from the working class. Hildur Ve, 'Ideals of equality in the school system of the welfare state', paper presented at the Tenth World Congress of Sociology, Research Group 32: *Women in society*, Mexico, 16–21 August 1982 (Bergen: Centre of Women's Studies, Institute of Sociology).

39 Herdis Alvsvag, *Har sykepleien en fremtid?* (Oslo: Universitetsforlaget 1981); Kari Martinsen and Kari Waerness, *Pleie uten omsorg?* (Oslo: Pax Forlag 1979).

40 E. F. Schumacher, *A guide for the perplexed* (Abacus, Sphere Books Ltd. 1978).

41 Schumacher, *A guide for the perplexed*, pp. 147–8.

42 P. Abrams, 'Community care: some research problems and priorities', *Policy and Politics*, **6**, no. 2, 1977.

43 Lynda M. Glennon, *Women and dualism: a sociology of knowledge analysis* (New York: Longman 1979), pp. 160–4.

44 Margaret Stacey and Marion Price, *Women, power and politics* (Tavistock Publications Ltd 1981), pp. 100–32.

45 Inger Hilde Nordhus, *Gammel og avhengig?* (Bergen: Dept. of Psychology, University of Bergen 1981).

46 L. Rosenmayr and E. Köckers, 'Propositions for a sociology of aging and the family', in R. Winch and L. Goodman (eds.), *Selected studies in marriage and the family* (New York: 1965).

47 Ethel Shanas, 'Social myth as hypothesis: the case of the family relations of old people', *The Gerontologist*, **19**, no. 1 (1979), pp. 3–9.

48 Marianne Gullestad, *Kitchen-table society: a case study of the family*

life and friendship of young working class women in urban Norway (Oslo: Universitetsforlaget 1984).

49   Lawrence Teeland, *Keeping in touch*, Monograph 16, (Gothenberg: Department of Sociology, University of Gothenberg 1978), pp. 170–1; Alvan Schorr, 'Current practice of filial responsibility', in R. Winch, R. McGunnis and H. Barringer (eds.), *Selected studies in marriage and the family* (New York 1962), p. 419.

50   This class difference among women is related to the descriptions of class differences in general. Researchers disagree in their interpretations of the working-class life-style, but many have pointed out the greater tendency to expressiveness compared with the middle class, e.g. Basil Bernstein, *Class, codes and control* (New York: Schocken, 1975); Richard Sennett and Jonathan Cobb, *The hidden injuries of class* (New York: Knopf 1972). To bring sociology closer to the realities both of working class and to women, we should cease to treat instrumentality and expressiveness (or rationality and emotionality) as two mutually exclusive qualities of action and should instead treat them as separate continua that vary independently and can be applied to a single action.

51   See Gullestad. The importance of the caregiving work of nannies and maids for children in the higher classes is nearly invisible in the research literature. Freud, for instance, when discussing the relation between mother, father and child, did not problematize very much what children's relations to nannies and servants could mean. As most of Freud's patients came from bourgeois or upper-class households, we can assume that in early childhood they were mostly taken care of by servants.

52   This statement was given at a seminar for representatives of different voluntary organizations and of the Ministry of Health and Social Affairs in Norway in 1976. In the published report from this seminar, no one expressed any objection to this view.

53   D. Bell, 'The measurement of knowledge and technology', in E. B. Sheldon and W. E. Moore (eds.), *Indicators of social change* (New York: Russell Sage Foundation 1968).

54   Eliot Friedson, 'Professions and the occupational principle', in E. Friedson (ed.), *The professions and their prospects* (Beverly Hills: Sage 1973).

55   Lowell S. Levin and Ellen S. Idler, *The hidden health care system: mediating structures and medicine* (Cambridge, Massachusetts: Harper and Row 1981), p. 1.

56   These figures are given by Levin and Idler (1981: p. 259) without rendering any account of how they are calculated. In documents from WHO not formally published, I found the same figures.

57   Alan Dawe, p. 414.

8 The circular trap: women and part-time work

Vicki Smith

Introduction

Part-time employment opportunities have been depicted as a beneficial option for women – offering them access to the labour market while allowing them the flexibility to fulfil their roles in the home as wives and mothers.[1] It is assumed that workers in this type of employment experience choice and autonomy: one personnel study concludes that,

> . . . [making a choice about part-time employment may] contribute to the quality and dignity of working life, offering workers more control over their working time and the ability to accommodate personal and family needs as well as work needs. They permit workers to be treated as responsible adults, and they may increase job satisfaction.[2]

Seen as an option that opens the way to alternative structures of employment and lifestyles, even feminists have suggested that profound and long-range changes may take place with respect to a fundamental sexual division of labour that has historically situated women exclusively in the home. Accordingly, *Ms.* magazine recently extolled part-time work as 'a way of humanizing the workplace and promoting equality; of permitting men to spend more time at home and women more time at the office',[3] assuming that men and women equally will take advantage of part-time employment opportunities.

This ideal depiction of voluntary choice obscures another reality: the reality that part-time work perpetuates the subordination of women in our society. In this chapter, this reality is examined from two sides: from the perspective of changes in the occupational structure, and from women's work in the household.

Part-time employment has emerged as a major labour market category for women only in recent years. It is a feature of a striking trend in women's labour market activity: the rapid and massive increase in the labour force participation of married women and/or mothers. Since the Second World War the number of working mothers in the United States has increased more than tenfold. In 1950, the labour force participation rates of married women (husband present) including full- and part-time workers, was 22 per cent; labour force participation rates for mothers (an overlapping category to be sure) in 1950 was 18 per cent.[4] By March 1982, 59 per cent of all mothers with children under 18 years of age (18.7 million mothers) were in the labour force; 50 per cent of mothers with preschool children (7.4 million mothers) were working.[5] This growth compares to the broader increases in women's labour force participation since the Second World War: in 1950, 32 per cent of all women aged 14 and over worked, while in 1981, 62 per cent of all women aged 18–64 years were workers.[6] The movement of married women and mothers into part-time jobs explains a significant proportion of this shift. In 1978, women with children under 15 represented 34 per cent of single-job, part-time workers, while they made up only 12 per cent of the full-time labour force.[7] In 1982, slightly under one-third of married women worked part time. Currently, women constitute 66 per cent of all part-time workers.[8]

In the following sections I focus on three phenomena. First, I introduce data concerning the proliferation of part-time jobs in which many married women and mothers work. I will illustrate that broad changes in the economy and the occupational structure led to the construction and growth of certain part-time jobs that are gender-specific. In this way, part-time work and the predominance of women in it is an important aspect of the contemporary accumulation of capital. Second, given the availability of these jobs, I examine the element of choice for women workers. I will argue that the choices women make about part-time work in a patriarchal and capitalist society importantly reflect the material and ideological constraints of our sex-gender system. Finally, I argue against the prevailing belief that access to this type of wage-labour, in and of itself, will be followed by an alteration of women's position in an historically rigid sexual division of labour. The availability of part-time jobs does not fundamentally change women's subordinate position within the family or the economy.

Rather, women's position becomes more firmly entrenched as a result of this labour market phenomenon.

Characteristics of part-time jobs: demand

The growth in regular and temporary part-time employment opportunities has been marked: in 1954, the first year for which systematically compiled data on part-time work are available, 15 per cent of all employees in non-agricultural industries worked part time. According to 1982 data, this figure was 21 per cent.[9] Indeed, various commentators have noted that deep and fundamental changes in the American economy will entail the continuation of this trend in part-time employment.[10]

Existing research on this trend is highly fragmentary. Articles in trade and management journals, and personnel policy studies, tend to focus on a small fraction of lucrative part-time jobs, such as those in the public sector, and in professional and managerial jobs in the private sector.[11] Such literature praises the part-time work option for its potential contribution to the qualitative enrichment of personal and working life. This optimistic representation of part-time work, however, obscures a very different experience shared by the vast majority of workers who engage in this type of employment. While the former are characterized by relatively high wages, pro-rated or regular benefits, relative control over schedules, and are often unionized, the majority of part-time jobs are located primarily in the lowest levels of the occupational structure with respect to wages, skill and control.

The rise in part-time employment is intrinsically connected to the expansion of certain industries that are now primary sectors of employment in our economy. Most part-time work is a key feature of two sectors that currently have the fastest growth rates: the services and retail trade.[12] Indeed, these two sectors alone provided over 70 per cent of all new private jobs created from 1973 to 1980.[13] Various low-level occupations within these sectors (at the non-managerial, non-professional level) employ the largest percentages of part-time workers: for example, according to 1977 data, in the service industries 40.8 per cent of total employees were part time, while 30.6 per cent of total employees in retail trade were part-time.[14] The third largest concentration of part-time employees is within clerical occupations: here, part-time positions, distributed throughout different industries, constitute 24.7 per cent of its total number of jobs.[15]

A significant proportion of the retail sales industry has been accounted for by the proliferation of fast food eating establishments. Between 1962 and 1975 the percentage of part-time workers in these establishments rose from 32 per cent to 51 per cent.[16] In the retail food industry (composed of grocery stores, supermarkets, specialty food and fast-food stores) part-time employment rates rose from 40 to over 50 per cent of the total work force between 1966 and 1977.[17] Temporary help industries, which hire part-time and temporary full-time workers out to other businesses, virtually exploded after the Second World War, from the employment of a few thousand people in 1946, to employing approximately 2 to 3 million people by 1974. Seventy per cent of these temporary employees worked in clerical occupations.[18] Much temporary and part-time employment, then, falls within the secondary labour market and the lowest strata of the primary labour market.

Of necessity, demand forces shape the manner in which such shifts will be organized. One example of the breakdown of jobs into part-time shifts is that of jobs that are geared toward the production of services rather than goods, where there is a cyclical demand for output (in relation to daily business cycles), where job tasks are routine and discrete, and which are non-managerial.[20] This organization ensures the co-ordination of production with irregular demand. Theorists of organization and dual labour markets point out that employers and managers need strategies to buffer the production process from such inconsistencies: the entrenchment of part-time work schedules facilitates a fit between employee flexibility and fluctuating demand.[21]

Service and sales jobs illustrate this tendency well. Almost all such jobs in the low-skill, low-wage strata are organized to respond to daily or seasonal fluctuation. Certain hours during the operation of a firm are distinctly busier than others; thus employees are required to respond to the changing influx of customers. This is particularly evident in fast-food eating establishments and retail stores. (In many retail stores a further breakdown occurs in which workers are hired temporarily in correspondence with seasonal and/or holiday rushes.) In an effort to reduce, or if possible, to eliminate, unused human effort, workers are systematically removed from a shift when at all possible.

Part-time work in clerical occupations is similarly organized around fluctuation, yet the fluctuation in these shifts can be contained and predetermined in a way that service work (organized around immediate consumer demand) cannot. So, for example, certain times of the month or year may predictably demand more labour than others. The variation in types of part-time employment are numerous, ranging from working regularly less than thirty-five hours per week, to being part of an internally regulated labour pool (available on-call in that company when needed), to the well-known 'temporary help' arrangements offered by such agencies as Manpower, Temporaries, Kelly Services and so forth.

The temporary help services in many ways demonstrate the organization and logic of part-time work structures. The primary way in which temporary clerical workers are used is to employ them during periods of peak business activity, thus decreasing the need for regular employees to work overtime. Further, a growing recognition of the under-utilization of full-time workers has contributed to structuring work schedules so that a minimum staff operates under normal conditions while temporaries are hired when the need arises. Companies save, on the average, 18 per cent of employee costs, in large part due to the impressive advantage of saving the cost of fringe benefits to these workers.[22]

Temporary workers notwithstanding, regular part-time employment rates of clerical workers have also increased due to a rigorous tightening, or paring down of hours involved in specific jobs. For example, at J. C. Penney's, a major department store chain, part-time clerical workers are used to cover peak periods of business activity. Many full-time positions have been cut in half to part-time positions in order to release more people for these periods. In addition, Penney's has a 'pool of people' to call on when needed; thus, their temporary workers are company employees who are familiar with documents, office procedures and management. Personnel directors comment that productivity is greatly increased with the use of this system because, 'After all . . . we have people here when we need them and they are not here when we don't need them.'[23]

Part-time schedules in these ways are rational strategies designed to pare away at any element of waste and under-utilization of labour. One full-time person may be augmented by a second or third person working two short overlapping shifts, rather than two or three full-time employees working a shift in which only one of them is busy for the entire period. Hence, any given job is fractionalized around the optimum utilization of necessary labour. The reduction of the wage bill for employers by paying for fewer total employee hours worked is thus a consequence of employing part-time workers.

Some industrial researchers maintain that part-time schedules are not cost-effective because of increased recruitment and training costs due to high turnover rates. These direct costs – as well as indirect costs such as organizational disruption, draining of management time and productivity losses – are argued to contribute to generally dysfunctional operations. However, the positive consequences of part-time employment *and* high turnover, although less quantifiable, receive less attention. For example, several personnel studies argue that two part-time workers tend to be more productive than one full-time worker, due to factors such as a reduction in fatigue, stress, 'burn-out', etc., and that there are lower rates of absenteeism for part-time workers.[24] Measurement experts claim that, 'Under-utilization of full-time workers may be as high as 50 per cent.'[25] Further, overtime will not be paid out to full-time workers; as part-timers take on excess work to be done, the level of continuous work for both full- and part-timers is intensified as the 'padding' of any shift is trimmed. Policies regarding part-time workers are frequently predicated upon employees working less than a certain number of hours so that employers may withhold benefits. Finally, continual turnover may be actively encouraged by employers in the secondary labour market to inhibit demands for increased wages and promotion.

The concentration of part-time jobs in the areas discussed implies female-specific demand. Sex segregation within sales, services and clerical work is pronounced; they are overwhelmingly 'women's jobs'.[26] Wages for these jobs are the worst. Wages in service industries are the lowest for any type of non-agricultural work; retail sales work is the next lowest category, with clerical work following with wages that are 8 to 9 per cent below the national average.[27] Part-time jobs in retail sales, service and clerical occupations resemble their full-time counterparts: they are primarily non-unionized; possibilities for promotion are low, if they exist at all; for the most part, they require little or no skill; and workers do not have access to fringe benefits such as company-paid health or retirement plans.[28] Statistics confirm the female-specific nature of part-time jobs more generally. Between 1968 and 1977 women accounted for four-fifths of the proportion of growth in part-time employment.[29] Indeed, 31 per cent of all new employment for women since 1966 has been voluntary part-time.[30]

That these jobs are primarily women's jobs, and that they are located in the lowest rungs of the labour market, suggest that part-time employment is an extension of occupational sex-segregation that continues to leave women in a severely disadvantaged position, and serves to heighten the exploitation of women as a source of cheap labour. Statistical forecasts confirm that our economy will experience vast growth rates in the dead-end (non-supervisory, temporary, part-time, non-unionized, low-wage) jobs which employ primarily female labour.

What are some of the ideological and material conditions that legitimate the reproduction of this massive secondary status experienced by women in the part-time labour market? Common assumptions about part-time work and the employment of women dovetail neatly into prevailing notions about the 'natural' relationship of women to the family, and about women's secondary status as wage-labourers. This is cast in the ideology of the male, 'family' wage. Men are viewed as the stable, primary wage-earners; their wages are purported to be adequate for the support of families. Further, women are seen as unpaid, home labourers. All women are structurally marginalized by this assumption. They are typically cast as secondary income earners, and are presumed to be workers for whom reduced working hours or fluctuations in employment due to slack business, recession, etc, are not as devastating as to men who are primary income earners. Women, it is expected, can fall back on the male, 'family' wage.[31] This belief prevails despite the increasing numbers of women supporting themselves and dependents.[32] For this reason, the subsidiary and often temporary nature of part-time jobs does not appear to place women at a disadvantage.

Both mainstream supply and demand arguments incorporate these assumptions into accounts of the growth of a female-specific, part-time sector of jobs. Most supply arguments concerning the increase in part-time work in the last two decades rely on a one-sided explanation: it is simply due to the increased labour force participation of certain groups based both on their desire for work and on demographic changes. The case of married women and mothers clearly exemplifies this shift. One economist has suggested that,

> . . . [the increase in part-time employment] is largely a result of an increase in labour force participation among the groups most likely to work part-time: married mothers.[33]

Certain lines of reasoning are employed in this framework of supply. Reference is made to historical demographic shifts in order to explain the massive entrance of married women and mothers in the labour force. Changes in fertility patterns, age of childbearing, attitudes, burden of household work and so forth, give rise to the proposition that demographic changes have been the primary cause in women's increased labour force participation.[34]

Employers thus explain and legitimate part-time work policies by pointing out that married women desire and seek out flexible types of work schedules. Because of this reasoning, certain part-time jobs are explicitly 'typed' around parental and marital status. Many employers organize jobs as 'mothers'' jobs, arranging part-time shifts to coincide with school hours and school holidays. Some firms have instituted four to five hour shifts known as the 'housewives'' or 'mothers'' shifts, so that 'the housewives can pick and choose which shifts they wish to work and which best fit in with their domestic needs'.[35] An interview with an assistant to the manager of personnel at a major department store in New York City proves illuminating in this respect:

> We are developing four shifts: nine thirty to two thirty; eleven to three; three to seven; and five to nine. The early shifts are mainly young mothers with school kids. The three to seven are high school and college students and people who moonlight.[36]

For this reason employers and policy analysts view part-time work as a functional labour market mechanism for incorporating married women and/or mothers into the labour market. This employment is seen as an ideal utilization of workers who are 'handicapped' in a variety of acceptable ways. For example, part-time schedules can be adapted to the demands of women who are constrained by the needs of their families.

The accommodation of women's paid work to their domestic demands is taken as axiomatic in their labour force participation. The fact that they can only work part-time is viewed as natural; one management journal claims that, 'A lot of the women are exhausted working four days after doing their homework. *They could never work full-time.*'[37]

Further, part-time work is posited as being advantageous to women in that, since most part-time work does not require skilled labour, women are not handicapped by a lack of training or education. Theoretically, they 'enjoy' access to this type of employment.

In the same vein, it is understood that teenagers cannot work full-time jobs due to their school commitments; the elderly and the handicapped are less able to cope with full-time, strenuous work. From this perspective, part-time work is viewed as a functional labour market institution that accommodates the needs of technically disadvantaged and restricted groups of workers. People who work part-time are identified as being socially, psychologically or physically ill-prepared to work full time:

People who hold (part-time) jobs are usually assumed to be intermittent workers without career ambitions, and the labour market has been structured accordingly.[38]

Thus the idea that part-time work is established to coincide with the defining characteristics of labour supply or the needs of particular groups has become an accepted explanation for this phenomenon. In other words, part-time jobs emerged as a labour market mechanism to meet the needs of an emerging group of workers. The benefits accorded to employers are overlooked in analyses extolling the benefits of part-time work for women.

Dual labour market theorists employ a functionalist framework of demand to explain the insertion of certain groups of people into part-time jobs. Piore and Doeringer, for example, argue that a part-time, fluctuating labour market is necessary for employers and managers to be able to meet unpredictable demand. This part-time fluctuation characterizes secondary labour market activity. Primary labour markets correspond to managed, stable demand forces, hence *requiring* a permanent, stable, full-time labour force. In this framework it naturally follows that people with tenuous commitments to work and personal reasons for being pushed and pulled out of the workforce (such as mothers and housewives) will fit into the lower strata of jobs.

Descriptively, then, the relationship between workers who are handicapped on the full-time job market, and the emergence of employment opportunities that are flexible to these handicaps, is accurate and important. From the perspective of workers it is crucial to be able to make a choice regarding full- or part-time employment. As will be argued later, shorter work schedules may be the only way to obtain additional income for households, as well as a singular means that many women have to overcome the limited access to the labour market. Furthermore, job structures do adjust to accommodate different labouring populations. However, these arguments as currently formulated, are uncritical of the particular interlocking dynamics of capitalism and patriarchy. They leave unexamined the relationship between the changing structure of occupations – the increase in demand for a female-specific labour force – and the gender relations and household structures that shape and determine the employment choices that women make in the work world. Barrett argues that

> . . . a model of women's dependence has become entrenched in the relations of production of capitalism, in the divisions of labour in wage work and between wage labour and domestic labour.[39]

It is the reproduction of this entrenchment that is illuminated by a more critical conceptualization of women's part-time employment.

Household strategies: women's employment choices

From the perspective of the household it has been increasingly difficult to maintain certain standards of living by relying on one wage – typically, the male 'family' wage. A second source of income has virtually been necessitated by the increasing inflation of recent years. Indeed, discussing the impact of stagflation on the lives of working families, Currie, Dunn and Fogarty suggest that the primary way in which living standards were maintained during the 1970s was by increasing the family labour pool: ' . . . putting more family members to work has become the key coping strategy for broad segments of the working class.'[40]

The struggle to maintain a reasonable living standard, while not the sole reason, has surely been one of the most pressing factors for the specific employment of married women and mothers outside the home in the last twenty years. In addition to inflation, 10 per cent plus unemployment and the indirect effects of 'Reaganomics', trap and pressure family income and domestic work.

Women who are female heads of household are affected by
the same structural pressures. For single mothers with secondary
labour market status this is especially tough: state and federal
cutbacks exacerbate the financial hardships of being the sole
income earner in the family. Overall, women in and outside of
families become trapped within the intersection of state policy,
economic conditions and the labour market. The rescinding of
federal and state supported services – both in terms of financial
assistance and indirect services such as community and school
activities for children, institutional care of older, ill and handicapped individuals – means that the care and reproduction of
family members rebounds on to women's shoulders, while the
need for a second income in the household increases.

Given this need for greater income, it is important to understand why women choose to work part-time rather than full-time
schedules. First, despite the fact that women and men engage
in paid work, it is women who continue to bear the greatest
responsibility for domestic work and childcare. Hartmann has
pointed out that even when married women are working full time,
they end up doing the bulk of unpaid 'home work'.[41] Clearly,
with household work placing concrete parameters on one's labour
market participation, the *greatest* constraint on women's labour
market activity is the presence of children. Childcare, of all
productive tasks in the home, is the least flexible: for mothers,
decisions made about any type of activity generally revolve around
childcare arrangements. For the woman who is earning low wages,
her paid work is 'cost-effective' only when her unpaid work –
childcare, cleaning, food preparation, etc. – does not become too
great an additional cost in her subsequent absence. Purchasing
childcare (i.e., paid daycare) would, in many cases, minimize the
contributions made by women's low wages; hence, women must
arrange part-time work around the availability of non-paid childcare. For example, women juggle part-time work around school
hours of children, and to some degree around husbands' hours of
work (women may be with children full time during the day, and
work part time in the evenings when men are home); women may
work seasonally (Christmas, summer) when older children may
take care of younger children; or they may exchange childcare
with neighbours and kin, working part time around these hours.
In such situations, women's part-time employment is considered

voluntary: they work part time by choice. However, the choice made is circumscribed by household demands.

Certainly there are situations that involve women part-time workers whose decision to work fewer hours more closely approximates being one of non-constrained choice. This would occur primarily where the pooled family income is high enough – whether by a male 'family' wage or via the wage of a woman earning higher wages as a worker in the primary labour market – that women may work flexible schedules of fewer hours. The important feature of such a situation is again the ability to pay for childcare from the total household income.[42] However, I argue that the majority of women part-time workers have highly constrained relationships to the labour market, *vis*. childcare costs and wages earned.

Several examples support this claim. Perhaps the strongest is the fact of extreme occupational segregation for all women, full- and part-time. Three out of four married women were employed in clerical, service, retail sales and operative work in 1978, strata of employment with the lowest wages for non-agricultural work.[43] The trap is a circular one, for if many women workers are employed part time in these jobs, it is clear that women don't earn enough to both contribute significantly to household income *and* cover paid childcare. Hence, job decisions must be made juggling domestic responsibilities with hours of paid work. Recent statistics on moonlighting provide more evidence for this thesis. Of women moonlighters (who comprise 30 per cent of multiple jobholders in the US) more than half had two part-time jobs. This has been attributed to the increased proportion of women who are primary income earners in their families.[44] This increase suggests great flexibility in the ways that women *must* arrange their paid work shifts to childcare responsibilities.

What does this limitation of choice mean concretely for women in their relationships to households? Clearly, having access to the labour market *is* important. Women make choices about bearing and rearing children, and about wanting to be their primary care-takers. They may prefer working part-time rather than full-time hours, where part-time hours allow them greater flexibility with domestic work. In addition, access to part-time work may mean the difference between confinement to the home and having increased contact with the social, public world. Certainly, the fact that their income is necessary for household survival gives women, in relation to men in the family, more status in and power over decision-making. In this latter sense, the option to work part time is an important one for mothers and married women who traditionally have had few alternatives to being full-time family workers.

Accordingly, the ideology about the benefits of part-time work for women expresses a certain reality. Yet I have argued that this ideology simultaneously obscures the reality of the paid and unpaid work of women. Only in the context of extremely limited options – i.e., women who are situated in a subordinate position within the sex-gender system of our patriarchal and capitalist society – can it be argued that contemporary part-time work opportunities are *beneficial* to women. Being 'able' to engage in a combination of exploitative part-time employment and unpaid home work is a dubious privilege. Zillah Eisenstein rightly notes that,

. . . freedom of choice is always an inadequate model for those who do not have power. The choices have already been limited for them. Women's choices exist within the political context of the sexual division of labour and society which defines women's primary role as mothers.[45]

While this situation is not as extreme as the situation of women who must work full time and handle family responsibilities, the phenomenon of part-time work represents a problematic and more hidden version of the hierarchical sexual division of labour. Part-time work is a concrete mechanism by which women's dual role in reproduction and as a source of cheap labour is maintained. It is an ideal labour market response to a certain tension in sex-gender relations, as an important means by which women can participate in paid labour, and yet retain responsibility for the rearing and care of children and household.

Family and work intersections

The utilization of particular workers – in this case, married women and/or mothers – in part-time work is, to a great degree, aided by the fact that they are structurally confined by their respective positions in the sex-gender system. A 'system' of part-time work is accordingly reinforced by the social stratification external to, but analytically integral to, the realm of wage labour. In this way, the relationship of women to the home prevails. While the justification of this relationship may be tentative and ideologically constructed, its foundation is decidedly material: a women's position in the home is reinforced by her lower status in the secondary, part-time labour market. Women are able to bring supplementary and necessary income into the family in order to maintain consumption, and to leave the narrow confines of the home. Nevertheless, a sexual division of labour is kept intact in so far as women may still organize the maintenance and reproduction of individual family members.

The availability of part-time work opportunities has important implications for the politics of women's labour market participation with respect to unionizing and demands for better wages and childcare arrangements. Given an entrenched ideology concerning the secondary work aspirations of women, there is far less chance of a challenge to the inequality existing between 'women's wages' and the male 'family' wage. The possibility that women, individually or collectively, will demand higher wages or look to the state or employers for affordable daycare facilities will be diminished as long as women *can* accommodate their paid to their unpaid work. This is especially pernicious given that the increased availability of part-time work is occurring in a context in which federal reductions in childcare programmes are extreme. (The current federal budget calls for a 25 per cent reduction in government-subsidized daycare slots.)[46] These reductions are occurring at precisely the same time that mothers of preschool children are the fastest growing segment of the labour force, with 66 per cent of mothers of school-age children currently working or looking for work.[47]

Possibilities for organizing around the issue of part-time work are undermined by the circular dynamics between part-time workers and the labour process itself. As has been demonstrated, women workers are subject to the worst conditions of employment, both in terms of wages and in access to skilled work. They are acknowledged to be a source of cheap labour and are readily hired for jobs which, by design, rely on the low cost of labour. Specifically, married women and mothers are highly desirable for part-time work because family restrictions increase the likelihood that they will accommodate themselves to employment of a limited scope. It should be added that the availability of part-time jobs undermines women's long-run possibilities for establishing themselves as permanent members of the labour force. Intermittent, temporary employment structured around women's family work prohibits them from developing the steady work record that would be valued by employers when women can finally join the labour force on a full-time basis.

Due to the nature of these jobs, this will be a transient, marginal labour pool with low expectations about or intent of challenging the structure of work. From the viewpoint of management they are ideal in so far as they do not and will not identify themselves as workers, with organized collective interests. Challenges are not made to the structured inequality of wages and benefits; yet, despite this inequality women will, at certain points in their working experience, want these jobs as their only viable work option. The constraints of the sex-gender system in essence reinforce the competitive, unskilled, transient characteristics of the secondary labour market.

Conclusion

I have argued that many employers need cheap, flexible labour for part-time work shifts, and that many individuals – in this case, women with primary household responsibilities – *must* seek out those very jobs. Hence, in so far as part-time work is often the most viable alternative for many women, it is a viability that has been acknowledged and embraced in the employment policies of businesses and firms. While the availability of these jobs is important to women in some respects, I have demonstrated that the secondary status women have in the part-time secondary labour market reinforces the economic dependence of women on men, as well as women's primary work in household reproduction. Part-time work shifts reconcile the conflicting needs of employers for cheap labour and of the sex/gender system for women's household/family labour.

What does this study suggest for change? At the most concrete level, policies that treat part-time workers differently from full-timers, such as hourly wage differentials, promotion possibilities, sick benefits and overtime policies – any way in which part-time workers are discriminated against *because they work fewer hours* – are targets for organizing. The excuse for such discrimination is frequently that real differences exist between full- and part-timers;

such excuses only legitimate the practice of hiring part-timers to save money. Such discriminatory policies are being investigated, for example, in Britain, where in 1976 women were 85 per cent of part-time workers.[48]

In addition, this discussion makes clear the importance of child-care for women today. Childcare stands as one of the most formidable issues influencing women's labour market status and must be used as an organizing issue for working women's organizations and trade unions that are unionizing women workers.

However, these strategies are problematic, as the phenomenon of part-time employment is structurally rooted in broader occupational and economic trends, and specific sex/gender arrangements. The expansion of part-time work cannot be attacked without understanding its connection to capitalist tendencies in general. As indicated earlier, most part-time jobs are located in sectors that are notorious for a lack of organizing and unionization. Further, as I have pointed out, the use of part-time women workers must be seen as a piece of a larger puzzle in which employers are striving for a cheap, exploitable labour force in the US. While the *specific* case of the utilization of women in part-time work has its own dynamic – particularly the factor of child-care, which will continue to circumscribe women's paid work – the *general* case speaks to similar tendencies in this labour process in advanced capitalism. In this light, teenage part-time employment must be systematically analysed, as well as the greater use of part-time workers in industries that have traditionally fought part-time schedules.[49] The increased use of part-time workers, as an employer strategy for increasing profits and exploiting workers must be understood in order to develop strategies which alter women's position.

Furthermore, as long as women are primarily responsible for childrearing and domestic work, these particular patterns in their labour market activity will be reinforced. Fundamental rearrangements in the unequal gendered division of labour must occur in order for women to participate more freely in the labour market.

Part-time work may, one day, provide a liberating alternative to a rigid and oppressive sexual division of labour. However, the system of part-time work in our society does not provide that alternative. Indeed, as it stands, this system serves to strengthen the bond between women's secondary economic status and their part in domestic reproduction. This is troublesome in our socio-economic and political environment. During a time of economic recession and moral–political conservatism, any mechanisms that serve to strengthen the sexual division of labour are suspect. The notion that part-time work is ideal in 'allowing' women to retain primary responsibility for children and home, obscures an important mechanism which reproduces women's subordination.

Notes and references

1   Accordingly, the overwhelming majority of part-time workers in the US are women who are classified as voluntarily working fewer hours. The category of part-time work consists of those workers who work part-time by choice: choice here refers to voluntary or non-economic reasons which people have for working under a specified number of hours or days. Involuntary part time refers to people who prefer to work full time; they work part time either because they are unable to find full-time work or for other involuntary reasons. Most people fall into the voluntary part-time work category. W. Deutermann and S. Brown 'Voluntary part-time workers: a growing part of the labour force', *Monthly Labor Review* (June 1978); E. Bayefsky; 'Women and the status of part-time work: a review and annotated bibliography', *Ontario Library Review*, **61**, no. 2 (June 1977).

2   S. Nollen and V. Martin, *Alternative Work Schedules*, p. vi parts 2 and 3, (American Management Association, (N.Y.) 1978).

3   A. Korpivaara, 'Will men legitimate part-time work?' *Ms.* (May 1981).

4   V. Oppenheimer, *The Female Labor Force in the US*, Population Monograph Series, no. 5, (University of CA., Berkeley, 1970)

5   *20 Facts on Women Workers*, (US. Dept. of Labor, Office of the Secretary. Women's Bureau 1982).

6   *Womanpower*, National Manpower Council (N Y.: Columbia University Press; 1957); also, *20 Facts on Women Workers*.

7   J. Owen: 'Why part-time workers tend to be in low-wage jobs', *Monthly Labor Review* (June 1978).

8   Calculated from Employment and Earnings, Table A–29 (US Dept. of Labor, Bureau of Labor Statistics, Dec. 1982).

9   Deutermann and Brown, and figures calculated from Employment and Earnings, Table A–29, (U.S. Dept. of Labor, Dec. 1982).

10 See especially E. Rothschild: 'Reagan and the real America', *New York Review of Books* (5 Feb 1981); see also H. Braverman, *Labor and Monopoly Capital: The Degradation of Work in the Twentieth Century* (N Y.: Monthly Review Press 1974).

11 See B. Teriet, 'Flexiyear schedules: only a matter of time', *Monthly*

Labor Review (Dec. 1977); J. Hedges, 'Flexible schedules; problems and issues', *Monthly Labor Review* (Feb. 1977); J. Hartley, 'Experience with flexible hours of work, *Monthly Labor Review* (May 1976).

12   See Deutermann and Brown, p. 6; Owen; R. Bednarzik and D. Klein; 'Labor force trends: A synthesis and analysis', *Monthly Labor Review* (Oct. 1977); also, R. Bednarzik; 'Involuntary part-time work: a cyclical analysis', *Monthly Labor Review* (Sept. 1975).

13   Rothschild, p. 12.

14   Deutermann and Brown, p. 8.

15   Deutermann and Brown, Table 3.

16   R. Carnes and H. Brand; 'Productivity and new technology in eating and drinking places', *Monthly Labor Reviews* (Sept. 1977).

17   J. Carey and P. Otto; 'Output per unit of labor input in the retail food industry', *Monthly Labor Review* (Jan. 1977).

18   M. Gannon; 'A profile of the temporary help industry and its workers', *Monthly Labor Review* (May 1974); R. Leone and D. Burke; 'Women returning to work and their interaction with a temporary help service' (Temple University: Center for Labor and Manpower Studies, May 1976).

19   M. Piore and P. Doeringer, *Internal Labor Markets and Manpower Analysis* (Lexington, Mass.: DC. Heath and Co. 1971).

20   Nollen and Martin.

21   See R. D. Barron and G. Norris; 'Sexual divisions and the dual labor market', in *Dependence and Exploitation in Work and Marriage*, D. Barker and S. Allen, (eds.) (Longman, 1976).

22   Gannon, p. 48.

23   G. Tevernier, 'New deal for part-time workers', *International Management*, **34**, no. 10 (Oct. 1979) p. 41.

24   Nollen and Martin; see also I. Kesner and D. Dalton; 'Turnover benefits: the other side of the 'costs' coin', *Personnel* (Sept./Oct. 1982).

25   Gannon, p. 47.

26   See L. Howe, *Pink Collar Workers*, (Avon Books, 1977); Table; 'Percentage of Female Workers in Selected Occupations'.

27   *US Working women: a databook*, US Dept. of Labor Bulletin (1977), Table 36.

28   Rothschild.

29   Deutermann and Brown, pp. 4–5.

30   Owen.

31   V. Beechey; 'Some notes on female wage labour in capitalist production', *Capital and Class*, (Autumn 1977) no. 3.

32   *20 Facts on Women Workers*, see also D. Pierce and H. Mcadoo; 'Women and children: alone and in poverty', Center for National Policy Review, Catholic University Law School, Washington, DC.

33 N. Barrett; 'Women in the job market: unemployment and work schedules' in R. Smith (ed.) *The subtle revolution* (Washington, D C: The Urban Institute 1979).

34 See Oppenheimer.

35 Tevernier. p. 10.

36 Howe, p. 78.

37 Tevernier, p. 44.

38 Barrett, pp. 84–5.

39 Michèle Barrett; *Women's oppression today: problems in Marxist feminist analysis* (Verso 1980).

40 E. Currie, R. Dunn and D. Fogarty; 'The new immiseration: stag-flation, inequality and the working class' *Socialist Review*, **10**, no. 6, (Nov–Dec. 1980).

41 H. Hartmann; 'The family as the locus of gender, class and political struggle', *Signs*, **6**, no. 31. (1981).

42 G. Stromstein; 'Part-time work as a labor market phenomenon', Working Paper, Institute for Samfunnforskning (Oslo, 1981).

43 B. L. Johnson; 'Marital and family characteristics of the labor force', *Monthly Labor Review* (March 1979).

44 E. Sekscensky; 'Women's share of moonlighting nearly doubles during 1969–1979', *Monthly Labor Review* (May 1980).

45 Z. Eisenstein; 'The state, the patriarchal family and working mothers', *Kapitalistate*, no. 8, (1980).

46 B. Ehrenreich and K. Stallard; 'The nouveau poor', *Ms.*, (Aug. 1982).

47 L. Cole-Alexander, 'Working mothers in greater numbers are in need of child-care services', in *Women and work: news from the US Dept. of Labor* (Jan. 1983).

48 'Women Workers: 1980', Report for 1979–80 of the T U C Women's Advisory Committee and Report of the 50th Women's Conference, (March 1980), p. 30; A. Sedley; 'Part-time workers and full-time rights', National Council for Civil Liberties (1980); V. Beechey and T. Perkins; 'Part-timers first jobs to be cut', *Rights*, **5**, no. 6.

49 Full-time workers in industries suffering from the recession are frequently faced with accepting part-time shifts as an alternative to widespread lay-offs. These workers fall in the involuntary part-time work category. We may be seeing a great increase in this category in the near future. The fact most often cited as contributing to qualification as an involuntary, part-time worker is 'slack work or material shortage'. It is worth expanding this qualification at length, primarily because it seems to place these workers in some type of residual category with respect to crisis conditions. In fact, data for the category of involuntary part-time workers, who usually would work full time, has risen from 2.6 per cent of the workforce to 4.8

per cent. 'Slack work is any suspension of full-time pay status because of lack of orders, model change-overs, taking inventory, plant break downs, shortages of materials and seasonal or temporary slowdowns and is often associated with economic downturns. In 1978, 6.4 million persons or 64 per cent of those who worked part time involuntarily named this as their reason for doing so. Workers in this category were usually employed at full-time jobs during the balance of the year (83 per cent). The majority were men (61 per cent), were primarily between the ages of 25 and 54 (59 per cent) and were blue collar workers (59 per cent). The remaining 3.7 million worked part time involuntarily because that is all they could find. They were most likely to be usually employed at part-time jobs (72 per cent), women (62 per cent), 16–24 years old (53 per cent) and white-collar and service workers (70 per cent).' S. Terry; 'Involuntary part-time work the new information from the CPS', *Monthly Labor Review* (Feb 1981).

9 Between public and private: the birth of the professional housewife and the female consumer

Gabriella Turnaturi

The rapid modernization that accompanied the second phase of industrialization in America at the beginning of this century brought with it profound economic changes. These in turn led to the development of an ideology of home and family as a haven from an external world in which the individual felt increasingly crushed and depersonalized. Home was seen as the place where traditional values were preserved, and as a refuge from the pressures of a threatening public sphere. Many writers[1] interpret this ideology as indicating the beginning of a divide between home and society and between public and private. Since the public and private worlds, according to this view, developed along separate but parallel lines, the role of women has often only been analysed in relation to the private sphere. This has meant that the links between women's public and private identities have been neglected, as well as the ways in which her traditional privacy actually represented an interaction with the public sphere.

In fact, this period was one of enormous flux, in which old concepts were breaking down, and the purpose and function of the home, the family, and of women's role within them, were all redefined against background of the entirely new dialectical relationship that was developing between private and public. Although superficially appearing to drift apart, in fact the public and private worlds of home and society were moving into an increasingly interdependent and structured type of relationship. Apparently contradictory phenomena emerge not only at the same time but as related parts of the same dialectic: the interventionist state and the concept of privacy, for example; the home as both sanctuary and as a cog in the social wheel; the ideology of the housewife and the social function of domestic work.

Thus we see state interventionism expanding beyond the economic sphere into the very structure of society, until it constituted a real intrusion into those areas of everyday life traditionally considered to belong to the private. At the same time, the strengthening of the private was seen as offering a defence against the invasive public domain which ultimately it only helped to consolidate.

Where exactly do women fit into all this? What are their new functions? What is the relationship between the newly emerging ideology of the housewife and the expanding sphere of state activity? And how does the spread of industrialization and its organizational methods – characterized during this phase by Taylorism[2] – affect the everyday running of the home? I shall attempt, however sketchily, to fill in the background to these questions, focusing on the situation in America in the early twentieth century as a specific historical context. My discussion will be limited to a particular group of women since the ideology of the housewife and of domestic efficiency were, initially, a peculiarly middle-class phenomenon. Even if this ideology subsequently spread to women of every social class, it remained fundamentally characteristic of the activities and attitudes of middle-class women.

The new family and the 'new' woman

By the beginning of this century the two most important changes to affect the family – the loss of a productive role and the transition from the extended to the nuclear family group – were already well established, and new factors were beginning to change the structure and function of family life. From the early years of the century the most characteristic features of the new-style American family were the introduction and extremely rapid spread of divorce, the drop in the birthrate, the trend towards later marriages and the widespread use of birth control. Many people believed that these changes heralded the imminent collapse of the institution of the family, a view which became widespread in American society. The ensuing panic mobilized people to save the family in its moment of peril. And it was indeed saved, through the neutralizing and institutionalizing of the very forces that appeared to be undermining it – in other words divorce, new sexual mores, and the radical change in emotional attitudes. In an ever more compartmentalized society, where the family had become the last remaining place for emotions and affections,[3] the only hope of saving and renewing the family seemed to lie in liberalizing the emotional and sexual life operating within it.

This perhaps explains why, after some initial opposition, both divorce and birth control came to be accepted and taken up even by the more conservative elements in society, such as the churches themselves.[4] In 1908 the American Sociological Society devoted its annual conference to the problems of the family, and set its seal of approval on the institution of divorce as necessary both to the freedom of emotional expression within it, and to the continued existence of marriage itself. Every divorce potentially implies that a new family can be created in which emotional and sexual drives can be contained, thus protecting society from the inherent dangers of theories of free love and the new sexual mores. At least these were the conclusions reached by the sociologists, and they were rapidly accepted by Americans generally. The question of divorce thus became part and parcel of the wider question of the state of the American family as a whole, and once moralistic arguments were set aside it simply remained to recognize and legitimize its practice.

Birth control, similarly, was viewed as offering the hope that sexual activity might once again be restored to the province of the family, thus giving it a new vitality and meaning. It was felt that a freer attitude to sex within the family would of necessity result in a stronger and more united quality of family. At the same time the practice of birth control appeared, at the beginning of the century, to offer individual families the opportunity of affirming their right to self-determination in the face of the needs of the state. The birth control lobbyists in fact found themselves in direct conflict at this time with several national campaigns aimed at stimulating the birthrate, particularly under the Roosevelt presidency. The new morality and new ideology of sexual emancipation received approval only because they served to reinforce monogamy and love between family members.

Paradoxically, the rapid advance of industrialization brought with it both romantic ideas about empathy and subjectivism as well as the rediscovery of instinct; as the theories of James on emotionalism and Freud on sexuality were accepted practically without question, it seemed urgent that the private sphere of the emotions should cease to be a matter of individual judgement and become regulated and given a social function. And since women are 'emotional beings' *par excellence*, the responsibility for the proper use of all this emotional baggage naturally fell to them.

But who were the so-called 'new women' described by contemporary writers, and what was their role within the new family? Culturally emancipated because of the greatly improved opportunities for schooling and education that became available for middle-class women around the turn of the century, they frequently found themselves delegated to organize and promote cultural activities which had little status in a predominantly pragmatist society.[5] At the same time the new woman was becoming urbanized, exposed to life in the public sphere as a result of her new role as consumer, ready to be influenced by the new individualistic philosophies and the reformist views of the Progressive movement.[6] The traditional virtues of dedication and self-sacrifice were becoming a thing of the past. She was now restless and dissatisfied to the point that contemporary writers dubbed her the 'uneasy woman', in search of a social role that would allow her to fulfil herself. Sometimes the tension between personal self-affirmation and a wider social role was thrown into extreme relief, as in the case of those emancipated women who were in some way connected with the masculine world of politics:

As it is now, if a minister speaks of self-sacrifice, the men think he is addressing the women; and when he speaks of any strong virtue he calls it manliness and the women know it is meant for the men. I believe you are a socialist. It seems to me that women are not ready for socialism. The wave of individualism that swept over the civilized globe during the last century entered every phase of life and work excepting the lives and work of women. During the present period of transition I believe it is wise to preach individualism to women, and Christianity to men.[7]

Looking beyond this, it is clear that powerful external pressures were fuelling the growing sense of dissatisfaction felt by women and their desire for a more active and committed role. The society they lived in was based, however, nominally, on principles of equality and social justice. The Progressive movement in particular made much of the vital importance of social commitment for the self-realization of the individual and of the real possibility of social change resulting from individual involvement. Middle-class women ended up feeling that they were useless parasites on society. They reacted by searching for their social identity through various kinds of social work (almost always in a voluntary capacity) or through their role in the home. Now that they no longer had any genuinely productive role to fulfil within the family, since by and large food and clothing were being produced outside the home and retailed in the market place, American women fell victim *en masse* to nervous illnesses such as hysteria and depression.[8] Nor were the more liberated among them spared the effects of this epidemic. Indeed, since no accepted role model existed to reinforce her self-image, a woman who was an intellectual felt herself entirely isolated in society. She was forced to work in a social vacuum, cut off from all but female society and the homes of other women. And although a woman who identified herself as an intellectual contributed to the cause of female emancipation, she did not achieve a particularly significant social role. Culture, after all, was not only held to be merely frivolous and amusing, but had already been handed over to women since the mid nineteenth century.

There was something peculiarly threatening and disturbing about women, traditionally the ministering angels of hearth and home, potentially turning rebel in their pursuit of a new identity. It was clearly high time they were given a new role, a new job. And so women found themselves the victims of a campaign of incrimination. Sociologists and the experts attributed the rising divorce rate to the heightened expectations of women, combined with their new egoism and rejection of the traditional feminine virtue of self-sacrifice.[9] Many women were themselves only too ready to agree: the changes they were experiencing often felt purely negative rather than part of a process of emancipation.[10] Moreover, the first decade of the century was a time when various tertiary occupations such as office and shop work became available to women from the lower and lower middle classes, giving them a measure of financial independence and offering them opportunities outside the home. Many were actually prepared to uproot themselves and move into the city, facing the inevitable problems of low wages and poor living conditions in order to experience freedom and self-determination. Coping with the world of work and life in a big city, they soon learned to be competitive: 'To walk through obstacles as if they didn't exist,' as Charlotte Perking Gilman put it, while 'looking the world square in the face and challenging it openly as if you wished everyone to the devil.'[11]

Inevitably all this played its part in reshaping women's

expectations and behaviour patterns, and not just for those who were employed outside the home. The years around the turn of the century saw the emergence of the General Federation of Women's Clubs (1899) and the first professional women's organizations such as the National Women's Trade Union League (1903) and the Women's Homoeopathic Fraternity (1904). The emergence of these new organizations demonstrated a far wider range of concerns than those connected with culture or literature. Women became engaged in a whole range of social affairs, from problems relating to the social services, to questions of legislation and to the central burning issue of votes for women. The sight of women organizing themselves and mobilizing their forces frequently caused astonishment, not to say hostility:

Monday, June 4th, in Milwaukee I attended the Biennial meeting of the General Federation of Women's Clubs. The Plankinton was their headquarters, a hotel frequently used for political conventions. As those fine-looking, well-dressed women from all parts of the Union filled the halls and parlors, and the streets, too, going bareheaded in streams between hotel and theater where they held their sessions, the men of Milwaukee gazed and wondered. They stood packed in the passages leading to the barbershop or the bar, staring and silent. Never had they seen women, *en masse*, going about by themselves, not with, for or to any man, but 'on their own' entirely.[12]

A sense of disquiet, then, and a desire for a more active role, were the chief characteristics of middle-class women during this period. But faced with the actual facts of their lives – their responsibility for the smooth running of the family and for its emotional stability, their recent promotion to the role of super-efficient sexual and emotional companion – what could the 'uneasy women' do other than turn back on themselves and search within their own homes for the answers to their questions and for the role denied them by society? But what sort of role exactly? A tame and domestic role, since it amounted to the containment of potential rebels. A role which would be totally new, without traditions, springing from the needs of a new social and economic order. But while apparently living as had their grandmothers, they would in fact inhabit a world in which everything had changed, and where every aspect of their domestic life required redefinition, not least by women themselves.

For many of them, this act of returning home had more a ring of victory than defeat; it was their authentic response as women to the processes of modernization. Far from being simply a surrender to some diabolical plan to force women back into the home, it was more a strong reaffirmation of the values of home and family, resulting both from a complex process of economic and social change, in which a Taylorist culture of efficiency became firmly established, and from the active participation of women themselves, particularly of the most emancipated of middle-class women. It was these who first claimed the right to play a part in the life of society and to share in its organization, even if only as housewives, simply on the grounds of being women, and proven administrators.

Expansion of the public sphere, birth of the housewife, the female consumer

It is not surprising that the concept of privacy and the ideology of the homemaker began to take shape at one and the same time, for both are essentially a function of the same limited, individualized and private world. It is, however, worth considering exactly why privacy and homemaking are most highly acclaimed just at the moment when the public and social spheres were expanding, together with an increase in the functions and power of the state. The new-style home, endowed with new dignity, should not, however, be viewed as antagonistic to society at large. What was taking place was much more a marriage of skills in which the home assimilated the procedures and organizational skills of structures in society and vice versa. Good household administration and the fulfilment of private life began to be seen as more an example of good management than as a way of separating family from society. The ideal model of the home changed from being that of home as sanctuary to home and family as both useful to society and complementary to it. This model emerged in the threatening context of a society whose development required the destruction of the old order and of old community structures, as the increasingly impersonal and paternalistic state continued its intrusion into every area of life, and as the economy became more planned and centralized, sweeping away all possibility of individual choice and action.

There was an urgent need to provide real protection from the effects of complex social changes that were felt to be too rapid and dramatic. Somehow or other an element of continuity between the old and new had to be introduced to hold society together and to promote active participation in the move towards modernization. A consensus needed to be constructed around the state's new economic policies and new legislation in so many areas – from primary and secondary education, to clothing, food and the social services. This consensus had to be rooted in the norms and organization of the factory which were offered as a basis for the norms and organization of society itself. Consent had to be gained, in short, for an erosion of individual rights and choices. What was needed were forms of joint management and compliance with the new socio-economic order, so that one of the principles of the American constitution, 'the consent of the governed', could be maintained and even extended, at least formally, to women, who up to now had no voice.

Both individuals and families were, in fact, rapidly losing any real power to influence their circumstances: new market forces and the trust company were sweeping away small-scale methods of production and consumption over which previously the individual had had some control, while a new paternalistic, interventionist state was taking over the organization of the family. And of all the rights and duties newly abrogated by the state, intervention in the area of adolescent education offered much the greatest threat to traditional family structures and responsibilities:

Division of labour and the cessation of the household economic unit has brought socialization; society lays claim to the child and refuses to recognize the parent's property right; parental protection of the young becomes less and less necessary and less and less possible as social parenthood gradually absorbs the old domestic jurisdiction.[13]

At the same time, with the development of technology and the social services, of applied psychology and educational theory, we see the emergence of the expert, whose ubiquitous and unfailing counsel and advice further undermined the essential functioning of the family.[14]

With the rise of the 'helping professions' in the first three decades of the twentieth century, society in the guise of a 'nurturing mother' invaded the family, the stronghold of those private rights, and took over many of its functions. The diffusion of the new ideology of social welfare had the effect of a self-fulfilling prophecy. By persuading the housewife, and finally even her husband as well, to rely on outside technology and the advice of outside experts, the apparatus of mass tuition – the successor to the church in a secularized society – undermined the family's capacity to provide for itself and thereby justified the continuing expansion of health, education and welfare services.[15]

There is no doubt that this invasion of the everyday life of the family appeared intensely threatening and disturbing, and before this led to social unrest and political opposition, measures were taken to allow for widespread participation in running society. This was only possible, first, by rebuilding a real sense of the autonomy and privacy of the family; and second, by involving large numbers of people in social management and by giving each person the responsibility of carrying out his or her particular job as well as possible for the benefit of society at large. These are the roots of an ideology of the home organized as a microcosm of society, an ideology which at the same time reinforced the image of society as one large family, run with the same rules and need for common sense as a small one. Only by strengthening the family as an institution, and by revalidating the private domestic sphere of people's lives so that personal privacy appeared vitally important both to the individual and to society, was it possible to create a basis of consent for the intervention of the state and the experts in the planning of people's day-to-day lives. Home and domesticity took on a new dignity and meaning while being effectively harnessed to social goals. Only women could guarantee the success of this operation, and only they could ensure both a close relationship between family and society and between family privacy and autonomy.

For the first time, we see women appearing in their new role as administrators and consumers, a role which derived not only from the real changes affecting the nature of work in the home, but above all from the ideological shift that had accompanied those changes. In fact, when the ideology of the housewife first emerged, it had a dignity and social value that have since been lost. The current scorn for domestic work is a comparatively recent phenomenon, resulting from a quite different phase in the relationship between public and private. The ideology of the housewife and the clear differentiation of roles and tasks within the family did not appear until the middle of the nineteenth century,[16] when the home lost its productive activities and a clear cut division developed between work carried out within the home and work carried out in the public sphere. In the middle of the nineteenth century the belief that home was the proper place for women became widespread, and the non-working wife and mother rapidly became a middle-class status symbol. As this idea took root, women accordingly found themselves forced back into the home to act out a role the very nature of which now marked out, for the first time, a clear division between middle- and working-class women. Right up until the second phase of industrialization women of all social classes were in some way producers of goods – food, clothing and so on – but the disappearance of genuinely productive work from the home and the movement of working-class women into the labour market created a new distinction between productive and non-productive women. There then followed a transitional period when staying at home appeared a mark of privilege, an indication of the essential idleness of middle-class women. It was only at a later stage that shrinking job opportunities and the expulsion of the female labour force forced a change in the ethos of the home to that of a place of great worth and dignity.

At the same time the first laws regulating the employment of women were just coming into force. While this was undoubtedly a significant advance in employment legislation, and provided a much needed response to the need for legal protection for the whole labour force, nevertheless one of the effects of these laws was to reinforce the idea of women as physically weak and unable to participate fully in the world of work. Dramatic descriptions began to appear at this time of the appalling conditions suffered by women factory workers, and of the damage inflicted generally on a woman's personality by any job at all outside the home. The effects of this anti-work campaign were far-reaching: even working-class women began to come under pressure to return home to domestic work. Thus female domestic work once again shed its class-specific character and, as we shall see, came to consist of an increasingly uniform set of tasks. Needless to say, this apparently single-minded surrender to domesticity was later revealed as a great deal more complex and contradictory than had originally appeared:

In the second half of the nineteenth century, the doctrine of feminine domesticity began to permeate downwards to the working classes. For working-class women, this doctrine challenged the economic facts of life: one parent's income could not cover the costs of childrearing, and many women had to work. . . . The idea that work outside the home for married women was a 'misfortune and a disgrace' became acceptable to the working classes only in the last decades of the nineteenth century. In the early years of the twentieth century working-class married women were increasingly likely to follow the middle-class pattern, choosing the role of non-employed housewife even in cases where their employment would have improved the family's standard of living. From the perspective of women's situation, this change to housewifery among working-class women is the most dramatic result of the industrial revolution.[17]

Shutting women back inside their homes was no easy task in the early years of the twentieth century, given the dramatic changes in social mores, attitudes and expectations that characterized the 'new woman'. Women who stayed at home had to be accorded social status, and their work stimulating and productive enough to be acceptable to women of all classes. The new functions of the housewife provided the answer. It gave women a social role that was complementary and presented as equal in importance to that of men. But in order to be fully accepted it was vital that home-making should subsume the full range of women's activities, from the provision of moral and emotional support and the exercise of consumer skills to the overall management and administration of the home.

Strengthening individual privacy, essential to the expansion of the public sphere, demanded an increasing sacrifice of time and energy for the emotional well-being of the family. Childrearing and education began to assume a new space and importance,[18] adolescence lengthened and husbands now required comfort, bodily refreshment and intellectual stimulation. For women this all added up to more work. They were expected to be constantly attractive and available, affectionate and intelligent, a source of spiritual as well as physical nourishment. One of the most distinguished historians writing on the family in the early years of this century speaks of the sharp dividing line between the sexes in both work roles and intellectual attitudes within the family, and of the new tasks confronting the woman:

Woman is the cultivated sex; for her the writer writes; for her the arts are carried on. As the man grows older he concentrates on business or politics while his wife is growing intellectually; the wife reads books while the husband reads newspapers.[19]

Thus women had to bring new energy and devotion to their tasks so that the home could become a place of privacy, peace and security.

The time and energy women have saved because they no longer perform a multitude of household tasks, or because they accomplish them more easily, have been put to use in a variety of ways. Many women found new work within the home. A glance at any woman's magazine testifies to the enormous importance of making today's home a place of beauty, culture, and spotless cleanliness; on keeping husbands contented and happy; and on insuring the sound emotional development of children. Clothing and linens that in 1890 might have been used for a week before laundering may now be used no more than a day. Interior decorating, gardening, preparation of varied and attractive menus, personal beauty care, and chauffeuring, entertaining, supervising, and otherwise catering to children – all take far more time than they used to. The focus of women's tasks at home has shifted. Less occupied with meeting the physical needs of her husband and children, the wife is now expected to help them pursue the elusive goal of happiness. Whether these new duties of women are properly classified as work is a matter of definition. There is no doubt that they consume time and energy and that society imposes at least some of them upon the woman who esteems her status as wife and mother.[20]

The new household duties described by Smuts, very much the same in the early years of the century as today, not only shift the focus of women's tasks but are all more or less connected with consumerism and the market-place. For instance, if she is to provide a continuously varied menu, she must keep up with the latest developments on the culinary scene, and with new products designed to keep a husband replete and satisfied. To look attractive and well groomed, she must follow the latest discoveries in cosmetics. The ideal home constantly requires new objects and furnishings which are, of course, kept clean and polished by the application of ever more powerful detergents and disinfectants. Women thus exchanged their role of producer for that of consumer, a role which requires commitment, responsibility and organizational skills. Women quickly learned to be 'rational' in the business of consumption. Vestal virgins in the temple of consumerism, they were convinced that they were engaged in an activity that was vital not only to their own home and family but to society as a whole. For while being a consumer was a private, even solitary business, it could only take place in the public arena and through the open market. The woman bought to supply her own needs, but in keeping a close watch over the price and quality of her merchandise, she was useful not only to her own family, but to the whole of a society dependent on market forces.

In this way what might appear at first sight as the most solitary and private of all activities was transformed into a 'socially useful' task in early twentieth-century America. Women were elected to safeguard the integrity and correct functioning of the market. Far from being a symbol of idleness, consumption was a deeply serious business if carried out with real commitment and for the good of society. The new large-scale market, offering a vast array of goods which are all produced according to methods and schedules that leave no room for individual choice or control, loses its threatening and alienating character once trustees exist who have been delegated to keep a close watch on its activities. Having been the subjects and the objects of the market, women are now also its guarantors. Their new activity as consumers is ennobled with social worth and dignity, as are women themselves; it helps them achieve a valid society identity – good consumption being socially useful – and to strengthen the structure and organization of the whole consumer system. In this way women are induced to take part in an activity of an essentially personal and individual nature, but which gives the illusion of offering them a real opportunity to participate in the economic and political life of their society.

The trend then is towards the privatization and fragmentation of people's lives, while, at the same time, the public sphere is strengthened by ascribing an apparent social value to these very processes. And the female consumer becomes another sign of the intricate relationship between public and private. Her new role as consumer was heavily backed by the current women's magazines – for instance the *Ladies' Home Journal* – and by the promoters of home efficiency. Ida Tarbell wrote in 1902:

The woman argues that her task has no relation to the State. Her failure to see that relation costs this country heavily. Her concern is with retail prices. If she does her work intelligently, she follows and studies every fluctuation in price and standards. She also knows whether she is receiving the proper quality and quantity; and yet so poorly have women discharged these obligations that dealers for years have been able to manipulate prices practically to please themselves, and as for quality and quantity, we have the scandal of American woollen goods, of food adulteration, of false weights and measures. No one of these things could have come about in this country if woman had taken her business as a consumer with anything like the seriousness with which man takes his as a producer.[21]

As guardians of consumerism, women not only assume a specific social duty, but they become the guarantors of the integrity and right conduct of society itself. As long as women are there, watching over and safeguarding the workers of society, what could there be to fear? Clearly the new atomized, depersonalized society could not be anywhere near as bad as had been feared. After all it was no different from a family, a large family certainly, but one presided over by the vigilance of its womenfolk. And woe to those women who, by failing to take their duties sufficiently seriously, would cause suffering to others and ultimately bring about the ruin and collapse of the American nation. Let them rather take proper thought not only for their own husbands and children, but for the whole of America. All this naturally helped to reinforce the pattern of associations that assigned to women the role of great universal mother figure, and as such she took her place alongside the new father figure of the state, supreme decision-maker and planner, her gentle counsel promising protection from any excesses of paternal authority.

If the Uneasy American Woman were really fulfilling her economic functions today, she would never allow a short pound of butter, a yard of adulterated woollen goods, to come into her home. She would never buy a ready-made garment which did not bear the label of the Consumer's League. She would recognize that she is a guardian of quality, honesty, and humanity in industry.[22]

This idealistic message was enthusiastically appropriated as the rallying cry of feminists and suffragettes who saw a chance of breaking into a man's world through the operation of their new joint role of consumer–manager; they saw women's right to the vote and to full citizenship in the public sphere as strongly reinforced by the special skills and experience they had acquired through their new domestic duties. In other words, this demand for participation was ultimately based on the woman's own quite specific qualities and on the changes that had taken place within the home:

Suffragists acknowledged gladly that the home was indeed woman's sphere, but they insisted that the spheres of men and women were not as separate as they had hitherto been. The historic sphere of women was more and more influenced by political life, as governments passed laws concerning food, water, the production of clothing and education. Thus the statement that the home was woman's sphere was now an argument not against women's suffrage but in favor of it, for government was now 'enlarged housekeeping' and needed the experience of the nation's housekeepers. As the functions which they had previously performed as isolated individuals at home became social functions, women's claim to political equality changed from a demand for the right to protect themselves as individuals to an assertion of their duty to serve society as women. They assumed that their training as cooks, seamstresses, house cleaners and mothers qualified them to help in legislation concerned with food inspection, sweatshop sanitation, street-cleaning and public schools.[23]

In this new society, where the state had assumed the function of a social welfare agency, the 'new women' were becoming, of their own volition, the agents and guardians of social well-being.

The factory and the home: the Taylorization of domestic work and the ideology of home efficiency

In the early years of the twentieth century large-scale industrial workplaces took over as the organizational blueprint for society at large. The widespread expansion of industry not only brought about social changes, resulting from changes in the economic structure, but also imposed new organizational models and new ways of thinking on every area of society. Productivity and efficiency no longer stopped at the factory gates, but now became normative principles shaping the whole of society, influencing the new way of organizing family life and domestic work.

Domestic work, in fact the whole daily routine, was gradually re-evaluated and restructured in terms of investment and production, input and output. Since there could no longer be any doubt that a significant amount of energy was invested in the running of the home, then clearly it should be put to the very best use and waste strenuously avoided. In other words this effort had to be used productively. But what precisely was produced in the home?

The product of domestic work could no longer be defined as a concrete object, using the normal categories of use or exchange value. It no longer had an intrinsic value that could be immediately recognized. It had value only if recognized as such beyond the confines of the home in society as a whole. The difference between the new product accruing from domestic labour and the product of all such labour up until the mid nineteenth century lies precisely in the loss of a sense of its having a value in and of itself.

The values of home-produced bread and clothing, for instance, prior to the second phase of industrialization, certainly did not depend on their being 'socialized' or specifically held up against the market as a whole. The bread that was baked and consumed within the home or exchanged within the same economically self-contained family unit for some other product retained its intrinsic value. But once the domestic product was transformed into emotional support, education of the children and the efficient use of manufactured consumer products, the way value was attributed also had to change. Home and family, or rather the woman who was responsible for them, were considered productive if what they produced could be used and consumed by the rest of society. The new demand for efficiency within the home was aimed precisely at encouraging this sort of productivity, thus making the woman a private producer certainly, but of public goods. The application of the standard of industrial efficiency to the home is bound up with the need to endow domestic labour with a higher dignity and to underline the housewife's social role. Organizational efficiency in the execution of household tasks was never an end in itself; it was legitimized by the resultant increase in productivity. By 1916 early proponents of home efficiency were writing:

Is there any way to judge of the home's efficiency except by its social product?. . . . And yet we need desperately to know just what proportion of money and brains and muscle are necessary to keep the average family group in a state advantageous to the community; and how if the home is under-supplied with any of these three, it can substitute one of the others; money, brains and muscle being interchangeable parts of the home running machine. For the home is properly a machine to make something with, not a self-sufficient, disassociated fact. It is efficient not through its own internal harmony, but its ability to produce something socially valuable.[24]

And so the home-machine turns into a real workplace, a small-scale factory in which the woman is both a worker producing the goods and a manager with overall control. Careful planning and organizing of her time and other resources were needed to make the home run as efficiently and productively as possible. And here the model available to her was the Tayloristic method of organizing factory work. So successful had it proved in bringing about improved productivity in the factory that it was increasingly being adopted as a pattern to be followed in any and every area of society. It was seen as a method that could effectively be applied to any task, so long as the prescribed rules and methods were strictly adhered to. In the second decade of the century, women's magazines such as *Good Housekeeping* and *Ladies' Home Journal* promoted the application of Taylorism in the running of the home. Thousands of American women learned its principles from Christine Frederick, one of the main advocates and an early theorist of home efficiency. Writing in the *Ladies' Home Journal*, she translated Taylorism into domestic terms, propounding a mass of simple rules suitable for use in the home.

The idea of job evaluation, planning, timing, classifying and recording every individual operation involved in any particular task, thus finds its way on to the domestic scene. Cooking, for instance, becomes a process that can be subdivided into its constituent phases: the assembling of utensils, food preparation, cooking, serving and clearing up. In the same way any cleaning operation can be analysed down into a series of processes which are then studied to avoid all possible waste of time or energy. The week is broken down into days each with different tasks and scrupulously planned not only from day to day but from hour to hour.[25] Having thoroughly organized her domestic work, the housewife is then expected in addition to run an efficient and well-ordered social life in which birthdays, anniversaries, and holidays are all programmed into her routine. She also needs a line in intelligent quotations, not to mention witty anecdotes and amusing small talk to use as occasion demands. Her home becomes one big planning operation: planned menus, planned timetables, planned festivities are the order of the day. Her work thus includes an intellectual dimension demanding both reflection and organization.

Once women were promoted to 'white-collar' status,[26] domestic work appeared quite gratifying.

It was by virtue of the element of organization and planning that domestic work was made 'stimulating' and transformed into a highly qualified profession involving both training and commitment. As they felt intellectually engaged and professionalized, women could devote themselves unequivocally to their domestic role, investing in it all their creativity, their ideas and their time. Accordingly the myth arose that home was the only place to fulfil oneself. Since improved working conditions and a good environment give rise to improved productivity at home just as much as in the factory, the housewife setting up home for the first time could show her skill and efficiency right from the start as she set about choosing the house that offered the best possible working environment. In an instant she was architect, ecologist, even sanitary inspector, as she carefully considered the suitability of the house from the point of view of brightness, airiness and the convenience of the layout.

As well as all this the new housewife had to shoulder the responsibility of safeguarding public health. According to scientific theories emerging at this time, many diseases, including TB, were caused by the spread of germs which were frequently present in household dust.[27] It followed from this that the house must be kept spotless, every nook and cranny obsessively scrubbed and polished and the utmost vigilance maintained in order to prevent a single grain of dust breaking through the *cordon sanitaire*.

By the second decade of the twentieth century the values of efficiency and productivity in the home along with the application of the Taylorist system were firmly established as models. Women's magazines by now were full of letters from housewives eager to share their daily routine or to ask for technical advice on how to improve their personal efficiency. The most influential book of the day was by the Gilbreths. He was a technical manager who had collaborated with Taylor, she a domestic science expert. *Cheaper by the Dozen* is an account of their family life – they had in fact twelve children – in which everything was run entirely on industrial principles. The children had to keep a strict account of all they did and the time spent on each activity, while their father gained time by such ploys as buttoning his shirt from top to bottom (three seconds as against seven the other way round) and shaving himself on both cheeks using two razors simultaneously (saving a good two minutes). Their mother in the mean time organized and supervised the whole programme.

Taylorism found its way into the homes and daily lives of families at every level of society, contributing to a similarity and predictability in the nature of domestic work whether the setting was a working-class or a middle-class home. The advent of household appliances such as the vacuum cleaner and the washing machine and the decreasing use of paid domestic labour meant that the job of the housewife became more uniform so that class differences were to some extent obscured. Even in middle-class households attitudes were substantially changing towards the employment of domestic labour, thanks partly to the new ideology of the innate worth and dignity of the housewifely role and partly to the diffusion of 'democratic' ideas labelling the employment of domestics as anti-democratic. In the name of democracy, the housewife ceased to employ domestic labour, and was subsequently able to invest the money thus saved in the purchase of household appliances and the many new consumer products just beginning to appear on the market – all of which, of course, had the merit of being not only efficient but perfectly 'democratic'.

But if women were so ready to apply Tayloristic methods of organization and the principles of efficiency to running their homes, it was certainly also due to their belief that this would result, as promised, in an overall reduction in the time they actually needed to spend on household tasks. Instead, domestic activities began to take up more rather than less time.[28] For one thing it turned out that all the new labour-saving devices needed constant upkeep and maintenance. And then the very business of organizing routines proved to be a labour in itself. Doing more in less time did not lead to increased freedom for the housewife. Rather, she had to fit more jobs and more activities into her role of ever-available, ever-loving wife and mother.

Home efficiency also proved to be severely limited by the absence from the home of one of the basic principles of Taylorism: the division of labour. The new housewife organized, planned, rationalized and supervised the whole domestic schedule, but on top of that she also had to carry out all the jobs herself. Somehow or other she had to combine the functions of labourer, skilled worker and manager: no small matter for one person. The little criticism that there was of organizing domestic work this way was on the grounds of a need for even greater efficiency. The ideology of the rational household was by now established practically without dissent.[29] It was further strengthened by the Women's Home Economics Movement. The roots of this movement in America can be traced back some fifty years to the emergence of theories of rational home administration, which maintained that women needed to study and learn about effective home management. Catherine Beecher and Harriet Beecher Stowe's *American Woman's Home* – soon to become essential reading for all American housewives – goes back to 1869, and in 1893 the Home Economics Movement was founded.

The real influence of this movement was not felt, however, until the first decade of the twentieth century. During this period, on the basis of strong support for both home efficiency and the dignity of domestic labour, it began to press for the introduction of domestic science or home economics into the curriculum of all girls' schools. Its two best known adherents, Ellen Richards and Christine Frederick, launched nationwide campaigns for the recognition of the productivity and dignity of domestic labour, arguing that efficiency and productivity in the home was not a matter for improvisation but was the result of serious study.

With the support of this movement and of women themselves, the new role of the housewife was established once and for all and with it the ideology of a perfectly functional relationship between home and society. The Home Economics Movement and Taylorization of domestic labour thus both contributed to tighten the links being forged in the early years of the century between the public and the private spheres. Organizing the home along industrial lines was just one way of affirming an ideology that presents society as a macrocosm of the family unit, and the home as vital to the smooth running of society. Once the factory becomes an established model, the organization and values of the home must change to adhere to it. And if the home is organized like a factory, women can even conceive of changing, transforming and influencing industrial organization itself:

She must democratize industry as we are striving to democratize government. If the truth were known Politics and Parenthood are pretty close kin. In a word the one answer to many questions is that the middle-class mother must stop soldiering on with her job . . . she must take up her share of the duties of citizenship. . . . Business is woman's affair as much as man's. The home is man's affair as much as woman's. What we need most today is the domestication of business and the socialization of the home.[30]

Women, as white-collar workers in the home management business, take on the task of both 'domesticating' society and socializing the private sphere. Standing at the interface between the public and the private and providing a vital link between the two, women were at last able to gain recognition for the work they did in the home. The price of this recognition, however, was their own acceptance of domesticity, and their relinquishing of any attempt to maintain a critical posture towards the principles of domestic economy, and hence by implication towards their own role as housewives.

Thus it was through the exercise of a role that they themselves had substantially created and justified that women were able to emerge as guarantors of the continuity between the old and the new order, and of the solidity of the private domain. This in turn made it possible for the expansion of the public sphere to continue with minimum conflict. In fact laws and regulations are established that bypass individual choice and decision-making at the same time as the private world is strengthened and endowed with a confident sense of the dignity and value of privacy. People responded to the threats posed by advancing modernization and the changing nature of the state by withdrawing into their own homes and their own private worlds to seek fulfilment for their needs, and confirmation of their individual and social identity. But the outcome of this was not only a reinforcement of the private sphere. This very process made it possible for the expansion of the public domain to be consolidated and legitimized. The reasons why women undertook an active role in this simultaneous consolidation of public and private spheres can perhaps be found, then, in the close relationship between the two. Perhaps the only possible and practical way open to a woman wanting to participate, albeit indirectly, in the public sphere, was to dedicate her energy and enthusiasm to giving a higher meaning and value to the private. And since nothing less than full-time commitment to the private world made her socially acceptable, perhaps she had no other recourse than to throw all her missionary zeal into promoting the public persona of the housewife for society. But, relegated to a private world which, faithfully mirroring the public world whose purposes it served, was neither her creation nor her property, she would end up overwhelmed by the role that should have given her the freedom of both public and private.

Notes and references

1   See, for example, C. Lasch, *Haven in a heartless world; the family besieged* (New York: Basic Books 1978).

2   Taylorism refers to the ideas of Frederick W. Taylor who developed techniques of 'scientific management' which came to be widely introduced in American industry. Aspects included job evaluation and a greater division of labour to increase efficiency.

3   On the internal revolution within the family see E. Shorter, *The making of the modern family* (New York: Basic Books 1977).

4   On the question of divorce in America in the early years of the century see, W. O'Neill, *Divorce in the progressive era* (New Haven: Yale University Press 1967).

5   See A. Douglas, *The feminization of American culture* (New York: Knopf 1977).

6   The Progressive movement was a broadly based reform movement in the US at the beginning of the century. It was concerned with a wide range of issues and ideas from the reform of city and state government to the regulation of food manufacturing. Diverse figures such as the labour leader Eugene Webs and the Republican Woodrow Wilson, later to become president, were associated with it.

7   Extract of a letter from M. Hoffendahl Jenny to C. Perkins Gilman in *The life of Charlotte Perkins Gilman, an autobiography* (New York: Appleton Century 1935), p. xxi.

8   Charlotte Perkins Gilman herself went through a serious nervous breakdown; see pp. 90ff.

9   A. Calhoun, *A social history of the American family* (New York: Barnes & Noble 1960).

10 An example of this process of self-incrimination can be found in L. Commander, 'Are the women to blame?', *North American Review* (1889), pp. 622–42.

11 An expression of Margaret Singer, the leader of the birth control movement in the United States.

12 C. Perkins Gilman, p. 279.

13 A. Calhoun, **III**, p. 158.

14 On the function and role of the expert, see R. Hofstadter, *The age of reform* (New York: Vintage Books 1959).

15 C. Lasch, *Haven in a heartless world*, p. 18.

16 A. Oakley, *Woman's work* (New York: Vintage Books 1976) is extremely useful on history.

17 A. Oakley, *Women's work* p. 50.

18 See E. Shorter, *The making of the modern family*.

19 A. Calhoun, **III**, p. 125.

20 R. Smuts, *Women and work in America* (New York: Schocken Books 1974), p. 28.

21 I. Tarbell, *The business of being a woman* (New York: The Macmillan Company, 1912), p. 64.

22 I. Tarbell, *The business of being a woman*, p. 67.

23 A. Kraditor, *The ideas of the Woman's Suffrage Movement: 1890–1920* (New York: Columbia University Press 1965), p. 67.

24 M. B. and R. W. Bruère, *Increasing home efficiency* (New York: The Macmillan Company 1912), pp. 10–11.

25 H. Hartmann, *Capitalism and women's work in the home, 1900–1930*, Ph.D. Thesis, Yale Univ. (1974), p. 223, reproduces this very significant schedule of the American housewife's daily activities in the early years of this century:

Wake: 6.30.
Breakfast: 7.00.
Dress the children, clear the table, take the dishes into the kitchen, air the beds.
Bath the children: 7.30, the baby sleeps from 9.0 to 10.00.
Wash dishes, prepare menus, cook and prepare for supper, 9.0 to 10.00 (the older child plays in the garden).
Make the beds, sweep and dust from 10.00 to 11.00.
Prepare lunch, sew for half an hour while playing with the children, 11.00 to 12.00.
Lunch with the children: 12.00. Leave the dishes.
Dress oneself, dress the children, rest for half an hour with the children, go to the shops or make a phone call.
Back home by 5.00: give the children their supper, prepare the dinner, bath the children and put them to bed.
Dinner with husband: 6.30.
Wash the dishes and prepare breakfast for the next day.
Finish at 7.30.

26 This expression is used by B. Ehrenreich and D. English in *For her own good* (New York: Anchor Press 1978.)

27 See Ehrenreich and English for detailed discussion on the germ theory and its effect on work in the home.

28 See H. Hartmann for calculation of the time taken up on the new type of domestic work.

29 The only serious critique of domestic work and the role of the

housewife was that of Charlotte Perkins Gilman, who clearly identifies the links existing between woman's economic dependence and her enforced role as housewife. See C. Perkins Gilman, *Women and economics* (New York: Harper and Row 1966, first edn. 1898).

30   Bruère *Increasing home efficiency*, p. 291.

10   Inside and outside the home: how our lives have changed through domestic automation

Hélène Strohl

When I set out to talk about domestic automation, I already knew what I would end up saying. It wouldn't be very original but it would reflect everyday common sense. After all, what else is there to say except that we love our own homes but we still want to get out of them, that these machines are unbearable but indispensible, that like it or not, do-it-yourself is a must? Furthermore, it is a matter of seeing if the major evolution of the relationship between life inside and outside the home – which today, for women, is lived essentially as a contradiction between motherhood and paid work – was linked to domestic automation or not.

To illustrate this jump into the past and present of domestic life, it seemed useful both to look at the introduction of electrical appliances in the 1950s and to interview a small sample of women from Alsace, where I grew up, and where there is a special tradition of being 'house-proud'. Here I discovered a whole atmosphere which has disappeared in our daily gestures and experience.

Chronicle of domestic activity: the housewife

Current discussions about the invasion of our homes and our kitchens by the paraphernalia of modern automation tend to focus either on nostalgia for what we have lost, or to eulogize about the technology we have gained.

At the beginning of the 1950s the first major influx of domestic machinery hit rural France, with its dank airless houses, unhealthy tenements and filthy farms. The function of the new appliances here was quite obvious. Acquiring a washing machine had a practical value that was directly proportionate to the relief gained from the backbreaking task of washing by hand in the sink. The purchase of a fridge brought other changes, as sooner or later all sorts of familiar skills and rituals disappeared – trips down to the cellar became unnecessary, the store-room needed to be completely reorganized and the whole apparatus for preserving food by larding, salting or smoking could be abandoned. The vacuum cleaner too was so quick, powerful and easy to use that its appearance was heralded as something of a marvel. People realized that things were changing, and that boring repetitive jobs, performed more rapidly and effectively by the new machines, would disappear.

Those of us who were born in the 1950s grew up in a world already bristling with electrical appliances, daily witnessing such simple realities as floors polished by Electrolux, carpets vacuumed by Hoover, dirty washing wedded ineluctably to the washing machine, milk and meat to the fridge. For us, any discussion of domestic appliances takes place without any memories of a pre-machine age. These machines have now earned an absolute and legitimate right to exist. They no longer have anything to prove. The question of whether or not to own them is no longer posed, or, if it is, it's either by the poor, in the fourth world of HLM estates,[1] where people are still a bit dazed by the whole business of family allowances, social policies, modern technology and the right to paid holidays; or by a certain critical fringe who allow themselves the luxury of taking a stand against machines, and criticize food processors, vacuum cleaners, dishwashers and washing machines, as they rediscover a means of reappropriating their own bodies and their own time and space by aping the old rituals – washing with cinders, for example, baking bread at home in the Aga, or cooking on the good old-fashioned stove used by our grandmothers.

Nor is this the only way in which our grandmothers are coming back into their own. In the early days Mère Denis[2] had to prove to our mothers' generation that washing machines were as effective as sweat and tears when it came to getting the clothes clean. The dream now offered to the women commuting home by tube, by an up-to-date Mère Denis, is all about vast fields flooded with sunlight. The whole thing has become rather a sick joke, since everyone in France knows by now that one detergent is exactly like any other, and anyway, who cares about a white that's whiter than white. Still, rather than testing, criticizing and generally giving these machines a hard time, wouldn't it be better, while we're considering the place they occupy in women's lives and homes, to look at the practical role they actually perform?

It's no longer possible to describe them, as Paul Breton did in 1950, as mere palliatives to certain forms of work. Today we have to consider them a basic constituent of our homes and lives, quite apart from their function. Of course they do have a function, but initially they are just there, so we use them. But it is the way in which we use them that provides the key to understanding the all-pervasive reality of our present machine world. Perhaps by decoding the everyday language of our repetitive, almost automatic actions, we can begin to break through the barriers of familiarity and arrive at an understanding of the real nature of their legitimacy. By describing the world of machines we can draw a line round the space they fill and, while feeling their rhythms, we can step back sufficiently to locate their exact place in a world that we can no longer view with detachment.

It's only when we have really faced up to and accepted the reality of domestic appliances in and of themselves that we can begin to make comparisons with a time before they existed. Of course this past has no reality of its own. It only exists from the point of view of the present machine age. It's a then-seen-from-now, a nostalgic exemplary past rather than a past consisting of any historic or logical reality. What interests us here is not so much how feminine or familial worlds developed from pre-automated days until now, but rather how today's women imagine the pre-automated past. The nature of this perception – however naive, however imbued with either enthusiasm or scorn for the old ways – can tell us a great deal about the present phase of our domestic life and, possibly, about how things may develop in the future. After all, the object of our nostalgia represents not so much a search for the past as a way of appropriating the present.

Having considered its specific grammar and its underlying mythology, a third way of understanding the machine-based domestic world would be in terms of its effect on the way the normal functions of the home are carried out. To do this we need to look at what one does in a home that has been taken over by batteries of machines, and what staying at home actually means when part of the activities normally performed there have been automated. We must ask, too, about the relationship between specifically domestic tasks and the other types of activity carried out in the home (those broadly concerned with education, recreation and leisure) and what sort of space/time allocation these rate in a world whose parameters are determined by domestic appliances and domestic science.

This line of questioning leads us directly to the relationship that exists between the automated home and the outside world of production and paid work – the whole problem of public versus private as it arises in a society that has grown up in the age of household machinery.

Four lines of enquiry are necessary, then, to describe the incursion of the machine into our homes. First, its everyday language and reality – its 'grammar'; second, its creation of a mythical past; third, the way in which the whole complex of functions associated with the home has been redistributed; and finally, the new relationship between public and private, between the world inside and outside the home.

The grammar of our machines: standardization and catastrophe

Everyone knows that there is no longer any difference between the various household machines currently available. Refrigerator motors are all made by the same company and only vary slightly in internal layout, capacity and type of plating. Where washing machines are concerned there are really only two possible choices: the straightforward, reasonably priced machine such as a Brandt, Hoover or Zanussi, with a built-in life expectancy of about five years; or the solid, sophisticated American or German models that will either fail extremely quickly as a result of their over-sophistication, or will last for ever. But having said this, you don't just pop down to the corner shop and buy a washing machine in five minutes. It's a purchase that takes a lot of thought and is often undertaken by husband and wife together, generally on credit. And it represents an investment, even if it costs no more than overhauling one's wardrobe, and probably costs less than a skiing holiday.

Most of us manage to get together a complete set of household equipment as soon as we set up home. Buying the cooker, the fridge and the washing machine often takes precedence over the acquisition of furniture since nowadays domestic appliances constitute the essential infrastructure of the home. In more or less standardized apartments one can now expect the basic furnishings and fittings to be similarly standardized.

But in spite of the fact that my kitchen is the twin of the one next door, within it my machines acquire an extraordinary degree of individuality. And perhaps it's significant that while basically all these machines are exactly the same as far as their technology goes, they do differ a certain amount both in their general appearance and in the quantity of knobs with which they are graced. If you suddenly find yourself in a totally strange kitchen, you feel at a bit of a loss. How do you light the cooker, for example. Does it have automatic ignition? Is there an electric gas-lighter, a box of matches . . . ? Somehow in other people's homes this very simple procedure is never quite clear.

We can take this further. After a few months in my care, a machine will assimilate the particular rhythms of my home. For instance, I had a very basic and fairly old washing machine. I was perfectly accustomed to its repertoire of noises and they didn't really bother me at all. Breakdowns acted as a simple reminder of my responsibility for its functioning. For instance, a marble left in someone's school blouse might block the pump, or the excessive use of high-lather detergent occasionally caused a flood, or the machine might suddenly come to life and make a quick sortie across the kitchen floor on its castors. But it only needed uncaring hands to be laid upon it – by a certain scornful American woman in brief occupancy of my house – for the breakdown, that up to now had been a sign of life, to turn into a catastrophe, marking its final demise. Once betrayed into alien hands it fell silent for ever. Even though no repairman has been able to identify the exact fault, it has never worked since.

Pierre Sansot once published a short piece in praise of the sounds of washing up by hand. For him the process was pregnant with a thousand little incidents and familiar habits. And of course this was followed by a diatribe against the dishwasher, seen as the force behind the destruction of this whole domestic language.[3] But does he realize, I wonder, that in fact no two dishwashers make the same sound, and that the particular sound of each one reflects the state of mind and the peculiarities of whoever filled it in the first place? Those whose masters are lazy or careless can be identified by the clinking of glass. The predominant sound in others is grating and clanking – a sure sign that they have been overfilled, due either to a desire to economize or to a general lack of organization in the household. Some come on in the afternoon, indicating a home where the daily routine is centred on the midday meal – in other words, where the mother doesn't go out to work. Others come on at night because their mistresses can only go to bed in a well-ordered house. And then again there are those that announce, each morning, that everyone is up and the day's business has begun.

In some homes the vacuum cleaner can be heard every morning at precisely the same time – a sure sign of a clean, respectable household – whereas elsewhere the vacuuming is done in long recurrent bursts on Saturday or even Sunday morning. And then, lastly, there are all those machines that work in an empty house, the only indication of life in a home that functions simply as a dormitory. One thing is certain: my machine, bought at the BHV,[4] a Nogamatic carrying a five-year guarantee, is not the same as my neighbour's. Domestic appliances behave differently in each home, and these variations communicate something specific about the intimate life of each household. I have no sympathy at all with the facile insistence that fitting our homes with machines has had a levelling effect on our life-styles. The machine remains in the affective sphere of our lives, representing our individual fantasies.

That's why in one sense breakdowns can't really be seen as technical hitches, descending on us shockingly out of the blue. They are much more an inevitable routine whereby we assert our individual authority over the machine. In the first place, the breakdown is often caused by an 'improper' use of the appliance: overloading, interfering with the programme selector, overriding the mechanism, breaking into the programme. And we don't experience the breakdown simply as an additional burden. Somehow it's entirely different from all the usual daily problems, the form-filling and decision-making. The breakdown is an event, and is experienced as such. At first, there are attempts at do-it-yourself solutions, to make the machine usable despite the fault. You try to dam the flood with strategically placed dishcloths (my neighbour has never done her washing without needing to mop up the little flood that invariably appears as part of her laundry rites), you bail out the machine or you operate the programme control by hand. But given time the breakdown can assume catastrophic proportions. Your neighbour's ceiling collapses, you succeed in blowing the whole electrical circuit, or you end up with a mixer on your hands that first glows red hot and then relapses into total blackness. In short you are witnessing the machine's final desperate cry for help.

At this point the real connoisseurs make their appearance. You have to beg them to turn out, then you have to lose a day's work to be there when they come, and of course at the last minute they postpone their visit until the next day. When they finally make it, the whole place is messed about. Having thrust the table and chairs aside, they shift the cooker and finally the offending beast can be hauled out and turned round. No one really knows what happens next, but invariably they are shortly to be seen triumphantly extricating something in the way of a bolt or rusty pump. They test run the machine, everything seems to be working, and they leave you with some discouragingly doom-laden prophecy, for naturally a visit of this kind heralds not so much the restoration of one's old familiar if admittedly cranky friend as the arrival of an entirely new member of the family. Sometimes their bounty extends to the gift of a catalogue, thus giving you plenty of time to dream about other possibilities. No matter what, their visit irretrievably alters the attitudes and loyalties that previously existed. No machine is ever repaired twice, and putting a new part in an old machine can only precipitate its final demise.

Bypassing automation

When we talk about the world of electrical appliances we mean something highly specific and individualized. We've seen this in what we might call the life and death of the machine. But a machine, my machine, not only works, but is used in a specific way. A machine is designed in the first place to save time and effort, to simplify the carrying out of a task and to enable a number of operations to be performed on my behalf. Consequently the only washing machines now being produced are automatics. To operate these all that is necessary is to load them, press a button and/or adjust the programme selector, add detergent, wait for the end of the cycle, empty the machine and hang out the washing.

Nevertheless, there are so many ways to disrupt this simple regime! I know some people who turn off the cold water intake,

collect the water from the pre-wash programme and use it all over
again for the main wash. Some real fanatics like to add an extra
rinse, even though it means maltreating the programme control.
You can cut out the pre-wash if you're washing wool, or interrupt
the cycle to allow the washing to soak for a while. You can stop
the machine before the final spin to take certain things out, or
alternatively you can repeat the final spin. No, however sophisticated they may be, these machines can't really do the washing
properly on their own. We have to compensate for their vagueness
and imprecision.[5] In fact many women strongly regret the disappearance of so-called semi-automatics. Indeed, the latest and most
sophisticated models (such as the new electronic Miele) no longer
offer the choice of different programmes, but provide a control
panel that can be used in different combinations to create a multitude of programmes entirely at will. If the conventional machine
can be likened to a television, its successor is more like a piano.
Perhaps now we can look forward to a new style washing machine
which, like Boris Vian's piano,[6] will mix us an aperitif while
simultaneously soothing us with amazing flights of fancy on the
keyboard. Alongside the normal outlet, a second hose will emit
a personalized and vaguely intoxicating liquid, while the built-in
television screen will allow us to assess the quality of our detergent
according to the colour of the dirty water leaving the machine.
The trouble is that even playing around with controls, albeit electronic ones, will never be quite so attractive as listening to the
grinding of a maltreated programme selector. Someone still needs
to invent a machine designed to cope with systematic abuse.

Oh for the happy days before we were swallowed up by these machines: or the myth of the good old days of domestic bliss

At the beginning of this discussion we put forward the hypothesis
that the existence of machines in the home was the proof positive,
the unavoidable everyday reality, of our modern domestic world.
True, the statistics tell us that there are still some French households that are not fully equipped – the market in dishwashers,
notably, gives scope for further expansion. Be that as it may,
there is no doubt that as far as the purchase of household
appliances goes, we're now at the stage where people are mainly

replacing worn out machines. Naturally the manufacturers continue tirelessly to introduce new products, altering the look of their machines, modifying the design or adding some new gadget or other. But in terms of the major items of equipment creative imagination seems to have dried up.

On the cooking front, perhaps, there have been a few new developments such as thermostatically controlled hotplates and microwave ovens. But look back at a 1950s catalogue and it's all there. I would go so far as to say that there has actually been a move in the opposite direction, away from technical progress in favour of functional streamlining. Compared to the ideal 1950s cooker – which consisted of two ovens, a drying compartment and hotplates of different temperatures, and which operated on two or even three different energy sources – the present-day cooker is desperately simple, doing nothing more than provide heat. The more sophisticated pieces of equipment – for instance the food-processor with beater, mixer and mincer – haven't changed. They just come in a cheap version now, which is not very efficient and wears out rapidly. Like all small electrical gadgets they have crossed the dividing line which separates essential domestic equipment from what are really toys. An electric tin-opener is certainly more exciting than a model racing circuit, an electric carving knife promises more thrills than a game of darts, and it's well known that switching on the oven light and watching the electric rotisserie turning is every bit as good as Guy Lux[7] on television, not to mention enjoying the cooking smells or the noise of the extractor fan as a bonus.

We are no longer talking about technical innovation or the disruptive incursion of the machine into our settled domestic world. By now, this world is comprised of the machines themselves, the fact of automation fully absorbed and digested. That's why, now that the first craze for machines has died down, the popular imagination is constructing a whole new mythology of the pre-machine era. And precisely because this response is very much a phenomenon of our times, we need to look closely at the current nostalgia for the days when everything in the home was done by hand.

What follows is not intended as an apologia for the past. It is simply an attempt to relate what people are saying to describe the loss experienced as a result of the incursion of machines. Let me be perfectly clear: we obviously have no real rational, logical or historical belief in the reality of this supposedly lost world. A return to it is neither desired nor possible. The yearning that we feel for a lost idyllic past simply enables us to come to terms with the machines that are today's reality.

When repetition had nothing to do with production

When I think back over the domestic world of my childhood I know perfectly well, as I've said before, that it was already populated by machines. Although my grandmother's cottage contained very few of these things, my mother had a gas cooker, a fridge, a washing machine, a vacuum cleaner and an electric floor polisher. Like all her generation, however, my mother used her machines in a rather topsy-turvy way. She had been brought up and disciplined in a non-automated world, and I think the rhythm and routines of our home had much more in common with those days than with the present. The early chaotic stages of automation were not yet governed by the inherent logic of the machine; this was allowed to play a part, but certainly not to impose itself rigidly. At the start the early machines were allocated space within the home according to entirely different criteria. The first washing machines were often installed in the wash-house, linen-room or cellar. The fridge, similarly, might be put in the cellar or store-cupboard. All the small gadgets such as food processors, mixers, electric carving knives, were kept in their boxes, tidied away in a cupboard. This, of course, meant that it took so long for them to be set up and operated that in the long run the old mincer or Mouli was much more handy and efficient. A period then followed when the machines seemed to be incorporated willy-nilly into existing domestic routines. In Alsace Monday remained washday, and that was when you laundered: adults' sheets every two weeks, children's every three weeks, two sets of children's underwear (these were changed on Thursday and Sunday), cleaning rags and towels (changed on Mondays). On Monday my mother would disappear into her laundry, and from then on the washing machine would be running all day. On Wednesday sheets, table-cloths, towels and cleaning rags were put through the mangle, folded and ironed. Thursday was mending day.

The routine for the rest of the housework was just as rigid. Tuesday was the day for serious cleaning of the dining room and living room, while on Friday they were given a quick dust round. On Wednesday the kitchen and bathroom were done out; on Thursday the children's rooms; on Friday my parents' bedroom and my father's study. On Saturday, attention shifted towards the outside of the house. The tiles in the front porch would be washed along with the stairs, and finally the pavement swept down. In addition, a daily rhythm supplied its own counterpoint: every morning the bedding was aired at the windows, beds were made, dishes washed and the kitchen floor given a quick mop down.

It didn't actually matter whether the room you were about to clean was dirty, whether the carpet you were beating was dusty, the sheets stained or the white tablecloth hardly used. Nor did it matter whether the curtains ended the month white or grey, or what state the windows were in. The appointed moment had come for cleaning to take place and nothing would prevent it. My childhood recollections contain only one real memory of cleaning having tangible results, when, twice a year, the smell, first of black soap and then of polish, swept through the house as the spring and autumn *gross putz* took place. These were times when everything was turned upside down and dust was seen to rise from places normally hidden from view. Drawers would be emptied, books dusted and shaken one by one, silver cutlery polished till it shone and all the best cutlery given an extra wash. But apart from this I don't believe I ever saw a dusty carpet being cleaned, an untidy room being restored to order, or a layer of dust disappearing. Housework had no specific purpose. It wasn't designed to produce a new state of affairs but rather to maintain things as they always were.

Nowadays quite the opposite is true: household tasks are only performed for a very sound reason. You suddenly notice the living room is extremely dirty so you get out the vacuum cleaner; or your feet stick to the kitchen floor so you reach for the mop. As you make your bed one day you decide the sheets need changing, and when the laundry basket is full you run the washing machine. I no longer wash because it's Monday but because I have five kilos of dirty washing ready for the machine. And instead of simply contributing a good deal of unnecessary noise, my vacuum cleaner now does a serious job of swallowing the dust. The washing machine only runs when its services are really needed, and the dishwasher is used not to mark the end of a meal but to replenish the supply of clean crockery.

It seems to me that the old days were a time before machines, and a time of adapting to machines, when the motivation for carrying out domestic tasks didn't come from practical necessity, but rather from ingrained habits that were still unquestioningly accepted. In popular mythology the old days were a time when the home was a haven of well-ordered tranquillity. Homes then were physically peopled and made functional by the unquestioning enactment of various time-honoured procedures, all of which were about life, not about productivity. Then the machine made its appearance and little by little took possession of this well-regulated world. It systematically took over by breaking down the life of the household into specific tasks, analysing the function of each and the operations involved in carrying each out, and assigning to each a desired aim or goal.

The home, then, has ceased to be the place where you live and spend time. It is becoming instead a set of clearly differentiated spaces, each of which have domestic problems which need to be solved. Life at home has been reduced to a series of tasks, which is precisely why the machine plays such a key role. While there was perhaps something demeaning about a vacuum cleaner going up and down over clean carpet, its inherent function is to mark out the difference between areas which are clean and those which are dirty. One could take this further and imagine a vacuum cleaner being designed with a transparent dust bag, so that we could actually watch the gradual accumulation of different varieties of dust, fluff, cigarette ash, breadcrumbs, splinters of glass, trampled toys and frayed threads. But what would be the point: everything our modern vacuum cleaner swallows so noisiiy is perfectly visible before it disappears before our amazed eyes. You can tell at a glance now when the housework has been done, whereas before you only saw when it hadn't. Today's home, with its functional kitchen, is structured by a growing arsenal of electrical appliances instead of by domestic life, and it's only possible to live there if everything is in working order.

What makes the past appear so idyllic?

The development of the housewife's role as we have attempted to describe it here certainly doesn't appear all that startling. One mode of repetition has been lost, only to be replaced by another.

So why do we constantly hear people talking about 'hand-made' and 'traditional' methods, as if they were harking back to a lost paradise? Those who are old enough to remember what it was really like will tell you that nostalgia is only for those who've never really got their hands dirty, or chilled to the bone in laundry water, or wrinkled and discoloured from peeling vegetables, and whose knees aren't calloused like theirs from scrubbing and polishing floors. And doubtless they are right.

Surely part of the nostalgia is to do with considerations that are more psychological than practical – the sense of fulfilment derived from doing something by hand, the sheer pleasure of physical sensation – but then beyond this I suspect another quite different need is being expressed. My own nostalgia, at least, is for the numbness of repetition, for the particular calm that results from a task carried out for its own sake, independently of my will or choice, for the stultifying and yet pleasurable rhythm generated by the passage of endlessly predictable days. I long for the unhurried happiness of a life whose rhythms are dictated by constraints outside my control. For instance I should much prefer it if I wasn't forced to vacuum because things were actually dirty, if the washing machine wasn't lying in wait for each new pile of dirty clothes, if I could simply cook all the time rather than for any particular occasion. Really what I should like would be for my home to exist independently of my will, independently even of the wishes of its occupants.

Machines have definitely not imposed uniformity on our lives or eliminated individual differences. Quite the opposite: the advent of machines has given every one of our actions meaning and purpose. It has been responsible for the creation of individual family units. Time and space are no longer structured by collective unconscious attitudes but have been replaced, thanks to machines, with conscious intimacy. Time is now broken up into separate identifiable periods. There is a time for everything, a time for work and for leisure, and for different activities, some exalted and some not. Before all this maybe you just existed, quite apart from any specific need or desire, and just got on with life, quietly accepting both its constraints and its satisfactions.

At this point perhaps I might speak a word directly to all you Noble Lords and Patrons of Domestic Science. You, my lords, have freely intoned the anthem of women's liberation. You have set us free from our most burdensome obligations and enabled our minds to be engaged in higher thoughts. You've ranked all our household duties and have ordained that washing clothes is sweated labour. Thank goodness that in fact Brandt and Ariel are there to do it for me, so that I can find fulfilment stitching away at some nice little piece of embroidery or – better still – use my freedom to go out and claim my true place in society as a fully-fledged and productive adult. However, I would have liked very much to stay here, in my own home, with its creaks and squeaks, flinging open the windows at precisely the same time each morning to air the bedding, setting off for the baker's every Monday to collect the Backeoffe[8] and meet all my neighbours, whose hands, like mine, would be rather the worse for scrubbing clothes. Perhaps this sort of life appeals to me just because, to quote my grandmothers, it was hard going, day in day out!

In 1920 an American woman declared that housework should be considered unconstitutional on the same grounds as slavery. At the same time, of course, she sang the praises of the advent of electrical appliances, domestic science and the rationalization of housework. Since then these ideas have gained general acceptance. Not that household tasks have been eliminated, but at least now everyone knows they're degrading. Machines have undoubtedly released us from a certain amount of hard work, but at the cost of making the tasks that still remain appear a real burden. Objectively speaking, it probably wasn't any more congenial having to do the housework every day, but, as my mother used to say, you simply didn't think in those terms. Maybe it's a longing for these very constraints which lies behind the hymns to the past and the condemnation of modern technology.

But that sort of past doesn't exist and has never existed

Yes, I know. I wouldn't even want it back nor, apart from a few ecology freaks, would anyone want to see the disappearance of all our extremely convenient – not to say dearly loved – machines.

Perhaps the main reason for this modest exercise in nostalgia is to point to a deep need for a new form of ritual that will enable us to make sense of our domestic lives. I use the word ritual in the sense of meaningless actions, the sort of actions produced by behavioural conventions, actions that are traditional in the sense that their origin and logic have been forgotten.

If the domestic robot, the home run entirely by computer

programme, the self-filling fridge, automatic cookpot or automatic dust extraction system holds such fascination, it may actually represent a first step, however tentative, back towards a home that generates a life of its own, independent of the efforts and intentions of its occupants. Perhaps all this is no more than popular fantasy, but then again perhaps it indicates a desire for a more passive, less individualistic life.

The advocates of domestic science had the very best intentions

The reading of the mythical past suggested here may possibly appear rather too idealistic and out of touch with historical reality. It seems about time then, if these assertions are to have an objective foundation at all, to hear what the gentlemen behind the scenes have to say for themselves.

Modern domestic science first appeared in nineteenth-century America as a direct result of the reaction to women's oppression. It was Catherine Esther Becker (1800–78) who both 'confirmed the American woman in the elevated nature of her task as mistress of the house, and made her understand that she had everything to gain from her housewifely profession'. She declared that domestic service was incompatible with the tenets of democracy,[9] offering in its place the systematic organization of the home.

The first household appliances were invented during the same period. 1869 was the year when the first patent was issued in Cincinnati for a conveyor belt system of dismembering and preparing pig carcasses. In the same year the first Pullman buffet-car was patented. The first 'standard' gas cooker was invented in 1851, the first dishwasher in 1865 (by James Francis) and the first electric cooker in 1893. Technical progress and an ideology condemning domestic labour had prepared the way for home automation, but another step was needed: the application of techniques of industrial organization to the problems of productivity in the home.

Writing for *Ladies Home Journal* in 1912, Christine Frederick had this to say about modern household organization in an article subtitled 'Taylorism in the Home'.[10]

As far as industrial machinery is concerned, the phase of simple invention was over by the turn of the century – machines tended subsequently towards specialization and differentiation by a natural process – attention being focused much more on the effective reorganization of available production methods. By 1910 exactly the same situation applied domestically. The modern industrialized kitchen would not exist if American housewives had not avidly followed the work of Frederick Taylor and Frank B. Gilbretti.

She continues:

Does this mean that the highly rationalized modern kitchen sprung into being at this time as a fully-fledged reality? In fact no, for even if housewives were familiar with the flow-line principle – the corner-stone of Taylorism – and ideas such as work planning, increased mechanization and achieving greater efficiency by the application of work study and method study techniques, nevertheless in attempting to organize their own domestic appliances into a workable flowline they rapidly came up against the practical problem of the enormously disparate shapes and sizes of the machines [at this time every designer had an entirely free hand] which wrecked every attempt at coordination. The problem of creating a functional kitchen would only be resolved in 1925 in Europe, when an essentially unified approach finally superseded the notion of the kitchen as a room to be furnished piecemeal.

Now that the home has become a sort of miniature factory, does it mean that women are reduced to mere shop floor workers? Not at all. While domestic work has undoubtedly been downgraded to the level of rationalized production and organized according to criteria of efficiency and productivity, this was to liberate men and women to fulfil their true purpose as civilized and cultured human beings, to savour the joys of the spirit and of relaxation.

In 1950, writing of the new spirit and ideology informing the practice of housewifely skills, Paul Breton had this to say:

The science of modern homemaking, arising out of the basic needs and unchanging desires on the part of men and women for greater well-being, strengthened by advances in science and technology, concerned to allow beauty its rightful place and to raise people's spirits, constitutes a mode of thought, almost a state of mind. It may not actually inspire a religion, but it certainly imposes a doctrine. . . .

In quoting these few fairly striking passages from some of the advocates of home automation, we are not trying to show that

the Machiavellian intent of the few imposed a particular way of
life on a whole generation. The point is the extent to which even
these discussions helped to create a mythology of the past – not
at all the past we remember and have described earlier on, but
one that seems based almost on images of primeval chaos. And
now this very chaos and formlessness is to be found lurking in the
shadows of our ultra-rationalized lives. When a whole section of
society is busy dreaming of equipping their kitchens with all sorts
of bits and pieces, reconditioning worn out machines, indulging
in unproductive rituals and generally wasting time, surely they're
not actually dreaming of the reality our grandmothers knew, but
of the vision of hell evoked by the advocates of modern domestic
science in the service of The Cause.

Motherhood is all very well, but what comes before, and after . . .

Time in the home has become chopped up, neatly sliced. One
slice is essential housework, one belongs to the children, one is
for leisure and one, frequently, for work. It's not so much that
women work harder than they did in the past, but that their lives
now have to accommodate a greater number of different roles.

If it's true that the real heart of the home is now to be found
in the people living there rather than the house itself, and if our
way of living there is now a matter of choice rather than tradition,
then isn't this another way of 'slicing up' our lives? These machines
are mine, and no one else's. I need no special skills to operate
them and in any case they are bound to be superceded. So what
is there left to hand on? What do our homes stand for now that
we've moved out?

In 1926 the Larousse Ménager, an illustrated dictionary of
household skills, opened with these words:

For centuries the practical understanding of household tasks was passed
on from one generation to the next almost unchanged: mothers handed
on to their daughters what they themselves knew. But in recent years
there have been such major technical developments in the home that the
time-hallowed tradition of the past has become inadequate, and daughters
now have to be taught what their mothers never knew.[11]

So what actually remains to be done at home? There's the

children's education, of course, but for the most part schools have taken over this responsibility. Then there's their initiation into the practicalities of life, but what sort of life will it be, having so little in common with our own? We may still stay at home, but we're sure to be bored and ultimately feel devalued if we do.

Can the relationship between people living under the same roof, between a mother and her children, be close without becoming conflicting and downright intolerable? Surely what we now need is to repair the damaged circuit, to re-establish links outwards (through clubs, extra-mural school programmes, cultural activities and sports) in order to re-create the process of mediation that the everyday wisdom of domestic life and skills used to ensure. Looked at in this way, domestic automation and home appliances have been more the cause than the consequence of women's new activities. What's left to be done in a home emptied by machines?

When I ask my 7-year-old daughter what I should do if I no longer worked, her answer is simple: 'You'd look after us.' But no doubt she doesn't realize that being at home used to consist of a great deal more than just looking after the children.

Can one ever have the best of both worlds?

We're told nowadays that it's a good thing for mothers who are housewives and who have some free time thanks to labour-saving devices, to take an active part in the life of their community. In fact, women already comprise 20 per cent of town councillors, and many run societies, sit on parents' committees, do voluntary work, attend all sorts of classes or become mature students at university. They can break out of their isolation and breach the walls of a home that has become a prison. Yet home hasn't always been seen as a place dispensing comfort and tranquillity, although, as we saw earlier, this was one of the fundamental aims of the founders of domestic science.

A quick look at domestic tasks will show us how women have been shut away since the beginning of the century, and why they now need to be released. If we take the key example of the preparation of meals, the phenomenon of tinned foods immediately comes to mind. Whereas, at the beginning of the century, the whole process of preparing daily meals for the household occupied much time and space, the modern housewife shuts herself up in the kitchen to prepare a meal. At one time she might have expected to go out into the garden to select whatever she wanted in the way of ripe vegetables, go down to the cellar or store-cupboard, dip into stoneware jars, visit the market, find time to gossip, prepare next day's soup and a mid-morning snack, and pause to chat with a neighbour bringing a gift of eggs, giving her in return a slice of tart for her elderly father. The smell of cooking permeated the walls of the kitchen and found its way out into the street. Round at the butcher's, where I often went with my mother, we could find out what Madame Walter or Madame Fritsch were going to eat, and I also discovered early on that one very hard-up, working-class family fed itself on *charcuterie*, that a farm labourer's family had a passion for braised beef, and that sauerkraut, only eaten in our household on high days and holidays, was an everyday dish for other families.

Going down the village street on my way to school each morning, I would always see Madame Blottier leaning on her bike, deep in conversation with Madame Schwach who would be shaking her quilt out of the window. I knew her next stopping place would be under the porch of the tower where she met Madame Bernard every day. For all these busy conscientious housewives the whole length of the street was punctuated by essential pauses during which they fulfilled their social role of village newscasters.

In country areas, stocking up on food has always represented a guarantee against the weather, never an intensive use of space. Fresh foods were bought or harvested the day they were needed, and the continuous rhythm of the housewife's trips from backyard to attic, from baker's to next-door neighbour's, gave the home a feeling of openness and accessibility.

Household appliances, on the other hand, were designed to rationalize effort, and eliminate any unnecessary actions. Each activity was to be classified and all unproductive time reduced to a minimum. And if you are counting every step, any time spent outside the home is time wasted. The kitchen, then, becomes the centre of operations in the home.

The most essential of household activities thus finds its way back, after many twists and turns, to the very centre of family life. Now and no doubt for many years to come the kitchen will remain as the mainspring of the home.[12]

The division of the house into hermetically sealed boxes – kitchen, living room, utility room, nursery – is all part of a general process whereby the home turns in on itself. Houses or apartments become fortresses. Every household task has its proper place inside. The housewife no longer needs the baker's oven, nor the public wash-house, which disappeared along with the tradition of doing a big wash every three months with help from neighbours – a custom that persisted in country areas right up until the 1960s. Already supplies may be fetched on a weekly basis and soon, thanks to the supermarket freezer, it will be monthly.

An organic unity, the modern home lives according to its own individual rhythms. Communal habits and the constraints exerted by community life are gradually disappearing. The common language of domestic experience is dying out, household tasks have lost their complexity, and everyone can cope by themselves.

In the 1926 Larousse Ménager, the process of doing the laundry was broken down into sorting, soaking, washing, soaping, rinsing, blueing, wringing, hanging out and folding. Even if by this time some of these operations could be done by machine, they were all complex, demanding individual thought and attention. Now you just fill the machine with dirty clothes, detergent and fabric softener and then later take out the dry laundry, ready for ironing. No skill is needed. The only place washing is discussed is in comic sketches and advertisements. There is a sort of knowing idiocy about Madame Dupont of Clochemerle who, in full view of a television audience, finally discovers that the solution to the problems her irrepressible children inflict on her in the form of grass and chocolate stains, is to be found in a packet of Dash (she says she's quite won over!). And while men discuss politics, business and serious things like that, what are the ladies to talk about now that the niceties of stiffening shirt collars and blueing the linen are long since forgotten? Shut away in their little boxes, where one activity automatically follows another, and where there is no longer any rewarding occupation overall, their role becomes that of baby-minders. Luckily, there are health centres – providing psychological, medical and educational help – which bring these fine mothers together to meet and compare notes.

Now that the ideal home – spotless, hygienic, comfortable and secure – has become a reality, women are discovering within themselves a deep urge to go beyond it and find fulfilment elsewhere. In France, the percentage of 'active' women hasn't really changed since the 1930s, but the type of work they do has. Productive work within the home, often connected to agriculture, has given way to salaried work outside. This change has both arisen from and reinforced domestic automation and the transformation of domestic life. Certainly women's desire to find 'outside' work isn't the only explanation for the increase in female activity rates. Urbanization, changes in production and consumption, the tendency for children to start school earlier, have all had the same effect. But women's rejection of political moves to send them back to the home reveals the real significance of the disappearance of the social dimension from domestic life. Childcare now represents the only generally accepted reason for 'giving up work' and staying at home. Apart from the few who hark back to a more gracious age, who would dare admit that they wanted to stay at home to polish the furniture, starch shirts, and spend their time cooking meals, making preserves or baking? It's not that these activities have disappeared or are impossible. In fact at the moment people are rediscovering in a big way the pleasure of making things themselves and recycling old materials. We are seeing a revival of taste and a renewed appreciation for the world of craft and manual skills.

But it wasn't any of this, really, that the machines destroyed. What they did away with for ever was the notion of the absolute and indispensible need for a woman to be present in the home. Obviously one can still try to make out that things are different and come up with all the old stories which say, as did nearly all the women we interviewed,[13] that the only real way to knead dough is by hand, and that certain things must be done in person. But really these are just games we play. There is no glory or meaning in domestic activity beyond the confines of the home, and not the slightest chance that it could lead to success or recognition. Only by looking elsewhere can we hope to become involved in real social interaction.

Not surprisingly, women who remain at home are discovering new skills and aptitudes. They take up plastering, upholstering, painting and decorating. They make clothes, repair machines and are generally capable of doing everything by themselves. And yet it's all fairly pointless since this tremendous outpouring of care and enthusiasm remains confined to their own homes and families. If ever I returned home as a housewife, it certainly wouldn't be to shut myself away. The front door would be wide open, I should come and go continuously and make myself as much at home in my neighbour's kitchen as my own. I should indulge in gossip and scandal as well as accepting the constraints of living amongst other people and other homes. If I returned home it wouldn't be to a house with a path that led away from the outside world. Mine would be a glass house, bearing the inscription 'come in' rather than 'keep out', a house open rather than closed to the outside world.

If we can really look forward to a future in which one's physical presence at work becomes unnecessary, and thanks to modern technology working from or running the home by remote control from a distance are real possibilities, then perhaps we may finally achieve a seamless union between home and the world outside. Perhaps . . . as long as we don't keep finding new boxes to add to the piles we've already stacked up so painstakingly.

Notes and references

1 HLM – *Habitations a Loyer Moderé:* low-cost council housing.
2 Mère Denis – a typical name like Mrs Smith or Jones to indicate the figure of an average housewife.
3 Pierre Sansot, 'La Vaisselle', *Nouvelles littéraries: Dossier sur la vie quotidienne* (December, 1978).
4 BHV – Bazar de l'Hôtel de Ville, a department store in the centre of Paris.
5 As early as 1926 the Household Larousse was warning its readers against following the growing trend of using washing machines too 'automatically'. Under the heading of advice we read:

> The housewife who uses a washing machine should follow the instructions supplied with it and may initially experience a few problems. For instance she may notice that some articles are not very white or have suffered some damage, or she may have to complete the work of the machine by hand, etc. . . . If you are having problems (though it must be said this is very unusual), then you should avoid following the instructions too literally. We suggest here various modifications one may introduce to improve matters (*Larousse Ménager. Dictionnaire illustré de la vie domestique* Paris: 1926, p. 155).

6 Boris Vian was an existentialist writer in the 1950s. He wrote about a piano which played by itself.
7 Guy Lux – a well known television presenter.
8 A dish made up of meat, onions and white wine traditionally cooked

in the baker's oven on laundry day in Alsace when the housewife was too busy to spend time cooking.

9 In *The American Woman's Home* 1865.
10 See footnote 2 on page 276.
11 *Larousse Ménager*, p. 1.
12 Paulette Bermege, *Petit guide de la ménagère* (Paris 1952).
13 In an empirical research project which was the basis for the ideas in this piece.

Index

308 *Index*